Project Management for Researchers

Project Management for Researchers

A Practical, Stress-Free Guide to Getting Organized

Shiri Noy

University of Michigan Press
Ann Arbor

Published in the United States of America by the
University of Michigan Press
Manufactured in the United States of America
Printed on acid-free paper

ISBN 978-0-472-03980-7 (print)
ISBN 978-0-472-22206-3 (e-book)

First published November 2024

To Digory Rascal Kirke Noy, who always managed to position himself just-so when I wrote. This book owes much to him, because no one dares disturb a sleeping cat when they're comfortably situated on your person.

Contents

Part IV: Final Notes

Acknowledgments

As I often share, I find sociology is so useful because it underscores the social nature of individual undertakings. I have benefited from the advice, mentorship, and goodwill of so many.

I am thankful for my many collaborators, mentors, students, and colleagues, who have all generously shared their experiences and tips with me over the years—leading me to realize how much we all have in common. I am fortunate to count among my professional contacts and friends people from across disciplines and in different professional settings: large firms, research institutes, small colleges, and large universities. Each have helped me recognize the ways in which the challenges we encounter in managing our research are distinctive but also share many commonalities, frequently organizational.

To people who generously shared examples, foibles, lessons, and stories— thank you.

As my friends and collaborators know, I only work with people whom I respect and admire on research, and I am fortunate to count each of my collaborators as friends, and some of my friends as collaborators. I am deeply grateful to have so many smart and generous colleagues and friends. I thank Joe DiGrazia, Randa Jabbour, Sarah Hatteberg, Jeff Kurtz, Ann McCranie, May Mei, Casey (Kathleen C.) Oberlin, Brian Powell, Nausica Marcos Miguel, Patricia McManus, Rachel Skaggs, Karen Spierling, and Linda Thunström for reading earlier drafts of this work and for their encouragement. They generously shared their insights and patiently talked through many of my questions and ideas. For encouragement and support of myself and my work I thank my immediate family, Dalia, Ronen, and Dean Noy, and my extended family, as well as colleagues and friends Jenn Agnew, Benita Bamgbade, Dave Chonowski, Susan Diduk, Nicole Fuller-Smith,

Melissa Huerta, Marina and Mike Landau, Lew Ludwig, Tim O'Brien, and Mandy Stewart.

In addition to reading earlier drafts, my ever-present and ever-supportive mentors, dating back to graduate school, Patricia McManus and Brian Powell have each been formative in my development as a researcher and scholar. I am fortunate to have "grown up" as a graduate student in Indiana University's sociology department—an intellectually generous and rigorous home, where I first had to think seriously about research. It was also where I began thinking about workflow because J. Scott Long shared his then in-progress book, and Patricia urged me, firmly but nicely in my first year, to attach a new subject line for emails on new topics, rather than continue to add on to a never-ending chain of unrelated emails.

I thank Katie LaPlant and the entire team at University of Michigan Press as well as reviewers for believing in this book and its utility and pushing me to make it clearer and more direct. I am grateful to Erin Ivy and her team for their work preparing the final manuscript. For helpful conversations and advice about the book I thank Laura Portwood-Stacer, for some early copy-editing I thank Tasha Bigelow, and for formatting assistance I thank Julia Petrie.

All errors that remain are, most unfortunately, my own.

Introduction: Who This Book Is For and How to Use It

As researchers, we receive training and education in the substantive, conceptual, theoretical, methodological, disciplinary, and other expertise we need to bring to bear on our research. And yet, we are rarely trained in the organizational, administrative, meta-organizational, and metacognitive skills required to manage our research projects. This comes at a cost: it increases stress and reduces efficiency, which can lead to delays and errors. It also has important implications for the scholarship itself: research that is not organized and well managed is more likely to be more challenging to replicate or reproduce, write up, and explain to reviewers and other audiences, and it may even lead to ethical and other issues. This, in turn, has implications for our employers and organizations.

This book is here to help.

My rationale for effective project management of your research is simple. First, it is good for you, the researcher. Second, it is critical for the research. Third, it is vital to the organizations where you work and the stakeholders of your research. I firmly believe that developing effective research management practices is, first and foremost, good for you, the researcher. It allows you to align your work with your goals, ethics, and priorities and reduce stress and worry. Research is a primary component of many academics', scholars', and certainly researchers' professional lives. However, we rarely receive formal training in managing and organizing our research (compared to doing our research), which causes many of us lots of anxiety and makes us feel disorganized. Developing a system helps reduce stress and opens up time and brain space for you to focus on the ideas and content of research. Further, it can allow you to respond nimbly to calls or requests for proposals

(CFP/RFP) for grants, papers, conferences, or chapters for edited volumes, for example. If your data and research are organized, you are well positioned to be able to draw on your data and analyses to take advantage of emergent opportunities.

Second, even if you do not get stressed about research, I argue that sound project management in research is important because it is good for research. Good project management for research, including good documentation and workflow, can reduce errors. Several disciplines are decrying a reproducibility crisis, with a concerted academic push toward open-access approaches. Research project management and organization can help. Sound project management for research contributes to your professional well-being and the research as it enhances the likelihood of achieving the project's goals, staying within budget and time constraints, and producing valuable and reliable research outcomes.

Third, effective management of your research projects is good for your employer, as one researcher who read an earlier draft and works at a large corporation emphasized. I wrote this book to make it worth your time and to benefit you. In economic terms, the return on investment (ROI) of the time and effort you spend working through this book and developing your research project management system should be high—to you, your research, and your employer. Effective project management for research is good for organizations or firms engaging in research in any scope and capacity. By organizing your (or your team's or organization's) research, you ensure that you can account for methodological and other decisions to your employer, supervisor, organization, reviewers, and funding agencies.

This book tackles the why, what, and how of managing your research. The *why* is likely the easiest to answer: to make your life easier and your work more efficient, to reduce stress and errors, and to improve your research. This book is for anyone managing research, encapsulating much of the *what*. The most challenging part is the *how*: this is at the heart of this book.

As researchers, we are immersed in the world of ideas and data, and we are experts on those. But we also live in the world of paperwork, budgets, and timelines. We need to manage our ideas and data but often have little guidance on how to do this. For many of us, research is only a small portion of what we are expected to do—alongside meetings, committees, teaching, presentations, advising, and other work. As such, we must use our research time efficiently and effectively. But whether research is only part of your job or the entirety of your workload, if you feel stressed by the disorganization of your research project(s) and not in complete control of it, this book is for you. It will help you develop a system to manage your research, reduce your stress and sense of overwhelm, and facilitate precise planning, execution, and adjustment.

This book outlines strategies, techniques, tips, and advice to demystify project management for research. I hope this can help you accomplish a few things. First, it will help you manage your research and yourself as well as anyone working with or under you in a way that is organized, more fluent, and accessible, reducing stress and enhancing efficiency. Second, it will help you with any necessary bureaucratic or other checks. When everything is organized, if you are audited or called to account (for example, by funding agencies, supervisors, deans, institutions, reviewers, or ethics committees), things will be cataloged and straightforward to access. Third, it will help you impose some analytic order on what is often a deeply personal, individualized, and sometimes ad hoc process. While we are typically meticulous in our research, we are often less meticulous about its metaprocesses, usually because we have not been taught those skills and have so many competing demands on our time and energy. However, living in disorganization and not having a system that works for us steals our precious cognitive and other energies that would be better devoted to our ideas and research.

Who This Book Is For

This book is for researchers.

It should be useful for *anyone* doing research. The book is likely most relevant for researchers with some control over their research. In the words of one scholar who read an earlier draft, this book adapts project management tools for researchers in charge of research (often called principal investigators or investigators). That is, this book is primarily for people doing, supervising, and managing research who do not have the luxury of a professional project manager: read, most academics (with lab managers in the natural sciences being an exception, though they are typically researchers themselves as well, though not the principal investigators).

Project management is an industry with specialized processes, vocabulary, and certifications. There are many jobs for project managers who are not typically in charge of the project but are instead hired to manage it. Increasingly, there are positions advertised for project managers on research projects even in universities, and many project managers work on research projects across the academic, corporate, non-profit, and governmental fields. Typically, these are not researchers but rather administrators, and these are often entry-level positions. That work requires essential skills and training, and this book is not a substitute for that, nor are those folks its intended audience. That is, professional research project managers will hopefully find it useful in thinking about the decision-making of researchers, but they will likely also have their own training in their field.

This book is appropriate for both novice and advanced researchers. If you are beginning graduate school, some things in this book may be unfamiliar to you as yet. Nonetheless, that is an excellent time to start thinking about managing your research: whether you are working on a closely related project of your advisor's or in a team or lab, common in some disciplines, or embarking on a master's thesis or dissertation. This book is also intended to be helpful for those who may have been doing research for decades but are not as organized or satisfied with their research management as they could be.

In writing this book, my starting assumption is that you are an expert or expert-in-training in your field and discipline and are doing important, exciting research but have many demands on your time and brain space. In academia, polychromic or multitasking work has increasingly become the norm (Mark 2023), underscoring the importance of organization. Further, it takes about 20 minutes to recover focus from an interruption (Mark, Gonzalez, and Harris 2005), and while some interruptions are not under our control, we can avoid interrupting our own work to search for something with good organization. Creating a system that works for you will help you and your research thrive, leading to better outcomes and experiences. Increased organizational efficiency will allow you to work on important projects and facilitate your peace of mind because your system has accounted for planning, execution, and possible setbacks and adjustments and is aligned with your priorities. Knowing that things are organized relieves immense stress. Clutter and disorganization reduce our ability to focus and tax our cognitive resources and abilities (Moacdieh and Sarter 2015; Whitbourne 2017). They also lead to emotional exhaustion, further sapping our ability to focus and think clearly—and enter that coveted state of flow that leads to breakthroughs in our research and ideas (Nakamura and Csikszentmihalyi 2014).

I am a sociologist who teaches and works with social and natural scientists. Therefore, many of my experiences relate to social scientists' work. That is, work that typically involves people, recordings, documents, spreadsheets, or other kinds of media. However, the ideas can be applied to other contexts, such as lab settings or archival work, including principles surrounding communication (with assistants, supervisors), documentation (of photos, specimens, papers), and people management (of yourself and others). Nonetheless, the examples in the book draw from the social sciences and may resonate most strongly with social scientists. The filled-out worksheets in the book are intended to provide you with examples rather than exemplars, and if their specific content is unhelpful or irrelevant to you, feel free to go straight to filling out your own! For blank worksheets, go to https://press.umich.edu/Books/P/Project-Management-for-Researchers and click on the Companion Website button for free resources and templates that accompany the book. Still, I hope the tools and strategies can be helpful for researchers across disciplines. I wrote this book because I wish I had it in graduate school and earlier in my career and as I mentored and taught people about research. In fact, I continue to draw on the resources in it as I refine my own system: entering into new collaborations, undertaking new data analysis strategies, and more. Both I and my work and its challenges change over time; that is the point of research, too: progress.

Further, I am an academic. However, I have worked to make the book accessible, and I believe its insights will also be valuable to those working in research institutes, government agencies, and corporate settings. I have included varied examples and considerations (e.g., organizations may dictate what software you can use) that speak to researchers' different work constraints, habits, and contexts across types of organizations, disciplines, and career stages. Nonetheless, as noted, the examples and some tools may resonate more strongly with social scientists and those who have a measure of control over their research, which may be more common in academia. I want to help you work more efficiently, and I offer this book as a guide, but it cannot change the systems in which we operate, with the pressure to always do more, faster, and better (more on that below).

Too often, I felt disorganized or lost sleep and focus as I randomly remembered I needed to do something but was unsure where or how to start. My experience, and that of dozens of academics I have helped with their projects and talked to more informally, suggests that I am not alone in this feeling. Even if you are not motivated by your personal concerns, effective project management will provide value and is a good investment for the organizations you work for and with, including your employer.

I regularly teach summer workshops via the Inter-University Consortium for Social and Political Research (ICPSR) on mixed methods research. (In the social sciences, mixed methods refers to methods that integrate or combine quantitative and qualitative data and analysis approaches). I have subsequently been invited to give other talks or seminars on this topic. Participants in these workshops have ranged from graduate students to research university deans, trained in disciplines from urban planning to medicine. They include academics, researchers and practitioners, and heads of academic and other centers. Many, from all career stages, confess to struggling to manage their research and data effectively and feeling overwhelmed by the idea of engaging with two different types of data simultaneously, even as they may have been doing award-winning, funded quantitative or qualitative research for decades. Further, even seasoned researchers working within a single method have reported struggling to manage their data and analyses. In the workshops, we discuss project management, supervision, software, metadata, and more. This is often cited as one of the facets of the workshop that participants appreciate most—the practical and meta-organizational advice and guidance. I have also been involved in formal and informal mentorship programs since graduate school and recently led a multi-week scholarship development seminar for junior faculty colleagues at my institution. A regular theme emerged: while many resources including books focus on writing or publishing or on particular research methods, scholars want information and advice on organizing and managing research.

When instructed on how to do research (whether in classes, by mentors, or by books), we are taught to collect and analyze data as the core of our disciplinary training. We often have dozens of instructive texts, general templates and expectations, guidelines, and canonical works on doing so. Plenty of training is available in software, methods, and disciplinary practices—from books, institutes, software companies, and universities. If we are lucky, we are trained in how to keep track of our research (research logs, for example). Still, management and meta-organizational systems are typically absent from graduate school research curricula, where most of us acquire basic research skills.

If it occurs to us, we often adopt organizational strategies learned from our advisors or out of necessity without building a broader system suited to us and our research, needs, goals, and lives. Further, collaboration is little discussed in the context of conducting research, even though research, on average, is becoming more collaborative (Henriksen 2016; Kumar 2018). I have several collaborative relationships, some lasting over a decade, and experience conducting cross-national, cross-disciplinary, and team research. The insights and recommendations come from my experience as well as many conversations and extensive reading about best practices but, as always, are intended to be tailored to your needs and priorities.

Challenges in Managing Research

Researchers encounter several perennial challenges when managing their research, which guide the book's structure and content. If you find yourself resistant to thinking about managing and organizing your research projects, that's OK—it's stressful, and we're invested in our habits. Those have served you well in many ways; you've come this far, haven't you? Rest assured that this book isn't trying to take any of that away from you; instead, I want to help you figure out what works for you and what doesn't and then optimize and systematize those habits and routines while thinking carefully about what serves your goals and what else would help you achieve them.

This book is divided into three main sections: planning, execution, and adjustment, with a fourth section on personalizing your research management approach to your needs and style. For each category, researchers sometimes resist the idea of organization and management. I address the most commonly cited concerns (and myths) surrounding each area.

First, the *planning* stage has several common barriers that researchers cite, and I think Chen (2019) makes some of these points particularly well as related to research (he is talking about engineering research):

1. My work is research, so I can't possibly plan it.
2. Committing to a schedule makes no sense; I don't know how things will go.
3. I don't have time to plan—I need to get my research done!
4. Things—people, software, the field—change too quickly; there's no point in planning.

Response: Research is an enterprise that not only allows planning but *requires* it. We are more likely to get lost if we don't have a map, as Chen (2019) notes (Chapter 1). It is only with a clear schedule, tasks, and a plan that we can iterate, pivot (the dreaded COVID-19 word that was often used as a euphemism for upending our lives entirely), or adjust accordingly in an informed and agile way while considering the bigger picture. Planning is the only thing that will allow us to keep our eyes on the goal and help us anticipate the pros, cons, and consequences of particular directions and resources needed (Chapter 2). A plan lets you understand the risks and trade-offs of specific decisions and enables more effective communication and execution. It helps you adapt to changes. Planning ensures that you are approaching your research with your purpose, goals, ethics, and priorities in mind, which will increase your efficiency and effectiveness and pay dividends for your well-being and the research itself—reducing stress and errors with clear documentation and a record of your decisions and transparent and reproducible decision-making (Chapter 3).

Second, for *execution*, researchers will often resist organization and planning by echoing the above and adding more concerns, often along the lines of the following:

1. There are too many moving parts and dead ends; keeping track of every little thing doesn't make sense.
2. I can remember the decisions that I've made.
3. If it's important, I probably wrote it down somewhere or can find it in my email.
4. I'm already mid-project; it's too late to create a management system for it.

Response: Any research effort has many moving parts, dead ends, and new threads, making it all the more important to have a clear organizational and management strategy. While you may remember many or all the decisions you've made (those with such an excellent memory are lucky!), calling on memory and keeping those things at immediate recall is cognitively costly and inefficient. You might remember a particular decision (e.g., why did I decide to code this variable this way?), but it is still helpful to put the decision in its appropriate context to understand what led to it and its consequences. In this example, that requires an organizational system with, for example, a record of the article that established the precedent for your coding decision and information on where to find the additional models you executed to check the robustness of the results when the variable was coded differently (Chapter 4). In terms of records—yes, you may have written it *somewhere*, but the question is where. By keeping your work tidy and organized, you won't have to root around, nor will you lose access if you change computers. Finally, you do not need to apply this system retroactively, though you are welcome to! I wrote this book from experience: mine and others. I therefore share examples and ideas. These are not intended to be perfect analogs for your needs but rather data points to help you manage your research project(s). As I recount in the book, in some projects lacking research management practices, specific documentation is limited; in others (Chapter 5), researchers have lost data because it wasn't backed up, and the stories go on and on. This may be incredibly challenging in collaborative relationships, where decision-making and work are shared and are not stored in a single person's memory! (Chapter 6).

Third, and finally, when discussing *adjustment*, researchers often voice more fear and concern than resistance:

1. What if things don't work out like I planned? How can I get back on track?
2. How do I incorporate new offshoots to projects into my plan?
3. When is a project over, and how do I know when I'm beginning a new one rather than extending it?

Response: The foundation of a system that matches your priorities, ethical commitments, and needs allows you to iterate, adjust, and accommodate change in a purposeful, directed way. Organization helps us to draw boundaries around projects, decide what tools best suit our system and goals, and adjust as needed with clear focus and reduced stress (Chapter 7). The book's third part focuses on adjusting, such as tackling unexpected (and sometimes unalterable—say, a pandemic for face-to-face research) circumstances. Not investing in crafting a system relies on the fallacy of sunk costs (or the sunk cost fallacy): just because you have invested significant time in doing research without a system does not mean you should not work to organize and systematize now to reduce stress! (Chapter 8). The book offers techniques to adjust specific aspects of your system. Planning and having a system allows you to adjust in an informed way and helps you see and work through the downstream and possible effects of deviations and adjustments. We often need to figure out how to manage offshoots and extensions of existing projects and incorporate them into our system. Generally, we think of a research project (or a project in general) as having a beginning and end date and including more than one task (Chapter 9). Still, the nature of research is that the results may be published years later—because of peer review processes or other considerations or delays—and you can think of the entirety of your scholarly trajectory as a project. Indeed, when we weave the narrative of our careers, we often have a clear sense (and are often required to account for it in tenure statements, grant reviews, job performance meetings, and interviews) of how our research connects across years or decades.

I argue that it makes sense practically to figure out our systems and organize projects by goals to accommodate outputs down the line. My system allows me to refer back to my project data and accompanying information (cleaned data, codebook, interview instrument, transcripts, documents, and media) that may have been part of a different paper but apply to a follow-up analysis as well and expand upon it (creating new variables, difference codes, running other statistical models). Having a clear workflow and system does not make our research inflexible. Instead, it allows us flexibility without additional stress or sacrificing documentation and organization.

Research is not linear, which makes it all the more critical that we are organized and have a system that suits us and our work to reduce stress and cognitive load, enhance efficiency, transparency, and reproducibility, anticipate necessary resources, adjust to new circumstances, and extend our research in exciting new directions. This book provides advice, guidelines, and templates to help you—no one size fits all, but specific principles and considerations will help you craft a system that suits you and incorporates best practices.

What This Book Is Not

This book cannot fix the structural issues that disproportionately affect the already marginalized and/or minoritized, and lead us to a persistent culture of overwork and framing increased productivity as a moral imperative. I want to clarify that my focus on efficiency is not so that you can necessarily do more—I do not buy into the neoliberal emphasis on always doing more. Instead, I want to help you enhance your well-being and ensure good research practices. I wrote this book to help you manage and conduct your research in a way that aligns with your priorities and goals, increases efficiency, diminishes errors and confusion, and reduces stress, but it cannot change oppressive systems.

Second, this book is not a product catalog listing all possible tools, software, approaches, and features. While I provide a non-exhaustive list of popular tools and will walk you through examples of selecting tools, this book will not tell you what software to use—this is often relatively niche and disciplinary, and software options are regularly changing. Instead, it is intended to help you identify what you want from software and guide you to find the best fit for you and your work. Again, this book is for researchers and will likely be most helpful to those with some control over their research.

Third, this book will not point you to specialized payroll services and software, for example, even though, as a researcher, you may have to hire and pay people. For most researchers, payroll services are something they cannot and do not control. Similarly, the human resources department (whether at a university or corporation) circumscribes hiring and requires conversations with human resources experts. If you are a research scientist or data analyst working in a lab or for a large company, you may not have any say in the project's timeline (Chapter 2), the software you use (Chapter 3), or bookkeeping (Chapter 5). Therefore, some of the advice may only apply in limited ways to your circumstances, but I hope the book can help you think about your organization (Chapter 4), collaboration (Chapter 6), and dissemination and replication or reproducibility (Chapter 9).

Fourth, this book is not a sermon. Your work is not your worth (despite the relentless messaging of late-stage capitalism that tells you otherwise), and your research is not your full identity. The contents of this book are not a chastisement of your approach to research, nor does the book claim some moral high ground or infallibility. Instead, this book is an invitation to construct and/or adapt your research project management system in a way that works for you. I wrote this book because I struggled mightily with managing my research, as did countless researchers I know. No one is perfect: coding errors happen no matter how well documented your work is. However, this book provides some strategies and information about navigating, minimizing, and, perhaps most importantly, avoiding mistakes as much as possible.

Finally, this book is neither a prescription note nor a magic bullet. Never believe anyone who tries to sell you an approach that argues, "Do this, and all your research will go smoothly forevermore!" Research is dynamic, as are people. The optimists among us believe that we are getting better at doing the work (research, science, scholarship), which leads to new developments and best practices that too are evolving. This means we're constantly learning. I am not prescribing a single model or answer. This book does not tell you what topic to study or what data to collect. Project management for researchers is about finding structure, not prescribing content. Instead, this book is an invitation to (re)consider your approach to your research project management and to develop a system that works for you.

How to Use This Book

This book is intended for use as a guide and workbook to help you plan, execute, and adjust your research. It provides a framework for you to manage your research in a way that aligns with your goals, ethics, and priorities and accommodates the demands of the structures and institutions you are embedded in—your workplace, granting agencies, peer review, journal reproducibility demands, and beyond. The information in the book is intended to help you develop your own project management style and system—introducing possible strategies, tools, and techniques to aid you in this process.

The book provides a practical guide to research project management from start to finish in four parts: the first section focuses on planning, the second on execution, the third on adjustment, and a shorter fourth part that gives some additional and more informal advice on finding your style. I recommend you start with one project in mind as you work through the worksheets and prompts so you don't get overwhelmed: the central research project you're working on at the moment, the one for which you are the primary person responsible (if you are collaborating with another researcher, you will need to develop a system that you both are willing to use). While the chapters are in conversation with one another and the material builds, each can also be read separately to address a specific issue or challenge.

Imagine three scenarios: one where you haven't started a project yet, a second scenario where you're gathering data, and a third where you're analyzing the data and writing. If you are in scenario one, you can start with Chapter 1 in the planning section, working through the book as you move throughout your project. If you are in scenario two, you may want to start in Chapter 4, in the execution section. If you are in the third scenario and the writing phase, you might want to start at the adjustment section in Chapter 7, or if you've finished writing, you might want to skip straight to Chapter 9 on dissemination, reproducibility, and replication. One scholar who provided feedback on an earlier draft recommended starting with Chapter 11, indicating it provided helpful advice they adopted to manage what they view as the most frustrating aspect of their work: email. Another researcher recommended starting with Chapter 8 because it shows that things can get back on track when they (inevitably) go sideways.

At some point, I recommend you read this book in its entirety—read it broadly and make brief notes about what you do that works for you, what seems interesting and important to you, and what intrigues you. This book aims to meet you where you are and to help you move toward a more organized, efficient, stress-free way to manage your research, whether you read it from start to finish, in sections or chapters. I have filled out the worksheets as an example in each chapter, with a different hypothetical project in each part of the book that draws loosely on the kinds of data I've discussed with other scholars. In Part I: Chapters 1–3, the worksheet examples refer to a hypothetical preliminary survey project on kindness—fictional but related to a project of mine; in Part II: Chapters 4–6, example worksheets draw from an imagined example of a focus group and interview project on community trust, while in Part III: Chapters 7–10 the example worksheets refer to a fictional media/article discourse analysis and survey on medical tourism. I include them as examples so you do not reach the worksheets and find yourself drawing a blank or wishing for an example. But do not be distracted by them—they are merely another data point! I recommend you utilize the blank worksheets available on the book's companion website to download and fill out as you work through your research. Finally, you can work through the book and/or any particular chapter separately for each project you undertake or work through it with your research team or collaborators for a specific project, downloading a new set of worksheets each time

Works Cited

Chen, Arthur C. M. 2019. "Introduction to Tech Communication & Project Management." Retrieved May 22, 2023 (www.scribd.com/presentation/296134188/Art).

Henriksen, Dorte. 2016. "The Rise in Co-Authorship in the Social Sciences (1980–2013)." *Scientometrics* 107(2):455–76.

Kumar, Sameer. 2018. "Ethical Concerns in the Rise of Co-Authorship and Its Role as a Proxy of Research Collaborations." *Publications* 6(3):1–9.

Mark, Gloria. 2023. "Advice | Multitasking Is the Enemy of Academic Productivity." *The Chronicle of Higher Education*. Retrieved August 15, 2023 (www.chronicle.com/article/multitasking-is-the-enemy-of-academic-productivity).

Mark, Gloria, Victor M. Gonzalez, and Justin Harris. 2005. "No Task Left behind? Examining the Nature of Fragmented Work." Pp. 321–30 in *Proceedings of the SIGCHI Conference on Human Factors in Computing Systems*. New York: Association for Computing Machinery. doi: 10.1145/1054972.1055017.

Moacdieh, Nadine, and Nadine Sarter. 2015. "Clutter in Electronic Medical Records: Examining Its Performance and Attentional Costs Using Eye Tracking." *Human Factors* 57(4):591–606. doi: 10.1177/0018720814564594.

Nakamura, Jeanne, and Mihaly Csikszentmihalyi. 2014. "The Concept of Flow." Pp. 239–63 in *Flow and the Foundations of Positive Psychology: The Collected Works of Mihaly Csikszentmihalyi*, edited by M. Csikszentmihalyi. Dordrecht: Springer Netherlands.

Whitbourne, Susan Kraus. 2017. "5 Reasons Why Clutter Disrupts Mental Health." *Psychology Today*. Retrieved July 2, 2022 (www.psychologytoday.com/us/blog/fulfillment-any-age/201705/5-reasons-why-clutter-disrupts-mental-health).

PART I

Planning

CHAPTER 1

Research Scope and Design

Research is enabled and constrained by researcher interests, resources, and other concerns. Research should also account for ethical, epistemological, and ontological considerations. You want to ensure that all of these pieces align in terms of your commitments and your research projects. In this book, I argue that ethical imperatives and concerns are embedded in not only our data and our writing but also our research management, whether this is funding, interaction with research participants, assistants, or otherwise. Often, our research begins with a question of design and scope, with their attendant distinctive organizational demands.

The Organizational Demands of Different Research Designs

Each research design and type of data has their own organizational demands. Some of these are dictated by the types of data and units of analysis, while others are about the scope and length of the project. Some research designs require more effort in the planning stage, others in execution or adjustment, and others still in the analysis and dissemination of results stage. I take the approach that writing, rather than what happens after we are done thinking, is part and parcel of the thinking process (Toor 2021), though what we think of as research writing (that is, writing up our results) happens toward the end of the research project. Similarly, planning is not just what happens before the research but is an integral ongoing part of the research process. As such, different research designs require different types of metadata, emphasis on the planning stages, and beyond. However, what is shared by all research projects is that they must be planned and executed, and relevant information must be collected and documented. In the social sciences, for example, there are differences in how we manage quantitative, qualitative, or mixed methods research. Within each, there are further differences; for instance, cross-sectional versus time-series data require different management and information on variables or respondent identification. As another example, analyzing and organizing images is different than text. In the following chapters, I will prompt you to consider what information you need about your data and project, allowing you to manage your research project effectively.

For any research project, at the planning stage, your focus should be on three primary research components in thinking about the scope and design: practicality, theory, and ethics. In the next chapter, I invite you to consider your research project's specific tasks and resources. At this stage, what we'll call project initiation, I invite you to think broadly about the practicality, theory, and ethical implications of your research project goal, outputs, and outcomes.

Practicality

The first issue you will want to consider carefully at this stage is practicality. Many of us have great ideas, but these are not always practical. However, before dismissing an idea on the grounds of impracticality, I recommend drilling down to the specifics to assess whether and how something can go from an idea to an action or plan. I find applying the SMART goal framework the best way to think about the practicality of my ideas and plans, big and small. The SMART goal framework is a common goal and task setting approach to creating **Specific, Measurable, Achievable, Relevant,** and **Time-Bound** goals (e.g., Leonard and Watts 2022).

Worksheet 1.1 invites you to brainstorm your project and go through a couple of iterations to ensure it is SMART (as a reminder, all worksheets are available in blank form for you to download and fill out and/or print at the book's companion website). The examples of worksheets in this book are here to serve as examples rather than exemplars; if you do not find them useful, skip to filling out your own worksheet. First, write your research project goal as you currently view it. It's OK if it's broad and vague. Then, let's use the SMART framework, asking and answering the following questions about your project in the worksheet: is the project **specific** enough to be clear to someone reading it? Is there some way to **measure** the project's success, that is, how will you know when the project is complete? Is it **attainable**, that is, is it feasible and possible to complete? Fourth, is it **relevant**,

Worksheet 1.1 *Project Goal Worksheet*

PRACTICALITY

PROJECT GOAL

Understand how Americans think about kindness.

DETAIL FOR THE GOAL ABOVE: WHAT THE MEASURABLE, TIME-BOUND, ETC. ASPECTS OF IT ARE.

SPECIFIC: I want to understand how Americans define kindness, and if there are actions they think are kind.

MEASUREABLE: Create a survey, with a combination of open- and closed-ended questions—field it to a representative sample of American adults.

ACHIEVEABLE: ~ 200 American adults for a preliminary survey.

RELEVANT: Create a variety of questions that get at how Americans define kindness, and what they think kindness "looks" like. I should be able to do this with part of the $5,000 I have in my research account.

TIME-BOUND: Complete survey construction by March, hopefully field full survey by December.

GIVEN THE ABOVE, IS THERE ANYWAY TO REFINE AND RESTATE THE GOAL TO INCORPROATE THE S.M.A.R.T. COMPONENTS ABOVE?

PROJECT GOAL REVISED

Develop and field a preliminary survey, combining closed- and open-ended questions, to a nationally representative sample of 200 American adults to examine how Americans define kindness and what behaviors they consider kind.

that is, does it do what you need it to do for your career, job, ambitions, organization, client, or whoever you are answering to or whatever mission you're trying to further? Finally, is it **time-bound**? When will the project be completed? Then, after doing so, let's rewrite our project goal, trying to integrate the answers to your SMART questions.

For the overall project, at this early initiation stage, you want to ensure your project is achievable, relevant, and time-bound. So, if your goal is to publish a *New York Times* (NYT) bestseller, that is a great goal, but it is not particularly **relevant** in conceptualizing a research project. It may be one of your desired outcomes, though I would argue that reaching a broad audience would likely be a better outcome to think through rather than fixating on a NYT bestseller. It may be **achievable**, but that, too, is highly uncertain given how little control we have over who buys our books. That is, try to focus on what is achievable from the perspective of the research information generated (e.g., a dataset, experiment, set of archival materials). Finally, you will want to consider your project as **time-bound** at this stage. I want to affirm how difficult this is: research is dynamic and uncertain, especially in the academic ecosystem, and we are sometimes bound only by our internally imposed, roughly estimated deadlines. If you are in charge of your research/lab/project, you decide the timeline, when to submit a paper to a conference, or when to send an article out for peer review. In this way, ensuring your project is time-bound is particularly important, and being as specific as possible is essential. In Part III of the book, we will discuss how and whether to adjust deadlines and tasks in response to circumstances both within and outside our control, which may include pandemics, other scholarly opportunities that we decide take precedence, and more. At this stage, however, we want to think of a practical and workable project. Generally, a **project** is a set of related tasks with a common goal and seeking specific results. A project also has a start and end date.

At the planning stage, your overall research project goal doesn't have to be specific (though it will have to get there at some point!). For example, you can have as a general goal to "understand Americans' views on kindness," but at some point, you want to get **specific**, for example, deciding what "views on kindness" means. **Measurable** means that you can measure it using a particular methodology or instrument, though making it even more specific and measurable would mean specifying, for example, the questions you would use in a survey instrument. I have provided an example of working through this in the following worksheet and follow this example (which is imagined but related to current a project of mine) through Part I of the book. A blank, downloadable, and fillable version of this worksheet and others in this book is available for download at the book's companion website so you can work through this for your project. Importantly, the below ends with a specific research goal that is adjusted for practicality; your overall motivation to "understand how Americans think about kindness" may remain unchanged!

A Note and Warning about Scope Creep

Determining the scope of any research project is important but challenging for various reasons. Some projects are decades-long and may encapsulate several smaller or even a few large sub-projects. For graduate students, you may be looking toward writing a graduate thesis. For early career researchers, your dissertation or thesis is often the largest project you have undertaken. Often, we think of our research scope in terms of the anticipated outputs, whether the data collected or the thesis, article(s), or book(s) published. The scope can then be measured in many ways: outputs or timelines or even broader goals the projects serve (tenure, promotion). In Chapter 2, we'll talk about time- versus output-based projects. We'll also think specifically about tasks and timelines. However, it is helpful as you start a project to think carefully about where it fits in your life. Sometimes, this is externally communicated. For example, if you are a research scientist or researcher working for an organization (corporate or otherwise), you may be given a research project to complete that has a specific deadline. In many parts of academia, it is more common for you to decide the project's scope, but even so, there are significant constraints, including funding, time, and effort. Further, as discussed in the book's third part, projects sometimes take longer or involve more resources or effort than anticipated, which might require adjustment.

When initiating a project, you'll want to think about what part of your work life the project will occupy. Again, this may be externally mandated (e.g., 40% of your work effort), and in those cases it might be doubly critical to plan carefully. Either way, if you anticipate this to be a two-month project, perhaps requiring ten hours/week for eight weeks if planning in terms of time, you will need and want to ensure that you are not spending 30 hours a week on project-related work for those weeks. While we'll talk about the specific tasks and resources required of projects more systematically in the following chapters, it would be helpful to think back to existing projects and project(s) you are currently planning to conceptualize how long you want or expect them to last.

It is also important to think about your project's goal in a specific way because of the dangers of **scope or mission creep**. Mission creep refers to constantly expanding goals, often in the aftermath of successes. While it was originally used to refer to military operations, it can be applied to various contexts (Fischer 2012). We can think of mission creep in the project context as scope creep; the project's scope keeps growing! The positive connotation of mission creep or scope creep is expansion, and who doesn't want more offshoots and exciting new developments in their research? This is not a problem as long as it is accounted for and planned around. Otherwise, mission creep happens almost unknowingly and is driven by factors other than our motivation and interests, for example, it seems silly not to collect such and such extra data or expand the research question based on such and such, but it might not be something we're actually interested in or the data quality may be low. As long as additions are done thoughtfully and with care, scope expansion is fine, and indeed, this is sometimes the most novel and exciting part of our research! But scope creep means you're working on things and tasks that you did not expect or plan for; this suggests that you will likely experience delays and need to readjust timelines and perhaps reduce resources devoted to the things you did plan for. This can be fine and tackled with adjustment (Part III of this book). On the flip side, it can also lead to stress and delays or lower quality and attention given to the original goals. This does not mean we should be inflexible and not expand our scope, but it does mean that we need to think carefully about the opportunity costs and tradeoffs of adding more to our plate mid-project.

Outputs and Outcomes

In addition to project goals, you'll want to consider your project outputs and outcomes. There are differences in how people use these terms, but we will treat outputs as concrete products for our purposes. **Outputs**, then, are "deliverables" in management speak: the reports, papers, datasets, and other "products" from your research. **Outcomes**, on the other hand, are more expansive goals and intentions, for example, policy change surrounding a topic or your own career development and advancement that, in many ways, lives beyond the lifespan of this particular project. So, while a dataset, publication, or report is an output, public outreach about your topic or a reorientation of understandings of a concept in the broader community might be a desired outcome. Notably, while outputs are concrete and measurable, outcomes may be a little more amorphous but often the "end goal." Perhaps the overall **outcome** you aim to achieve is to affect policy or social change in a particular area. How your research project might culminate in distinct **outputs** and how your outputs relate to different outcomes should help you begin to think about how your project fits into your broader goals and mission. Worksheet 1.2 invites you to restate your goal, which you can refine further from the previous worksheet or keep as it was, and then prompts you to think about anticipated products and outcomes or outputs and outcomes.

Worksheet 1.2 Project Outputs and Outcomes Worksheet

OUTPUTS AND OUTCOMES

PROJECT GOAL

Develop and field a survey, combining closed- and open-ended questions, to a nationally representative sample of 200 American adults to examine how Americans define kindness and what behaviors they consider kind.

BELOW, BRAINSTORM SOME PROJECT OUTPUTS OR SPECIFIC PRODUCTS AND SEPARATELY THE BROADER OUTCOMES OF YOUR PROJECT. YOU MIGHT HAVE JUST ONE OF EACH OR SEVERAL.

OUTPUTS	OUTCOMES
1. preliminary quantitative dataset on kindness	1. tenure and promotion, of which this is a part
2. academic article focused on definition of kindness	2. launching a new research stream: empirically based, sociological definition of kindness
3. grant proposal for a larger survey or mixed methods project	3. refining theories of morality in light of the concept of kindness
4. presentations at [name] and [name] conferences	
5. blog post on findings on [name] blog	

For me, one of the most stressful parts of a project is communicating the scope and expected outputs of a project externally to what I'll call stakeholders or gatekeepers, such as in annual plans or proposals. Personally, when communicating about final products or deliverables, I tend to under-promise and over-deliver when talking to those "in charge." I suppose it is the mark of an anxious personality. As such, I will, for example, not mention some papers at the planning stage in annual work updates or to colleagues. Personally, this is just how I work—and I want to give myself some leeway in case I decide not to publish something I began work on or that gets rejected (I will say, I've abandoned several papers along the way in my career for a variety of reasons, and I never felt too bad because I learned essential skills. I've always had so much exciting work in the pipeline that this was not too great a "cost" for me, but again, no one size fits all, and I know many people who never abandon a paper or project! I agree that every piece can find a home, but I moved on to other projects because the effort spent on finding that home was not "worth" it to me then and I had moved on intellectually. Again, your calculus and considerations will vary.)

However, I want to be clear and transparent that my approach has a cost and that this practice is likely gendered (Bornmann, Mutz, and Daniel 2007; Burns et al. 2019). We live in a time where flashiness and self-promotion in research are popular, and talking oneself up is also valued (Cain 2013). Therefore, many find it essential to promote and self-promote in myriad ways, and whether and how you do so depends on your goals and personal practices. In addition, though, and more practically, there is a lot of benefit to sharing intentions, drafts, and information with at least some trusted others, which I do. But I do not do it with gatekeepers. I am getting better at self-promoting and sharing "finished" (typically, for me, this means published) products, so that's progress!

Many researchers who share intentions widely and sometimes even publicly find that it creates accountability and a feeling of responsibility to deliver or that they receive important formative feedback. In some positions, sharing such plans may be required. Similarly, it is helpful to workshop research at many stages to get feedback regarding the scope across stages: including during planning, data collection, data analysis, write-up, and revision. What, whether, and to whom you communicate your outputs and outcomes at the planning stage depends on many situational and personal factors. For now, I invite you to write them down for yourself, and then you can decide what, when, and with whom to share then.

Theory

When we think of managing and organizing our research projects, we typically think of how to manage our data and analysis. However, it is essential to keep the role of theory and other factors (ethics, practicality) front of mind here. Beyond deductive (top-down) and inductive (bottom-up) research approaches, researchers have identified "abduction" as a particular approach that is neither strictly top-down nor bottom-up. Abduction notes that it is essential to recognize where ideas come from and when and whether they emerge from the data versus outside of it (Swedberg 2017). Often, we think of theory and method as separate endeavors where the practical challenges of research are defined by method.[1] However, theory and method are in many ways inseparable, as methods are guided by ontological and epistemological foundations about how we can know or learn things about the world—research.

In project planning, you will want to consider your discipline's or subfield's particular theories and understandings. A deep dive is beyond the scope of this book, but I briefly note that for those of us in sociology, for example, our theories of how humans think and live have significant consequences for how we measure those same things. In the social sciences, we draw on developing an understanding of human cognition to think about how to study people. One of my favorite things to teach in mixed methods seminars and other methods courses I offer is dual process theory. While the theory has a long history, I encountered it as elaborated by psychologist Jonathan Haidt and expanded upon in sociology by Steve Vaisey and others in regards to moral cognition. The theory (this is, naturally, a summary; you can go straight to the source(s) and their bibliographies for the full richness of this approach!) suggests that we undergo dual processing for information (Haidt 2006; Vaisey 2009).

They use the metaphor of our cognition consisting of an elephant and rider, where the elephant is slow moving, set in their ways; this is our automatic processing self. On the other hand, the rider is active, constantly thinking, and can decide and expend effort to change course. They argue that particular methods may be differently suited for capturing the elephant and rider, respectively, and that this understanding of what insights different methods yield can influence our answers to research questions and theory development.

As an extension, the elephant may be best attended to via survey questions; for example, when you ask people about their self-rated physical health in a survey, they are given response options such as "excellent," "good," "fair," or "poor," allowing them to provide a rapid answer by selecting one of the options. That is, many people have a basic and typically immediate sense of how they view and think about their health and an answer that seems to capture their overall or average state of health with little difficulty. There, you are capturing the elephant (which you can tell by question response times, for example, where if respondents spend a long time on a question, they are no longer engaging the elephant). However, suppose you engage a person in a conversation about their overall health, perhaps via a semi-structured interview, in a focus group, or in the context of ethnographic observation. In that case, there is much more complexity and ambivalence about how people rate and think about their health. People may bring up acute versus chronic conditions that may involve flareups, sleep, exercise, or other nuances. Dual process theory suggests that neither of these answers, which the same person might give separately in response to a survey versus an interview, is more or less "right" or "true" (the possibility of ever knowing what is true notwithstanding, and something we leave for philosophers). Instead, they each reflect some facet of reality and capture different parts of our complex and wondrous cognitive processes and can in turn be suited for different types of research questions, goals, inferences, and purposes.

The above example is intended to demonstrate that theory has an essential bearing on method and vice versa; different methods (note, not just different "data" or "cases") may reveal different facets and ideas that may require us to revise our theory(/ies). That is the beauty and, to me, one of the most exciting things about research. Dual process theory in its development was not intended to be about methods but rather understanding cognition, and yet has enormous methodological implications.

All this is to underscore that much is baked into your selection of research methods and approaches and the management and use of this data. The more carefully you think about this at the planning stage, the easier it will be to ensure you align your project management practices with your research goals. Most relevant to the nuts and bolts of project management are that your theories may also guide what information you should collect and keep track of (e.g., response time in surveys). Theory may also guide your choice of the appropriate unit of analysis (e.g., individuals, families, cities) in addition to helping you decide what kinds of associations, variables, markers, themes, or data you want to focus on. This, naturally, varies widely by discipline, but the importance of selecting the right unit of analysis for the issue you are going to study is a cross-disciplinary concern (cf. Beyene et al. 2009; Gross 2019; Kainulainen, Puurtinen, and Chinn 2019). This is something you should consider, and the most fruitful conversations and information about this will likely be found in your discipline-specific literature, coursework, and conversations with mentors and colleagues in your area. I make this note here as a reminder of how vital theory is for crafting your project plan and as a reminder to engage in these conversations!

Ethics

In this book, I argue that understanding and incorporating your ontological, epistemological, and ethical commitments are essential when selecting methods and data. Research integrity is not just about data and analysis but also about social responsibility regarding topics and data and their management. **Ethical decisions and repercussions** are embedded in our research and writing and their management. I invite you to reflect on your ethical priorities in Worksheet 1.3. These likely relate to your intended outcomes, which you can revisit from Worksheet 1.2. Thinking about these at this early research project initiation and planning stage will allow them to serve as a "north star" where you can consult these principles in thinking about your decision-making, recognizing that decisions, even (seemingly or actually) minor ones, have important ethical implications.

I invite you to consider instances of ethical questions or challenges you have encountered in your research and think back to the values and underlying priorities you want to guide your research in Worksheet 1.3. If you struggle to think of different values, you can search for "core values list" or "personal values list" online to see some lists and examples. We can hopefully make these salient and explicit by thinking about this at this early stage. I hope this can set the tone for how you feel about your project management, from dealing with data to dealing with people, as we discuss in the following chapters.

Worksheet 1.3 *Ethical Considerations Brainstorming Worksheet*

ETHICAL CONSIDERATIONS

CONSIDER INSTANCES IN YOUR RESEARCH WHERE YOU HAVE HAD TO MAKE DECISIONS YOU FOUND MORALLY OR ETHICALLY CHALLENGING. WHAT HAS GUIDED YOUR DECISION MAKING? WHAT KINDS OF VALUES WOULD YOU LIKE TO UPHOLD IN YOUR RESEARCH?

1. Respect and consent
2. Giving and sharing credit
3. Accountability

Above, I provide an example of a filled-out worksheet on ethical considerations. My **ethical priorities** in my research (and in other situations as relevant) are: first, respect for and fully informed consent from participants, collaborators, people working for me, and anyone else involved in research. That means that I am careful to disclose and discuss the upsides and downsides (as I understand them) of any work people do, whether as participants or collaborators; second, giving and sharing credit, which means I work to actively include and acknowledge people who work with me, for example, by inviting them to co-present or co-author and provide them other opportunities as I am able; third, accountability, where I focus on making sure that I use data that I myself have collected involving participants and publish it so that it is shared with the broader scientific community given the funding, time, and effort that has gone into it, remaining accountable for my decisions and actions and apologizing and correcting course as needed. That is, all data that I have collected for my own projects that has involved effort from participants (surveys, interviews) has been analyzed and published in some form. (The papers I mentioned "letting go" of earlier relied on secondary data or other people's data, or used data I had published with elsewhere.) I hope I never have to because that would make me feel unaccountable and misaligned with my values.

My decisions are guided by these priorities. For example, I am driven by protecting the privacy and confidentiality of my research participants and their data, but that is more specific than the general principle that guides me, which, for me, is respect. Our priorities and values guide each of us. You likely have other ethical priorities you adhere to, and it would be helpful to write them down. For example, one of my friends and colleagues is guided by an ethos to "maximize equity." While this likely means different things to different people, for this researcher, this is the lens that guides all decisions they make, including, for example, publishing almost exclusively open access, as they see this as an issue of equity in terms of access for researchers across different types of institutions including other countries, but also public access to information.

In the next chapter, we will examine what resources are at your disposal and what resources your project requires. That is, based on the outputs and outcomes you identified in this chapter, I will ask you to think through the tasks and resources associated with your planned research project. Taking stock of the resources at your disposal and those that you might need to accomplish your goals helps you understand where there may be areas for rethinking, editing, and planning most effectively.

Note

1. Note that some scholars distinguish between method and methodology, where methodology is seen as the strategy and rationale for the research, including theories, and method is a specific tool, approach, or procedure such as archival research or interviews (Swedberg 2021), but here I use them largely interchangeably.

Works Cited

Beyene, Joseph, David Tritchler, Jennifer L. Asimit, and Jemila S. Hamid. 2009. "Gene-or Region-based Analysis of Genome-wide Association Studies." *Genetic Epidemiology* 33(S1):S105–10.

Bornmann, Lutz, Rüdiger Mutz, and Hans-Dieter Daniel. 2007. "Gender Differences in Grant Peer Review: A Meta-Analysis." *Journal of Infometrics* 1(3):226–38. doi: 10.1016/j.joi.2007.03.001.

Burns, Karen E. A., Sharon E. Straus, Kuan Liu, Leena Rizvi, and Gordon Guyatt. 2019. "Gender Differences in Grant and Personnel Award Funding Rates at the Canadian Institutes of Health Research Based on Research Content Area: A Retrospective Analysis." *PLoS Medicine* 16(10):e1002935.

Cain, Susan. 2013. *Quiet: The Power of Introverts in a World That Can't Stop Talking*. New York: Crown.

Fischer, John Martin. 2012. "Responsibility and Autonomy: The Problem of Mission Creep." *Philosophical Issues* 22:165–84.

Gross, Daniel R. 2019. "Ecosystems and Methodological Problems in Ecological Anthropology." Pp. 253–63 in *The Ecosystem Concept in Anthropology*, edited by Emilio F. Moran and Susan H. Lees. New York: Routledge.

Haidt, Jonathan. 2006. *The Happiness Hypothesis: Finding Modern Truth in Ancient Wisdom*. New York: Basic Books.

Kainulainen, Mikko, Marjaana Puurtinen, and Clark A. Chinn. 2019. "Historians and Conceptual Change in History Itself: The Domain as a Unit of Analysis." *International Journal of Educational Research* 98:245–56.

Leonard, Kimberlee, and Rob Watts. 2022. "The Ultimate Guide to S.M.A.R.T. Goals." *Forbes Advisor*. Retrieved April 11, 2023 (www.forbes.com/advisor/business/smart-goals/).

Swedberg, Richard. 2017. "Theorizing in Sociological Research: A New Perspective, a New Departure?" *Annual Review of Sociology* 43:189–206.

Swedberg, Richard. 2021. "What Is a Method? On the Different Uses of the Term Method in Sociology." *Distinktion: Journal of Social Theory* 22(1):108–28.

Toor, Rachel. 2021. "Advice | Scholars Talk Writing: Tressie McMillan Cottom." *The Chronicle of Higher Education*. Retrieved July 31, 2023 (www.chronicle.com/article/scholars-talk-writing-tressie-mcmillan-cottom).

Vaisey, Stephen. 2009. "Motivation and Justification: A Dual-Process Model of Culture in Action." *American Journal of Sociology* 114(6):1675–1715.

CHAPTER 2

Taking Stock

Planning requires some setup in itself. In particular, it's helpful to take stock of your needed and available resources: infrastructure, time, and other resources you already have access to and those you might need to procure or request. There are several ways to approach planning; one is what I like to call outcome-based, and the other is time-based. However, these are "ideal types." Much as introductory textbooks often describe the research process as a linear and neatly prescribed process—read literature, devise hypotheses, design study, and so forth—in reality, we often flip between "stages" of the research process. In the same way, time- and output-based are ideal types, and our planning is often a combination.

Planning to Plan

Output-based planning focuses on, unsurprisingly, the output(s). These are sometimes more challenging—for example, it's hard to plan to write a book before even starting research, though this is less true in some fields or projects than others. But some projects are very clearly output-based; for example, a dissertation is a clear output at least in form, if not in content. **Time-based planning** is determined more by the time constraints than by the product, per se. So, we may have an interest in a particular topic and a semester or four months to devote to it, or two hours a week for some number of weeks. Of course, many projects are some combination of output- and time-based. Time and output plans and constraints are significant to note and can be empowering. Self-directed research is exhilarating because it's a blank page: we can study many things in many ways, and many tools are available. Boundaries help with the practical, facing the blank page, and putting some sketches down.

Despite the best-laid plans, as I discuss in Part III of the book, it is important to be open to change and flexible. But I argue that having a clear and thought-out plan makes flexibility easier and more effective. You might think that coming up with a detailed and elaborate plan is a waste of time, given that plans inevitably change, especially with something so emergent and unpredictable as research. There might be such a thing as over-planning, trying to micro-manage each hour of each day, from project start to end. But generally, when you have a set plan, with clear outcomes and outputs, and to use corporate-speak planned "deliverables," you are much better positioned to be flexible and responsive to changing dynamics and circumstances.

The first thing that is involved in planning is a clear overall goal. This can take several forms in research: your goal is usually to answer a research question or address a research aim—to investigate a particular issue. This is the goal you started refining in Chapter 1. However, you may have other goals that might be more specific and are outputs, for example, publishing an article. In planning, we will consider these goals as subsets of the overall goal: tasks to be accomplished in the project's broad scope. Some might argue that these "deliverables" and other hoped-for outcomes or outputs might be beyond the scope of the research; that is, they are a summary or result of it rather than part of it. But I argue that dissemination and conclusions of research are part of the research, just as writing is part of the thinking rather than solely the culmination of it.

Output-Based Projects

For **output-based projects**, you will want to work backward from the output. Again, research is unpredictable and hopefully exciting in its emergence, and you may find strands and insights you want to pick up mid-project. Wonderful! Plans can be adjusted. The point of the plan is not for it to control you but rather for your plan to facilitate the organization of your project. This is especially important if you have people you are accountable to, for example but certainly not limited to supervisors, clients, granting agencies, dissertation committees, and tenure requirements.

Time-Based Projects

Time-based projects are a little different, and between time- and output-based, there's not so much an either/or but rather an "and." If you are less time-constrained (and perhaps if you are applying for funding or talking through plans for a project with a supervisor or advisor), it helps to focus on the outcome. On the other hand, if there is a strict timeline, this necessitates figuring out what precisely can be accomplished in the time frame given your project goal. This may be more common in corporate and non-academic organizational settings but may also be the case for research projects that are "handed down" from either a supervisor or advisor. Time-based planning may also be important in the context of planning a research project during a sabbatical or fellowship period, for example. It is essential to be realistic, and again, the best way to do that is to rely on your own experience, have some conversations with those with experience in the type of research you are planning, and perhaps the most useful approach, described below, piloting the project.

Taking Stock: Project Tasks

As a first step, you will need to think about the **primary tasks associated with your project**. You may find it hard to balance being too fine-grained and specific (decide on the specific survey or interview question(s) to measure such and such concept) and too general (do the research) in the planning stage. It will likely be easier for you to identify the primary tasks if this is a type of project/method/data you are familiar with and have used before. Even for seasoned researchers, however, it may be helpful to do a "brain dump" of everything you can think of that you will need to do for your research project. In Worksheet 2.1, I first invite you to list all possible project tasks, big and small. Then, see if you can sort them into "primary" or "big" tasks and sub-tasks. Finally, list the big tasks. Worksheet 2.1 provides an example of a "brain dump" and lists primary tasks associated with the same imagine project on kindness reviewed we began with in Chapter 1 and that we will work through in the first part of the book. The worksheets in this book are here to serve as examples rather than models to follow; if you do not find them useful, please skip them and move to filling out your own worksheet.

Taking Stock of Your Resources and Constraints

Before starting, **taking stock of your resources and constraints** is essential. This is a little different if you're applying for a grant since you're asking

Worksheet 2.1 *Project Tasks Worksheet*

TAKING STOCK: PROJECT TASKS

PROJECT GOAL

Develop and field a preliminary survey, combining close- and open-ended questions, to a nationally representative sample of 200 American adults to examine how Americans define kindness and what behaviors they consider kind.

BRAIN DUMP

LIST ANY PROJECT TASKS THAT COME TO MIND.

Contact different survey fielders for quotes—Prolific, Qualtrics—can I have Prolific field a survey entered on the Qualtrics framework?, figure out budget and exactly how much I want to spend, look up existing kindness questions, adapt survey, brainstorm kind behaviors based on literature, write instrument, consult with [name] and [name] about survey, IRB approval, decide what socio-demographics to collect, clean data, analyze data, write papers.

BIG TASKS

GROUP THE ABOVE INTO TASKS AND SUB-TASKS. BELOW LIST THE BIG TASKS ASSOCIATED WITH YOUR PROJECT, FOR EXAMPLE, SURVEY DATA COLLECTION.

1. IRB application
2. Instrument development
3. Data collection
4. Data cleaning
5. Data analysis
6. Write paper(s) and presentations

for additional resources, but it's not a bad idea, even in that case, to figure out whether and how you can accomplish your project with a fixed set of resources. It's also helpful to figure out the minimum you need to complete project tasks, how and whether you can scale up if given more resources (data, time, research assistance, etc.), and how that might affect your timeline.

Before starting project planning, you will want to take stock of your resources: those you have and those you need. People have different approaches to doing this, but the best way to think about resources, in my experience, is in five large buckets: time, skills, money, equipment and tools, and approval/buy-in.

Time

The first bucket is time. In short, you will want to consider the **time require-ments** of research project components: how many hours/weeks/months do you have to devote to this project? You can also consider how much time it would require and think in tandem about what resources you *have* and what resources you feel you *need*. I recommend you think about hours per week as a starting point because research suggests that working consistently in short chunks is better than binge work (Boice 1990; Redelfs, Aguilera, and Ruiz 2019; Rud and Trevisan 2014), not to mention that the luxury of several uninterrupted hours much less days without meetings, emails, and other tasks are hard or impossible to come by for many of us. Even worse are the lies we tell ourselves, including the dreaded "I'll do this in the sum-mer when I'm not teaching" or "It's OK, I'll give up weekends if I need to" or "I'll start this next month when my workload is lower." I discuss time management, developing a consistent work habit, and rest in more detail in Chapters 10 and 11. By considering hours/week, ideally you can figure out an average, or perhaps a minimum, if you find that more useful, of hours available, which will help with planning. If you work collaboratively and manage others, this requires discussion and communication. Of course, this is an estimate, and estimates change. Worry not; this book understands the need for flexibility, and the third part discusses how to adjust thoughtfully in response to unforeseen circumstances or inaccurate planning.

What I mean by inaccurate planning is planning that you are doing at an information deficit: it might be you are starting a project that is different in scope, stakes, or content than what you're familiar with, which makes esti-mation difficult. For example, if you've never done an interview, you might have difficulty estimating how long it will take to transcribe or code an inter-view. Another good approach that many researchers I know use is to rely on colleagues and other experts to help estimate. Yet another researcher always multiplies any estimate by 1.5 whenever trying to anticipate how long things will take. This builds in time for delays as well as iteration. Still, my general recommendation to deal with this will always be to do a pilot component/ pilot project before the overall project, especially if this is a method that you are less familiar with. As I discuss below, this has several significant benefits, not least giving you a realistic and experienced ability to estimate project and task time needs.

Skills

Research requires skills. Many of our **skills** have been hard-won from years in undergraduate and graduate courses, learning by doing, whether in our projects or assisting and working for and with others, or doing additional reading and training, and practice. It's important to remember our abilities and proclivities are not all created equal, even when we're well trained.

When I teach mixed methods research, one of the first questions I always ask participants is which kind of data and methods they feel more comfortable and familiar with. This is because social scientists typically encounter quantitative or qualitative (rather than mixed methods) training first. Moving past our most dominant training or the methods we are most comfortable with is challenging. Research projects should be driven by the research question, not by the skillset of the researcher. Of course, the kinds of questions and topics we're interested in are shaped by our training and skills, but it may be that our project requires skills we either don't have or are not as comfortable with.

Determining what skills are at your disposal at the beginning of the process is helpful because: first, it may require we reorient the scope/focus of the project if we are conducting research alone or with similarly trained others and we are limited to those skills. Second, it brings into focus the skills we may need and helps us think through in the planning stage how we may go about acquiring them, with examples including bringing on collaborators or research assistants, investing in training for ourselves, hiring consultants, or bringing on external dissertation committee members with the requisite expertise. These are just some ways to bridge a skills gap, but the first step is figuring out what skills we have at our disposal for a given research project, either independently or as a team.

Money

Research requires financial resources: **money**. As a faculty member, some research I can do without money beyond my salary for my position, which in my case includes an expectation of research and scholarship. There are some components for which money and time are trade-offs. For example,

I can transcribe interviews myself if I have little or no funding. However, that may not be the best use of my time if I can secure funding to help. Other things that cost money can sometimes be resolved via "trade." For example, manuscript peer reviewers might request information about intercoder reliability as part of quality checks and assurance on content analysis projects that will require an additional coder. Trade is another way to save money. You can offer to code (or otherwise help) with someone else's project with the agreement that, in return, they help you by double-coding some of your documents or other content analysis materials or assist in some other way.

On the other hand, some things require money that cannot be replaced by time or trade, such as participant compensation for those of us conducting research with human subjects, or travel. Participant compensation will require you to secure funding alongside figuring out the conventions in your field, the requirements of any ethics committees (in the U.S., the Institutional Review Board [IRB] if you are working with human subjects), and your own values, priorities, and ethical commitments. (Participants are also referred to as respondents, subjects, and interlocutors—terms that are sometimes used interchangeably but may vary. For example, I use respondents or participants in my own research, but subject is often the descriptor in experimental research, while anthropologists are most likely to use the term interlocutor; in this book I use them interchangeably.) There is typically no adequate non-monetary substitute for compensating research participants, meaning money (often in the form of gift cards) must be considered. In my many conversations with researchers across rank, discipline, topic, and methodological approach, many argue that there are certain situations in which not compensating participants may make good sense. For example, in some types of evaluation research of a particular program or when interviewing elites, but this is something you will want to think carefully about and plan for.

Equipment and Tools

Another set of resources you want to consider is **equipment and tools**. They may include your personal/professional computer on which you work as well as software and data analysis programs and data storage (and backup; much more about this in Chapter 3). In the natural and physical sciences, you might have expensive microscopes or lasers, while, the fine arts may require advanced cameras or instruments; our equipment in the social sciences and humanities is typically more limited, but this is not always true (e.g., scanners, supercomputers, and so forth). Computers with ample storage are expensive. If doing interviews, you need a means of recording. Software often requires upgrades. Some lab equipment and tools require replenishing and upkeep. Similarly, you'll want to ensure that for collaborative projects, relevant team members have access to necessary **tools**, for example software (and the same version for everyone working with the data!). Overall, thinking carefully about the equipment (hardware, software, possible space) your project entails is important as you begin and manage it (more on this in Chapter 3).

Approval/Buy-In

Thinking about **approval or buy-in** as a resource in the planning stage may seem silly or premature. Why think about approval when you're still thinking through your research aims? And, after all, isn't research all about discovery? Nonetheless, I argue it is imperative to consider who possible gatekeepers, integral partners and stakeholders, and participants might be in the planning stage. These can range widely. For example, for many people conducting research involving collecting data from/with people in academia in the U.S., you will need IRB approval or at least review. If you work with non-human animals, you will likely need approval from an animal protection committee. You will want to factor that into your planning and perhaps even have preliminary conversations early on so that you can integrate that into your timeline. You may need space to store a particular piece of equipment at your workplace. Thinking about and having conversations with gatekeepers and other people whose buy-in you will need in the planning stage can save much time and frustration later. It will also help to consider possible contingency plans for approval/buy-in. While it is impossible to anticipate all the obstacles you may encounter, considering alternatives at the planning stage is a good start. We will discuss adjustment in more detail in Part III of this book.

I invite you to complete Worksheet 2.2 to take stock of what you have and could potentially commit to a project and what you anticipate the project needs. Some of these may be set; for example, the timeline for a project may be dictated by the supervisor at your research institute or organization. Alternatively, a budget might already be identified and externally mandated. In those cases, asking for additional resources or applying for a grant may still be possible, but some resources or parameters may already be decided.

Worksheet 2.2 Taking Stock of Resources for the Project Worksheet

TAKING STOCK

NOW, PUTTING ASIDE THE SPECIFIC TASKS, TRY TO ESIMATE THE TIME, SKILLS, MONEY, ETC. NEEDED FOR YOUR PROJECT COMPLETION. NOTE: ONE OF THESE MAY HAVE ALREADY BEEN DECIDED FOR YOU, FOR EXAMPLE, YOU MIGHT HAVE A SET BUDGET OR TIMELINE.

DIMENSION	NEED	HAVE
TIME	Maybe a year if I work for 10 hours/week in summer and 5/week in semester, with some breaks and leaving some wiggle room	No clear time limit on this, but I would like a paper to go out for review within 2 years from this data ideally, and to present at [conferences] in [year]
SKILLS	Programming into Qualtrics, data analysis, information on existing kindness survey questions	Have the technical skills, need to do reading and find existing surveys to adapt items from
MONEY	I want to spend about $1,200 since this is a preliminary survey	$5,000 in my research account
EQUIPMENT/ TOOLS	Qualtrics, Stata, maybe AtlasTI for open-ended	Have access to all, I will likely need to buy an updated Stata license if they move to the next version, but I have research funds for this
APPROVALS/ BUY-IN	IRB, talk to [mentor] about this as my next research focus	IRB, talk to [IRB committee member]

Below, I provide an example based on the same fictitious kindness survey discussed in Chapters 1 and 2. As you can see in terms of timeline, I'm anticipating how long ethics/IRB approval might take and how long field-ing the survey might take based on my experience. You may not have a very accurate sense, but it is better to estimate if you can; this is also a reminder to me to ask whatever survey firm I want to work with how long they think it will take to reach my desired number of responses.

Next, we want to categorize our **resources by task**. Worksheet 2.3 invites you to do so, and this exercise serves several purposes. First, it helps you align the resources with tasks, which might help you tweak or figure out whether other options are viable. Second, it helps ensure you are not missing any significant project components as related to necessary resources. Third, it enables you to understand what tasks are particularly resource-intensive and which require fewer resources. This lets you get an overview of the most time, skill, money, and other resource-intensive tasks and assess priorities and timing. In response to Worksheet 2.3, you may need to adjust your plan and tasks and figure out where and how to gain access to more resources required.

Piloting the Project

The importance of **piloting a project**, in my experience, cannot be over-stated. Piloting does several things for you and the project.

First, it allows you to establish **proof of concept**—that is, you were able to access the population/sample/group/location/information that you need to or get the data you need. This allows you to provide evidence that the project is viable and feasible. This is important for your own confidence and credibility as a researcher and scholar but also for granting agencies, dissertation or tenure committees, clients of your research firm, or other stakeholders. It indicates that you have done some preliminary work successfully. This helps establish your authority vis-à-vis those that provide resources and approvals, and strengthens your case.

Second, it lets you work out the kinks, speaking informally or in more formal terms, and **refine your research approach and instruments**. That is, piloting the project allows you to very clearly and in real time understand what is working, what's not working, whether the data you're getting is useful, and try some adjustments or tweaks and see if they work better. Again, this is important for planning because you might need to adjust the resources devoted to any particular task. Some examples of realizations researchers have had as the result of pilot projects are learning that you need to reorder interview questions or replace some, realizing you need a more powerful (e.g., higher-resolution, higher-capacity) equipment, or discovering the sample generated by a data collection firm is not representative.

Worksheet 2.3 Taking Stock of Resources by Tasks Worksheet

TAKING STOCK: TASKS

BELOW, FILL IN DIMENSIONS, BUILDING ON THE ABOVE FOR EACH OF THE TASKS YOU IDENTIFIED. THIS WILL HELP YOU ENVISION BOTH THE SPECIFICS AND THEIR RELATIONSHIP TO THE OVERALL PROJECT.

	TIME	SKILLS	MONEY	EQUIPMENT/ TOOLS	APPROVAL/ BUY-IN
OVERALL PROJECT	1.5 years	Stata, possibly Mplus, Qualtrics, might need to read more on survey building	$3,200	Computer, software	IRB, surveys, presentation and publication outlets
TASK 1: IRB application	6 hours	Have certification, can be PI	None	Have	IRB approval
TASK 2: Instrument development	16 weeks at 4 hours/ week for survey development	Need to consult [names]	None		
TASK 3: Data collection	8 weeks	Need [research firm]	$1,200	Have institutional access to Qualtrics, Google forms	Survey research firm
TASK 4: Data cleaning	12 weeks at 10 hours/ week for data analysis and first draft	Can do in Stata	None	Have	
TASK 5: Data analysis	12 weeks at 10 hours/ week for data analysis and first draft	Can do in Stata, might need to spend time refreshing memory of mPlus	None	Have, might need to talk to [name] about mPlus if needed	
TASK 6: Write paper(s) and presen- tations	12 weeks at 10 hours/ week for data analysis and first draft	Can do	$1,000 per presentation		Conference organizations, reviewers, editor

Third, piloting your research gives you a reasonably good (and often conservative, since it is the first time collecting that particular type of data in that specific context) **estimate of how long things take** and how demanding they are of resources, especially if the methodology is new to you. How long did ethics committee/IRB approval take? (And hopefully, having secured approval for pilot data will make it easier to gain approval in the future!) How long does transcribing an interview take you? Jotting down field notes? Cleaning data? The list goes on.

Fourth and again related to the first and second, collecting pilot data **allows you to back out of your project**. Sometimes, projects are not viable, or at least not possible in their original form. This requires entirely reworking the project (sample, type of data, or analysis plan) and rethinking the project or timeline. Encountering potential roadblocks and obstacles at the pilot data stage means you can back out of a project with less investment than starting a more extensive project, after devoting more time and effort in planning and preparation, only to have it fall apart.

I generally recommend following some variety of the 10% rule, depending on the circumstances and time commitment. So, for example, if you plan on conducting 20 in-depth interviews, pilot your instrument with two to four interviews. If you plan on insect sweeps in 20 agricultural plots, try a sample of one or two. The worksheets in Part I of the book discuss a preliminary survey with a sample size of 200 (some may consider this is a pilot if the plan is for a survey with a larger sample size in the future). But, if the research project for the moment is to do this preliminary survey with a sample size of 200, I would ask some friends or research assistants to take the survey online just to be sure the flow and formatting are good (that is, to vet the instrument) and send me any comments or issues they encountered before sending it out to my research sample, which may be considered a pilot with a convenience sample. Of course, this will vary for different disciplines and types of data, and some piloting may not be possible, for example, without a costly piece of equipment. But generally, this rule can work across different types of project contexts. Examples from other researchers include pre-testing a survey, even with a convenience sample, doing a short visit to a field site or archive, or something similar. This will, again, ensure that you can accurately budget time, money, and other vital resources you will need to consider for your more extensive project. Further, results from pilot studies may be publishable in themselves, especially for folks interested in measurement, which can result in standalone outputs.

Time-Charting

Piloting your project is an excellent way to learn how long things take you. If you can do any pilot research—whether data collection, cleaning, analysis, or some other aspect of your research—before planning the larger project, I recommend you do so. When charting a project's duration and tasks, Gantt charts are a popular tool. A **Gantt chart** (named after its creator, Henry L. Gantt) is a visualization tool popular in project management and grant applications. It presents work completed or planned over time. The vertical axis lists tasks, while the horizontal axis indicates time (often in months, but this can be in weeks, years, quarters, semesters, or any unit of measurement). It sometimes resembles a bar chart or can look more like a table. Gantt charts can be created in a variety of software programs. Below, I provide an example of a timeline for a project. I make my Gantt charts in Microsoft Word as a table by shading in particular cells (Figure 2.1A,

Figure 2.1A Example of a Gantt Chart in Table Form

	Summer 2020	Fall 2020	Spring 2021	Summer 2021	Fall 2021	Spring 2022
Preliminary survey development						
Interviewee recruitment						
Cognitive interviews						
Interview transcription						
Interview analysis						
Refine survey instrument						
Survey instrument pre-testing						
Survey pre-test analysis						
Finalize survey instrument						
Survey fielding						
Data cleaning and analysis						
Write-up results						
Presentation and dissemination						

charted by semester) or in Excel as a figure (Figure 2.1B, charted along months; this requires customization of data in a spreadsheet to make it into a figure/chart), though, of course, you could also create it in table form in a spreadsheet rather than a table in a document.

It is also helpful, at this stage, to think carefully about and build in or indicate milestones and deadlines. While some deadlines are flexible, others are harder and faster, especially if you are not entirely in charge of your research. For example, if you are a researcher working for someone else, you might need to deliver a certain number of interview transcripts within a particular time frame. Or you might have deadlines that funding agencies or clients dictate or ones that you decide on with an advisor. Clearly understanding milestones and deadlines, as appropriate, will allow you to diagnose and iterate, troubleshoot, and adjust accordingly (Chapters 7 and 8). You may want to build in external deadlines (e.g., a draft report or conference abstract) within the Gantt chart if they are known as a reminder to yourself and so that you can, at a glance, understand where you are in your timeline and what needs adjusting if and when the time comes.

Figure 2.1B Example of Gantt Chart in Bar Graph Form

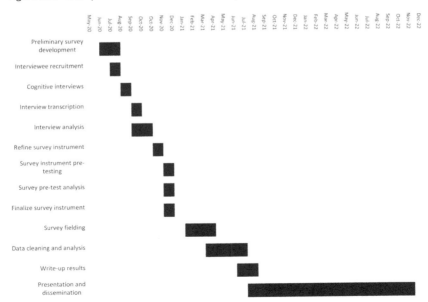

Building a Data Management Plan

In the previous worksheets on resources and tasks (Worksheets 2.2 and 2.3), you already began to think about your data collection, but data and its management require particular attention. A **data management plan (DMP)** is a formal plan that discusses how you will handle your data across your research project both during and after, including collection, storage, and sharing. Data management plans are often required by funding agencies and sometimes by ethics committees (e.g., IRB) and other regulatory bodies. While DMPs differ, they should all have several elements. While granting agencies often require these, they are helpful for you to have (and amend as needed) so you can think about your data as you plan your research. I find it helpful to create a DMP and revisit it regularly, and we'll discuss the issues of data sharing, reproducibility, and replication in additional detail in Chapter 9.

A DMP should have several core components: it should contain information about data collection and analysis, a description of the data, and information about how it will be stored, shared, and accessed. Figure 2.2 includes prompts to get you started working on your DMP for the various dimensions of data management.

Ethics and accountability in research are not limited to between-people relationships during the "doing" of the research (e.g., with research participants, archivists, or collaborators, clients), as discussed in Chapter 1. There is also the question of accountability to the broader research community. Data management plans prompt you to think about some of these issues carefully. Worksheet 2.4 invites you to answer the questions in the Figure 2.2 prompts to get you started on the road to developing your DMP. It should also prime you to think about your research project management system, tools, and workflow, as we will discuss in Chapters 3 and 4. At this point, you may not be sure about the answers to many questions, for example, what software you want to use, which we will discuss in the next chapter, Chapter 3. Nonetheless, I recommend you brainstorm to the best of your ability and make notes to yourself about things to return to as you make your way through the book. You should revise and revisit your DMP in the planning process and also consult it during and at the end of the project when the time for data sharing and longer-term data storage arises (Chapter 9).

Figure 2.2 Data Management Plan Prompts

Plan Element	Questions to Ask Yourself	Product
Data collection	What data do you plan to collect? How will the data be collected?	A clear and comprehensive description of the data to be collected, managed, and shared. This should take the form of a general overview of the types and amount of data.
Data analysis	How will you analyze the data? What tools will you use?	Information about what tools are needed to analyze the data, to allow others to use the data, and to support replication and reproducibility.
Data description	How will you ensure that the data can be interpreted, read, or used by others/in the future?	A description of the documentation related to the data needs to be constructed and provided: data formats, dictionaries and codebooks, and other data documentation, such as sampling.
Data storage	How will you store the data?	This will begin as a plan and timeline for data storage and access—including deciding where it will be stored, where it will be available and identifiable, and when and how it will be made available to other users.
Data access	How will you manage access to the data?	Describe what (if any) data you intend to share and how you will deal with privacy, security, informed consent, and other ethical concerns that might affect access or distribution.
Data management and sharing	How will you share the data? Are there data that you will not share? How will you handle ethical/legal issues and implications of your data? Do you have IRB approval to share? Will access be restricted? Is there an embargo on data before you share it? If so, for how long?	In addition to the question of access, this will require information about how the plan will be monitored.

Worksheet 2.4 Management Worksheet

DATA MANAGEMENT

DRAWING ON THE TEMPLATE PROVIDED IN THE CHAPTER, ANSWER THE QUESTIONS FOR EACH PLAN ELEMENT BELOW.

ELEMENT	PLANS
DATA COLLECTION	Survey data from about 200 respondents. They survey will include open-ended short answer questions, socio-demographic characteristics (age, race, gender, etc.). and information about how respondents define kindness and what acts they consider kind.
DATA ANALYSIS	Data will be analyzed using Stata, descriptive and inferential statistics. Significance tests and regression models.
DATA DESCRIPTION	A codebook will be created for a cleaned version of the data, and a replication package for any data that will be presented/published will be generated.
DATA STORAGE	The data will be stored in Dropbox folder, in a password-protected account on a password-protected computer.
DATA ACCESS	Access to the data, at this stage, will only be available to the principal investigator.
DATA MANAGEMENT AND SHARING	A limited dataset that includes variables used in any publications will be shared with corresponding analysis files upon request.

Pre-registration

Pre-registration has become increasingly popular in the natural and social sciences. Pre-registration is the process of publicly indicating your hypotheses or expectations and expected results before data analysis. That is, sharing a pre-analysis plan. The idea underpinning the practice is that hypotheses should be decided before data collection and that pre-registration of research can reduce the practice of "p-hacking" in quantitative analyses: running lots of tests and models until you find something statistically significant to publish. Some disciplines and their national associations (i.e., economics and the American Economics Association [AEA]; psychology and the American Psychological Association [APA]) strongly promote pre-registration alongside some journals that encourage it (Munro and Prendergast 2019; The Journal of Politics 2023). Pre-registration is argued to improve the quality and transparency of research (Nosek et al. 2018), though there are debates about whether and how its utility for experimental research extends to observational studies (Coffman and Niederle 2015; Dal-Ré et al. 2014).

You will want to determine your discipline's research conventions and field/area. You can do this by examining your professional association's website and having conversations with advisors, supervisors, colleagues, mentors, and peers. You can also review submission guidelines in leading journals in your field and other venues (e.g., conference proceedings) where you hope or plan to publish or share your work. Appendix A contains some information on where you can pre-register your studies.

Measure Twice, Cut Once

The importance of planning can't be understated. When possible, it's much better to catch any issues or errors at the planning stage. If you, like me, become very excited about your research and are eager to get started, it's sometimes hard to make yourself stop and plan carefully. However, as we learn in our methods classes, even the fanciest methods cannot correct for insufficient or poor-quality data. To borrow the analogy from carpentry, all this is to say, measure twice so that you only have to cut once. If you mismeasure, you must cut a second time and possibly use a second piece of wood to achieve the desired outcome. For example, if you don't double-check and proofread your survey more than once, you may accidentally omit an important answer option to a critical question in the survey (you mismeasured and miscut). Then, you might need to pay for a new sample to re-field the survey (a new piece of wood, so the metaphor goes). This is much more costly than measuring carefully and double-checking before cutting your wood or starting your research.

Works Cited

Boice, Robert. 1990. *Professors as Writers: A Self-Help Guide to Productive Writing*. Vol. 190. Stillwater, OK: New Forums Press.

Coffman, Lucas C., and Muriel Niederle. 2015. "Pre-Analysis Plans Have Limited Upside, Especially Where Replications Are Feasible." *Journal of Economic Perspectives* 29(3):81–98.

Dal-Ré, Rafael, John P. Ioannidis, Michael B. Bracken, Patricia A. Buffler, An-Wen Chan, Eduardo L. Franco, Carlo La Vecchia, and Elisabete Weiderpass. 2014. "Making Prospective Registration of Observational Research a Reality." *Science Translational Medicine* 6(224):1–4.

Munro, Kevin J., and Garreth Prendergast. 2019. "Encouraging Pre-Registration of Research Studies." *International Journal of Audiology* 58(3):123–24. doi: 10.1080/14992027.2019.1574405.

Nosek, Brian A., Charles R. Ebersole, Alexander C. DeHaven, and David T. Mellor. 2018. "The Preregistration Revolution." *Proceedings of the National Academy of Sciences* 115(11):2600–606.

Redelfs, Alisha H., Juan Aguilera, and Sarah L. Ruiz. 2019. "Practical Strategies to Improve Your Writing: Lessons Learned from Public Health Practitioners Participating in a Writing Group." *Health Promotion Practice* 20(3):333–37.

Rud, Laura Girardeau, and Michael Trevisan. 2014. "Jumpstarting Junior Faculty Motivation and Performance with Focused Writing Retreats." *The Journal of Faculty Development* 28(1):33–40.

The Journal of Politics. 2023. "The Journal of Politics: Pre-Registration Guidelines." *The Journal of Politics*. Retrieved August 4, 2023 (www.journals.uchicago.edu/journals/jop/pre-registration?doi=10.1086%2Fjop&publicationCode=jop).

CHAPTER 3

Systems and Tools

The third core part of planning after selecting a design and goal (Chapter 1) and taking stock of your resources (Chapter 2) is selecting your tools and developing your research project management system. At its best, research project management is a framework for organizing your research projects. This chapter will help you build your system or framework and consider the necessary tools to conduct and manage your research. Now that you've thought about your available and required resources as well as the scope of your project, it's time to plan in detail for the "doing" or execution, which will comprise the Part II of the book. Expertise in tools (e.g., software programs, equipment) can be classified as a skill and should be counted among your resources, but you can also learn how to use new tools. As you venture into new research areas and projects, you will likely need to update your toolbox over time. The tools may also change, including discontinuation or updated capabilities or new functions requiring adaptation. This chapter outlines the distinction between systems and tools and guides you in selecting your tools and conceptualizing your system.

What Is a System?

A **system** is a set of relationships among tools, actions, and plans essential to effective project management and organization. A system organizes (systematizes) information, data, and activity (analysis). You will likely have systems within systems (e.g., a coding system within a broader system to analyze qualitative data), which must be organized. You can also have overlapping systems—for example, an overall system for email (both personal and professional) that overlaps with your project management system inasmuch as you are communicating with participants, supervisors, administrators, granting agencies, or collaborators over email but you may also email with your students, doctors, and family over the same medium. As another example, the storage location of your research files (e.g., computer, desktop, the cloud, in paper folders in a filing cabinet) may also likely include materials for other aspects of your life (e.g., tax documents, photos), for which you might have a different categorization and system.

The most important thing about a system is that it *works for you*.

Your system needs to be reliable, legible, and efficient: that is, you should be able to quickly find what you need consistently—**reliability**—and easily, without stress—**efficiency**. Your system should allow you to organize information in a way that makes it understandable to you and those you are accountable to (perhaps journals, for replication or reproducibility, or co-authors)—**legibility**. In my experience, your system will require trial and error and will need to be updated occasionally to accommodate new tools, actions, demands as well as changing preferences and other developments.

Your system should allow you to find things you need in shorthand and dictate the relationship between things—like a map showing location and distance. However, your research project management system is not the research, just as the map is not the territory or landscape, simply a scaled representation of it. If you include all the research details in your research log, it is not a log but the work itself, a bit like drawing a map in real scale—of little use!

The following chapters will tackle the "execution" phase of research. Workflow is an integral part of your system (Chapter 4), as are bookkeeping (Chapter 5) and managing people (Chapter 6). In this chapter, we'll work to help you select your tools and develop your system and the components and relationships therein.

Systems and Tools

Tools are part of the system, like people, actions, or documents, but they are not synonymous with the system. Tools range from specific to general (a digital calendar app, a paper planner, a piece of paper, a set of sticky notes, writing on your hand—each can be, and for me sometimes are, tools to manage your weekly calendar) but also from simple to complex (Notepad, Microsoft Word, or LaTeX for writing) in terms of their capabilities. Tools are technologies (in the broad sense) that allow you to accomplish goals, as compared with a system that manages tools and is more meta-organizational.

Systems can work with different tools (Manaher 2023; Trentman 2021) and manage the relationships between various components of the system, including tools for research that aid in data collection, analysis, and other research tasks.

Tools should be responsive to your demands: different tools can produce particular types of outputs, but they respond to the user/manager/programmer. In our profoundly digital reality, it is essential to remember that tools, like objects, have particular affordances, the possibilities of actions allowed by tools' specific properties or features. That is, an affordance is a feature of the relationship between the user and the object rather than solely a property of the thing itself. Most simply, we can say that a chair affords sitting (Bloomfield, Latham, and Vurdubakis 2010) or an elevator button affords pressing (Interaction Design Foundation 2022). But a chair can also afford laying the next day's clothes (or last week's clothes) on. Similarly, tools have particular functionalities; some are obvious to a general user, while others require some "digging" or training to discover. For example, qualitative coding software may allow you to create codes via centrally located buttons, but the capability to connect the codes across documents may be hidden in a sub-menu.

Several factors may limit the tools available to us, such as our operating system (some tools are only available on some platforms), budgets (some are more expensive, others free), or our institutions (some institutions limit which software can be used on their servers, by their employees, or may subsidize or freely provide other software). Furthermore, tools may change in that they add, subtract, or alter features in ways that work better or equally well for us or render them less useful for our purposes. For example, a writing tool may remove integration with citation management software. If you have a clear sense of your goals and what you wish to accomplish— underscoring the importance of planning!—it will be easier to adapt and decide whether you need to change the tool, whether it can still perform the necessary functions you need, or whether it might need to be supplemented or its use amended to make it work for your goals and system.

The Difference between Systems and Tools

Understanding the differences between systems and tools is critical to effective project management. You can change tools without changing your system, just as you can change the order of actions or timing in a system without losing the overall system. For example, as we'll discuss in the context of communication in Chapter 7, you can decide if you need to check in with yourself and any collaborators or research assistants about project progress weekly, bimonthly, monthly, annually, or at some other interval. However, checking in and accountability remain part of your system regardless of changes in frequency. Similarly, when writing, you can use Microsoft Word, Google Docs, a sticky note, napkin, or notebook, and so forth. These are tools, but writing is the action; a system is how you put that writing and the tool used for writing into conversation with other information—how you name, store, and organize it so that it is accessible and legible to you and others working on a project, how your writing tool works with a citation management system, and so forth.

Much like "seeing like a state" (Scott 1998), seeing like a manager of your research project requires systemization and standardization to make information legible and enable a comprehensive view. Scott argues that seeing like a state makes things uniform in ways that may stifle uniqueness, promote conformity, and privilege a "top-down" and "bird's-eye" view. Similarly, many of us believe that research—as a creative, emergent process—cannot, and perhaps should not, be carefully organized. After all, so many unexpected events and insights occur, and organization may hamper creativity. Scott argues that winding roads and non-systematized names and identifiers for people, as a couple of examples, have historically been legible to people living in such communities and, therefore, are not less "effective" for locals than standardized systems, for example generational surnames and streets on a grid. This is true: states need to control, but so do research managers to a certain extent. To take the analogy further, reproducibility and sharing data and analysis (see the discussion of pre-registration and research management plans in Chapter 2 and dissemination and data sharing in Chapter 9) require it to be legible not only to you. Again, however, the level of "gridiness" rather than "windy roadiness" of your system will depend on your style (Part IV and, in particular, Chapter 10), the nature, scope and design of your project (Part I, in particular Chapter 1), the resources and tools available to you (Chapter 2), and demands of your discipline, gatekeepers, and more. But, whatever your system, it needs to be, at the very at least, easily accessible and understandable to you.

Your "products" and creations do not need to be uniform (think field notes and sketches and brainstorming documents), but they should be organized (labeled, and metadata about them produced) in a way that makes them accessible and legible to you over time and across different tools. Importantly, standardization does not mean that they need to be legible to anyone and everyone. But if you are working on large-scale projects with collaborators and employees, they should be legible to those people at least. Your research project management system needs to be accessible and readable to you in a way that reduces stress and diminishes the probability of mistakes and loss of information.

Your system helps you coordinate the relationship between tools, actions, products, outcomes, and timelines and keeps the project moving; the tools constitute and support that system. With no underlying system, the tool doesn't necessarily work as part of a broader framework or serve any particular goal. For example, using quantitative software to analyze data is a good tool application. Still, it leads nowhere without information on which models to run, which, in turn, should be informed by methodological literature and the broader research project with research questions, goal, directions, and so forth.

Conversations with researchers and my own experience suggest that people often confuse systems and tools; so many of our tools are powerful and used so often that we confuse them for systems and treat them as such. This may be limiting. Tools have particular affordances and capabilities that may direct some of our work; we need a system to guide their use and control their inputs (e.g., survey data, to keep with the example of quantitative data analysis), outputs (e.g., statistical model results), and their relationship with overall project goals and desired outputs and outcomes. This is what effective research project management does: create a system that draws on tools and subsystems to organize and coordinate action to reach goals.

What Kind of Tools Should I Use?

The tools you need depend on your goals and tasks. Broadly, we typically need several types of research tools: first, for data collection and analysis and storage; second, for writing, perhaps presentation, and dissemination; third, for communication (whether it be with colleagues, granters, participants, or others); and, fourth, for administration (such as research logs or budgets). In subsequent chapters, I focus on workflow and building your system. This chapter introduces advice and considerations to aid you in selecting your tools.

A list of tools is included in Appendix B. Notably, the tools discussed in this chapter are not exhaustive. You may require others for your specific needs (e.g., security tools or lab equipment). To inform your tool selection, it's crucial to determine what resources you have and need (Chapter 2) and your project goals, scope, and design (Chapter 1). Finding the correct tools might require some research and conversations, especially for some kinds of (disciplinary, sub-area, or specialty) analyses and data. Some methodological traditions and disciplines have specialized tools that are not widely known but that you have hopefully encountered or will be introduced to via course-work, conversations, reading published work in your sub-field, and attending conferences or other professional development events.

At this stage, take some time to brainstorm your **tasks and priorities** in Worksheet 3.1. As a reminder, all the worksheets in the book are available for download at the book's companion website. The versions in the book are intended to provide you with an example rather than an exemplar, and if it is unhelpful or irrelevant to you feel free to ignore it—just go straight to filling out your own! Base your tasks on the worksheets you completed in Chapter 1 and take a moment to brainstorm the priorities for tools for each task, which may include any number of considerations, such as the follow-ing: do you already know how to use a particular software? Does the task require collaboration? Do you know if your collaborators have access to it?

Selection Considerations

Selecting your tools relies on several considerations. Before beginning, espe-cially if you work for an organization that limits the software you can use for collaborative or privacy or other reasons (this includes many corpora-tions but also some educational institutions, government agencies, and non-profits), you may want to request a list of software that the organization allows or if there are any limitations on software use. In academic settings, many universities provide either free or subsidized access to some tools, though you are often free to use and purchase others if you choose.

Your **goals should help you select your tools**. In many cases, your train-ing and skills may decide your tool. If you need to switch tools or are at the beginning of your research career, your goals should guide those decisions. When you develop your project management style and system, that too will help guide your tool choice. Further, tools may be chosen for us—for example, the email platform our work uses or software that is available via institutional subscription. I use Stata for statistical analysis; if Stata were not available for me via my institution and I lacked research funds to purchase it, I might consider switching to a tool that was available. Further, some researchers prioritize consistency, and if they're in positions that include both teaching and research, like to work and teach in the same software, and may be willing to switch and work on their research in the program their

Worksheet 3.1 *Tasks and Priorities Worksheet*

TASKS AND TOOL PRIORITIES

RESEARCH PLAN TASKS AND TOOL PRIORITIES

BELOW, LIST YOUR PRIMARY TASKS AS OUTLINED IN CHAPTER 1 (E.G., DATA COLLECTION, OR MORE SPECIFICALLY SURVEY DATA COLLECTION, ETC). AND THEN LIST THE PRIORITIES FOR THAT TASK (E.G., INTUITIVE, EXPORTABLE TO EXCEL, ETC).

TASK	PRIORITIES
IRB application	Need a full survey written that I can share with IRB, they can approve on Qualtrics or, if needed, as a document
Instrument development	Ideally something shareable with respondents so that I don't have to copy it elsewhere increasing the probability of errors, also something that can transfer results into at least Excel
Data collection	Online availability with a shareable link, needs to not collect individually identifying data (IRB), can I find a firm that works with Qualtrics interface even if not Qualtrics itself re above? I want data output in Excel or Stata
Data cleaning	Something that allows me to clearly rename and label variables, something that can import from Excel and export back out, something that allows me a script file for reproducibility
Data analysis	Allows me to do regressions, possible latent models
Write paper(s) and presentations	Allows headers, sharing, track changes of editing, work across several computers

department mandates for teaching to maintain consistency and facilitate student collaboration. Importantly, your system should *help* you select tools but not necessarily dictate them. For example, if your system involves to-do lists, you can use a notebook, Word document, email, calendar, or some other tool. As another example of goals determining tools, if you need multiple eyes on a collaborative group to-do list where not everyone is local, it will likely make sense to choose a shareable place (rather than, for example, a single physical notebook).

There are benefits and drawbacks to each choice in how to organize information, and we are often faced with particular types of decisions: spreadsheets versus documents, by hand or on a computer, local versus cloud storage. Appendix B offers you a non-exhaustive list of tools but does not discuss each of them in detail—remember, this book is not a product catalog (see the Introduction). This is partly because tools change (sometimes quickly) but also because preferred tools vary by discipline, organizations, research goals, and more. As a contemporary example, nearly no one in academia knew what Zoom was or used it regularly before COVID-19 and now it is ubiquitous. This chapter and Appendix B are presented as a starting point and an invitation for you to do some research, have conversations, and figure out what you want from tools and then select them. Sometimes, you cannot select your tools (e.g., your institutional or organizational email program). However, even in those cases you can often save emails and store them elsewhere (as discussed in Chapters 4 and 5).

Writing with Pen and Paper versus Digitally

Generally, you should digitize any non-disposable writing and figure out how to store it so you can find it later, even if you prefer to primarily work with pen and paper. As we discuss in Chapter 4, to-do lists may be disposable to you once they are complete, so you may not want to digitize those. However, most of the writing we do is non-disposable, and we often want to refer to it months or years later, whether this writing contains ideas we brainstormed or write-ups of results, so I recommend you digitize it so it remains accessible and so it can "live" alongside other project materials.

Beyond digitizing writing to preserve it, some tools (tablets such as reMarkable, see Appendix B, or other programs available on computers and tablets) allow you to handwrite and recognize text. The benefits of digitizing writing so that the text is recognizable (whether you convert handwritten notes into typed ones, take notes in a Word document, or use a tool that digitizes your handwriting) is that it is **searchable**. This should allow you to find what you need easily within the text (though the question of locating where that text or document might be is a separate question we'll get to when discussing naming conventions and research logs later this chapter!).

Document versus Spreadsheet

Another decision we are often faced with is whether to use a spreadsheet or document to store information. For numeric information, spreadsheets or matrices are often the intuitive choice. But for other information that needs indexing, the decision is not so clear.

The primary benefit of spreadsheets is that they are easily **sortable**. They make it easy to sort by date, length, cost, ID number, or any other variable or attribute. On the other hand, the primary benefit of documents is that it is easier to see and organize longer swathes of text. Therefore, if I need something sortable and want to see it at a "snapshot," I typically use a spreadsheet, for example for metadata on interviews, expenditures, and administrative data (see Chapter 5). On the other hand, when I need to include additional details and account for less clear-cut characteristics, I will use a document, such as for brainstorming, research logs, or communication. Furthermore, I like to make my to-do lists in a document (pen and paper or Google Doc); this is not because they are particularly long or detailed but because documents allow certain features—different levels of headers, checkboxes—and these are instances where I don't need to manipulate the stored information extensively, just check it off.

Local versus Cloud Storage

You'll also need to decide how and where to store your digital information (that is, you can't store specimens digitally, but you can store photos or information from or about them digitally). Local digital storage is physically in your possession—whether it be in the computer or in an external hard drive or thumb drive, which makes it more secure in some ways, and it is not subject to the whims of a corporation providing cloud storage. On the other hand, local storage is vulnerable to hardware glitches, loss, and physical destruction in a way that cloud storage is not. Cloud storage allows simultaneous access across machines and to collaborators or others across time and space, which may facilitate collaboration and sharing of data. However, it also costs money, and the price may change. You might also be limited by what data privacy demands (e.g., IRB or Health Insurance Portability and Accountability Act [HIPAA] guidelines for research with human subjects or health data) allow, or cost. Again, you will want to think about your priorities and goals when deciding what and whether to store locally versus in cloud storage.

How Do I Choose Tools?

In short, tools should be chosen to *work for your goals*. Tools should be able to *work as part of your system*—alongside other tools—and, ideally, should be intuitive and pleasant to use. Unfortunately, the latter is not always possible given the sometimes limited universe of tools often required for our specialized research and work.

Generally, if you are not using your tool very much and finding ways around it, it is clearly not working for you—whether that is because it does not have the technical capabilities that you need, it is glitchy and/or unreliable, or you just don't like to use it and therefore won't. As one example, I bought a pen that used special paper that could digitize my writing as I wrote; the pen could also record audio during interviews as I took notes and sync them with timestamps. However, I hated writing with the pen, even though it had many features that I needed and wanted, so I never used it beyond that first time. While nothing was wrong with the tool per se, it was not working for me.

A necessary condition of a tool being good *for you* is your willingness to use it. That is not a sufficient condition, of course; just because you're willing to use a tool does not mean that it will yield information or products that are useful, but a tool simply won't work if you won't use it. An example from another researcher: they bought a tablet for reading and had hoped to be rid of their reliance on paper and pencil. However, they ended up not using it—they simply found they could not do their "thinking while reading" in the form of margin notes on electronic articles in the same way they did with paper and pen. While more environmentally costly, they printed articles and scanned them after annotating them—using their printer and pen as tools and the scanner as a third—to re-digitize them. Of course, if they had been willing to use the tablet, it could have saved the printing and rescanning, just annotating in Adobe PDF or another program, but that didn't work for them. That's OK; it's essential to know yourself (Chapter 10), which should not dissuade you from trying new things, but it's also OK to stick with what works for you.

Your research projects will likely require a multi-pronged and multi-tool approach. It helps to think about the different functions your project and system need. For most projects, researchers will need tools for the following activities: writing, reading, brainstorming, project management and organization, and data collection and analysis.

Below, I provide some principles for your consideration and adaptation for tool selection across the main components of the research process. As we learned with the pandemic, the tools we rely on may change quickly, so I do not discuss particular software programs per se. However, we know that the devil is in the details when selecting an appropriate program; each has its own pros and cons. Appendix B contains a list of some possible programs and technologies. It includes many of the tools we use for data analysis, storage, and management but also tools for communication and project management. However, the list is not exhaustive, and these tools may change quickly and no longer meet your purposes. For example, I was an avid Twitter user (I left before it became X) and got a lot of professional information from it, including about new publications, debates among researchers in my discipline, and information about pre-prints and presentations. Therefore, while it was not part of my research project management system, it was an important professional tool to aid in keeping updated on happenings and debates in my field. X no longer allows me to do that, and so I use other tools (RSS feeds and listservs, while other researchers have reported becoming active on Mastodon or Threads). Remember that the tools are not the system but instead work in service of your system and goals.

The following considerations should be relevant for those doing a wide variety of work across disciplines or areas—for writing, reference management, and project management. For particular actions or tasks, the tools you have been trained in or what your outputs demand (e.g., a journal may require article submission in Word or LaTeX) will help determine what you use. In addition, your decisions may be guided by the limits your employer sets, price, what your institution provides you free, or what your collaborators and colleagues have expertise in and/or are willing to use.

Writing and Focus

Deciding on your writing tool(s) is typically a two-step decision (as are many of these): first, will you use pen and paper, a program (e.g., Google Docs, Microsoft Word), or a combination of both? The most important concern if you use both and/or more than one software is how you will keep track of what you do in each.

Many different tools are available. I rely on pen and paper, Google Docs, and Microsoft Word for different types of writing. I like to use Google Docs for to-do lists and planning (it has handy checkboxes) and it allows for collaboration in real time and "thinking together" in written form (e.g., note-taking during meetings). You may also want to think about tools for "focus" (which is often discussed in the context of time management and finding time to write). I use a timer to write and the Pomodoro method (Collins 2023) of writing in intervals with breaks; each Pomodoro is then 30 minutes—25 minutes of work, and a five minute break. After four Pomodoros (or poms) you take a longer break, often 15 minutes, and then repeat as you are able given the time you have. I use an online timer but have recently bought a 30-minute hourglass with bright pink sand that I am enjoying using; another scholar I know uses a kitchen timer (a tomato, which is what the word "Pomodoro" means in Italian, and a tomato-shaped timer was the inspiration for the method), while another uses their phone. Mac users I know (I'm a staunch PC) like Flow, which is limited to Mac users (these tools are listed in Appendix B). For limiting distractions, one scholar I know uses a dedicated program—RescueTime—to manage their computer and writing time and to gather information on how long tasks take (time tracking; more on this in Chapter 11). Yet another scholar I know turns off their internet while writing, and another uses Freedom to limit apps and internet distractions.

I like to do my research writing (as compared with meeting minutes, which I do in Google Docs) in Microsoft Word. Partly this is because this is what I am used to, but I stick with it because it works for me and is readily available. I particularly like using the "Navigation Pane" feature to have outlines I can see as I'm writing that can help me navigate different sections on the document (Google Docs offers a similar capability); I develop my own "Styles" for headers and, overall, find Word the easiest to work with. Other researchers I know are LaTeX devotees, using editors or "wrappers" such as Overleaf. This is particularly true of researchers I know working with lots of equations or images, such as my mathematics colleagues. Your tool choice will likely depend on how much effort you need to expend to learn it versus how much utility it adds.

Pen and paper are very effective for brainstorming, writing, and making lists. However, paper has a tendency to get lost or misplaced (or have coffee spilled on it or have kittens you are fostering nibble on it—I speak from experience on both counts), so you'll likely want to create a digital copy or a physical system (e.g., a folder or filing cabinet) to keep track of necessary paperwork (e.g., decisions about models, idea brainstorms, outlines, or even full drafts if you like to write them with pen and paper). Furthermore, personally, my handwriting is hard for even me to read, so I convert it into digitized text—at least, the things I need to keep track of (not the doodling or smaller to-do lists!). Any project notes that have to do with decisions about data analysis need to be centralized. My recommendation is to do so in a research log. That log, which I keep in a Word document, and its contents, is further described in Chapter 4.

As another illustration of picking the wrong tool for me (in addition to the digital pen): I got very excited about Scrivener. Scrivener can break your writing into chunks that can be moved around, you can store images on it, and there are outline and notes functions. I immediately downloaded and bought it after hearing about an author using it on a podcast. It turns out this is not the right program for me. It seemed perfect for how I think and write, drawing on diverse ideas and documents and moving arguments and points around. Despite watching a tutorial on how to use it and giving it a good-faith effort for two weeks, I never got used to it. In addition to the usability barrier for me, syncing it with citation management software is more challenging than Microsoft Word. Yet, if I found Scrivener easier to write with, I would have probably written there and then added citations afterwards or worked harder to figure out how to sync it with Zotero (my reference manager of choice, described below). Unlike situations in which a program might be the only one that can do the particular job you need (e.g., a particular type of visualization only a specific package in R can do), I can and do write elsewhere.

Considerations and recommendation: Where and how can you write in a way that makes sense for you, and what tools might suit your different writing needs? How can you keep your writing safe and organized? This should help you determine what needs to be saved versus what is disposable (to-do lists may be disposable while article drafts need to be saved). Relatedly, what do you need to work and write effectively? Would you benefit from a dedicated program to limit distractions?

Reference Management and Reading

I strongly recommend that you work with a reference management program. This is particularly important in the age of inter- and multi-disciplinarity—using a reference management program means I can convert the citation style from MLA to Chicago to ASA in seconds, depending on the target journal or preferences of conference organizers. Note that you will still need to review those citations (or have a copyeditor do so), as these programs are wonderful but imperfect.

You will want to decide where and how your notes and readings will be filed (I describe my folder and project structure in Chapter 4). Many reference management programs also allow you to take notes on each citation and link to the reference itself, which is an excellent way to manage your reading notes (I use Zotero, and Appendix B lists additional options; further, more specialized citation tools exist, such as Juris-M, for legal and multilingual citations, Obsidian, Zettlr, and JabRef). But some of my colleagues have shared that Zotero does not work for many history scholars, for example, who find that it does not accommodate primary sources that require including information about both the archive and collection.

Some researchers I know prefer annotating more extensively within the reading in Adobe Acrobat or another program, though this can be linked in Zotero as well. In contrast, others may like to keep their notes in a document dedicated to readings specific to any one project. Just be aware that such a file may become unwieldy; the benefit of centralizing this in a reference manager is that you can copy or draw on readings from one project for another without difficulty locating the notes on that piece in a previous project.

To keep up with what to read, I utilize an RSS feeder to receive tables of contents from journals in my area (I use Feedly; RIP Google Reader, which I used for many years). Other scholars I know use various sites (one researcher friend calls this "social media for academics"), including Google Scholar, ResearchGate, and academia.edu to keep updated on new papers. These sites highlight papers that may interest you, and you can save and "follow" articles and authors. They can provide alerts or information on when authors of articles you have read publish something new and papers that may be similar to others you read. Google Scholar allows you to set an alert for specific researchers (including yourself!) or specific topics (e.g., "sociology of science"). Some programs can create a map of relevant literature, finding connections via citations and other strategies for you (see Appendix B). These may be especially useful as an exploratory tool if you are engaging in a new area of research.

Considerations and recommendation: Invest time in selecting and learning a reference management program if it can accommodate your sources, unless you're really committed to writing out your references by hand (and I know some people are! Again, a tool is only useful if you are willing to use it). Many citation management programs will also allow you to store your notes alongside the reading, which helps to organize reading notes in a centralized way. A citation management program will enable you to transform your citation style within minutes for resubmission or if you change your mind on venue.

Communication and Brainstorming

I primarily rely on email for communication, although I use Slack for projects where the group requests it and Google chat for brief discussions with some collaborators, not to mention texts and phone calls. I primarily use pen and paper for brainstorming but have also increasingly turned to Scrapple or LucidChart to map out my ideas (some additional programs are listed in Appendix B). One researcher I know has a large chalkboard, another a whiteboard, and a third uses an elaborate system of sticky notes on a wall that they move around to brainstorm. For communication, I often find nothing like a face-to-face meeting or a phone chat (I personally don't prefer videoconferencing to a plain old phone call but others love it) to talk through an idea with a collaborator or mentor or work through a particularly sticky (research) wicket.

I primarily use Gmail to communicate, and my advice is to have three email accounts to start, though you might want a separate, dedicated email account for a large project, and so forth. Your employer may also have its own communication software that it mandates employees communicate on. In terms of email (more on how I manage email in Chapter 11), first, I have a personal account (for friends, family, online shopping, library card, insurance). Second, I have my institutional or organizational account (and you may have more than one if you work for several institutions) with my .edu ending, which I use to communicate with students and institutional colleagues (mine is in Gmail, but my previous institution had Outlook; this is one of the things you cannot typically control). Third, a key part of my research project management system is a non-institutional professional account (mine is shirinoyphd [at] gmail [dot] com; feel free to email me to tell me about your experience with this book and research project management!). After moving institutions, I began relying on that account in earnest when I realized I had lost some communication along with my previous email. When moving, it was hard for me to figure out what needed to be transferred, and I didn't have time to do it all given the demands on my time while handling my move, work, and life. This email is the address I use for manuscript reviews and submissions, and to correspond with collaborators on research projects. Despite having to do some things on my institutional email, such as for IRB or budgeting reasons, if I am able, I CC myself on my professional email (e.g., not when corresponding with participants—for privacy reasons, as my institutional email has additional security built in—but when I'm paying for transcription, for example, so I have the receipt and record on an email account that I control, rather than one that my institution owns).

I also use the Gmail tasks pane for some information I need handy, for example, my university ID number. I have a Google document with a weekly plan—my to-do list by week that I organize Friday afternoon for the following workweek, and another with a strategic/semester-long plan that I create each semester organized by week, a practice I learned from the National Center for Faculty Diversity and Development (NCFDD 2022), and that I describe in additional detail in Chapter 4. Those are my personal lists, although, as described below, many project management software will allow you to share to-do lists.

To organize my emails, I use the tagging feature in Gmail and the archive function. My tags are by project and not further subdivided. That is, I don't have tags like financial or drafts within projects, but these would be appropriate for those managing very large projects or those handling large volumes of project-related email. Like the naming conventions I describe in my workflow (Chapter 4), this reduces my decision fatigue and cognitive burden. Every email gets read and dealt with immediately and only emails that require action live in my inbox—I archive it if I don't need to take action, for example, some announcement that doesn't pertain to me or information I've read and don't need anymore; if it's an event I want to attend, I put it in my calendar and then archive the email; if it requires a response, I either respond to it immediately or leave it in my inbox until I do or calendar it (Gmail calls this "snooze") for a later date if I plan to reply in a few days or a week. My email system means that I am not met with hundreds or thousands of unread or read emails every time I open it and that anything actionable is top of mind. This aversion to having many emails in my inbox encourages me to unsubscribe from listservs I don't use and create Gmail "filters" to sort emails (e.g., I can automatically send emails containing any word or from any person to another folder—more on how I manage my email in Chapter 11).

Considerations and recommendation: In cases where you have choices, communication decisions need to consider scale. You may need a program that allows group communications or opt to communicate on an editable document or over email. It depends on what function the communication serves. Regardless of how you think about communication, you will almost surely be forced to engage with email. I recommend a professional email not tied to your organization where your professional accounts and communication are routed (with authors, vendors, journals, and beyond).

Tools for Project Management

I do not use dedicated project management software for managing my research, primarily because I've found that a combination of tools I like and am comfortable with—Microsoft Word, pen and paper, Google Docs, Gmail tasks—accomplish what I want to do without a separate platform. Furthermore, for collaborative projects to be effective, everyone needs to be on board with a shared platform (which sometimes requires payment).

However, many researchers I know use Trello, Asana, or Monday to manage their own tasks or to-do lists, and you may find that you also like these tools, even if you are not using them to manage other people but only to organize your own work, or not even limiting their use to research management but rather for "life" management. That is, some people who use them report they use it to organize their home and family tasks, not just work or research tasks. If you are interested in a program with project management capabilities, take a few minutes to visit the websites in Appendix B to get a sense of what they do. If you are managing a large team—research assistants, a lab, a research group—where you can require that people use this software, many have found a dedicated platform to be an excellent central location to facilitate brainstorming, task assignments, timelines, communication, and more. However, each program has specific pros and cons, and you certainly don't need one to manage your research (Alston 2023). After reading the next chapters (Part II, Chapters 4, 5, and 6) and figuring out your system, you will likely want to revisit whether such centralized project management and organization tools serve your purposes, goals, and system.

Considerations and recommendation: Your decision(s) should be guided by how much you like having everything in a centralized platform, first and foremost. Another important consideration is how many moving parts—primarily people—are in your project that need coordination that might make a centralized software desirable, and can you get everyone on board with using it? If you have many people to coordinate you may be more motivated to use a project management program, but whether it is worth the cost and learning curve and whether you can get buy-in (and how much authority you have to mandate it) are essential to consider.

Storage and Backup

You will want—I would actually characterize this as a need—to have a backup of your research, inasmuch as possible (e.g., of your statistical datasets; while you cannot have a backup of specimens or sculptures, you can back up images of or data about them) whether in the cloud or on a physical external hard drive. The benefit of a cloud-based service is that it is not physically in the same geographic location in case of a fire (knock on wood) or similar catastrophe. (I also say this as someone who no longer has access to some files because an external hard drive I kept them on was corrupted; my laptop had died but I wasn't worried because I had my external hard drive! I got another laptop and forgot to reload those files; when the external drive stopped working a few weeks later, for reasons unknown, I lost access to all files on it). However, some consider it less secure. I have used several platforms, including Box and others listed in Appendix B (as always, there are more, such as IDrive and OneDrive) and settled on Dropbox for my work.

My rationale for choosing Dropbox is that I use three computers regularly and installed Dropbox on my phone to back up photos (not typically related to research, but sometimes when I run across inspiration!). I wanted storage that could "live" physically in all three machines and online. I like its selective sync option (for example, backups of old laptops or completed projects are online but not on my machines' local Dropbox and therefore do not take up local drive space but "live" only in the cloud). Furthermore, it has excellent security, which my IRB has approved for data and file storage. Several researchers I know love and use Google Drive, citing its much easier ability for collaborative work, especially when working on the same document, with clear indications of who made changes when and the ability for simultaneous work. One researcher I know uses Box because that is what their institution uses and is the only one approved for IRB purposes. Another researcher has a laptop used by several members of their lab; they have each assistant log in separately for shift work, and they use Backblaze to back up the multiple accounts on a single machine.

Storage options also raise questions about file ownership. While storage is not synonymous with ownership, if you are using an institutional program, you may be limited in who you can invite to collaborate as well as who can restrict access to the files, and you may lose access without institutional affiliation. One researcher shared that they lost access to their storage and email associated with their university within two weeks of leaving an academic position in the summer. They temporarily lost access to all of their research. They thankfully were able to work with their previous institution's IT department to regain access for long enough to download all of their files, but it took another week and while it was being worked out: panic. In this way, sometimes our tools are not under our control; instead, we must adapt to them. It behooves us to think about this carefully and have a backup, or at least a plan.

Considerations and recommendation: You will want to ask yourself whether you are comfortable with/able to store your data or other documents on a cloud storage program. If not, how can you ensure your work is backed up? How important is your backup to be automatic and stored in a separate physical location versus in the same place as where you work on it primarily (often a computer)?

Selecting Your Tools

For each of your tasks, as outlined earlier, you should now be in a position to begin thinking about specific tools. I invite you to fill out Worksheet 3.2 for each task you identified earlier in the chapter, which should help you decide on the tool you'd like to use. For some of your tools, there might be no question—that is, you know you will use Gmail or Outlook to email and communicate with graduate students or co-workers because that is what your organization uses. For others, this will require more work. Part of selecting tools is learning about what tools are available. I have provided a list to help you get started in Appendix B, but there are many ways to continue to learn about new tools and new (to you) features of tools you already use. I'm still learning about features of Stata and Gmail—some are new, some I was simply unaware of—that help me do new things or can help me do what I already do more efficiently! If your organization hosts workshops about new tools or has a technologist (at universities, these are often instructional or educational technologists or dedicated librarians) or other points of contact, these might be good sources of updated information about tools beyond conversations with friends, colleagues, blogs, social media, podcasts, and beyond.

I recommend you take this opportunity to think about communication more broadly and whether you might be interested in exploring another tool that I listed, or one that you have heard of, and whether you are using your current tool(s) in a way that works well for you. Might including tags or using filters or other features in your email program render it a more a more effective tool for your use? What benefits would that have, and what might that look like? Might you want to separate communication out, for example creating a Slack channel for each project, in addition to email? If you want a more centralized communication platform that would accommodate a team, exploring listed project management software in Appendix B would be a good idea. Many tools provide a free trial for a week or more, allowing you to play around with the features before making a decision. Worksheet 3.2 invites you to brainstorm tool selection. (As a reminder, you can download and print as many blank copies of the worksheets as you wish on the

Worksheet 3.2 Tool Selection Worksheet

TOOL SELECTION

TASK: Data collection

TOOL BRAINSTORMING

Possible Tools	Notes
Google forms for survey link	Available online, easy to use, can get data in Excel, I think IRB will approve based on nature of the data, can ask IRB chair
Qualtrics for survey link	Available online and we have an institutional subscription, easy to use, can get data in Excel, can give me feedback about question construction and might allow more different formats than Google Forms, can also tell me the average time of the survey, can send straight to IRB for approval inside the Qualtrics application
[survey firm 1]	There have been some questions about data quality based on [reading], maybe talk to [name] who uses them frequently
[survey firm 2]	I recently heard of someone using them at a conference, but not sure what their prices would be like

IS THERE AN OBVIOUS CHOICE?

YES: Qualtrics for survey link, need to do more research on [survey firm 1] and [survey firm 2]

IF NO, LIST THE TOOLS YOU WANT TO EXPLORE FURTHER BELOW

1. [survey firm 1] get quote
2. [survey firm 2] get quote

THEN, PUT A 45 MINUTE SLOT FOR EACH IN YOUR CALENDAR FOR THE NEXT TWO WEEKS. SEARCH FOR EACH ON THE INTERNET AND SEE WHAT PEOPLE SAY, EXPLORE THEM, ASK OTHERS IF THEY'VE

USED THEM AND FOR ADVICE, CONTACT WHOEVER MIGHT IMPACT
YOUR CHOICE (E.G., IRB), AND TAKE NOTES BELOW:

Possible Tools	Notes
[survey firm1]	Got a quote for $1,050, I've worked with them before, they assured me I can include socio-demographic quotas which should help with data quality
[survey firm2]	Got a quote for $1,300, [name] said they found both firms equally reliable as long as you check the data and set quotas on particular demographics

FINAL DECISION

TOOL FOR TASK: Qualtrics for link/instrument, [surveyfirm1] for data collection

book's companion website—I recommend you go through the process of tool selection for each of your primary tasks.) Above I use the example of the "data collection" task from Worksheet 3.1.

Why Do I Need a System?

We need a system to help us find what we need and to make our research process more efficient and reliable. For example, many scholars have shared with me that they feel hard pressed to find the file that replicates an article's results if someone asks for it five years later, they're not sure which draft contains that insightful paragraph they want to use for a grant application or another paper, or they can't locate a photo they scanned at an archive when someone asks for more details. Personally, as an early stage graduate student, I found it fairly easy to rely on my memory to keep track of my projects and decisions, since I was focused primarily on a single project: my dissertation, with little distraction from other research endeavors. (Note I said fairly easy; I have the working memory of a raisin, as I joke with my friends, so I still had to slowly retrace my steps more often than I care to admit). Especially as we take on more projects and advance in our careers, we cannot store all the information in our minds (not to mention amid other teaching, service, and personal, family, and other details vying for precious memory and executive function space!).

So many books geared at academic researchers are focused on writing. Deservedly so—communicating and sharing our research is challenging and vitally important for disseminating the research to interested audiences via publications, grants, reports, and so on. This book serves as a complement to this literature. As a reminder, I believe writing is not what comes after thinking or research but is part of it. I argue that if your research is organized, it's easier to write up your findings, results, data, insights, and so forth. Further, organization can leave more time for writing on a regular basis (for more information on developing a daily research and writing habit, see Chapter 11). Finally, writing is easier when you are less stressed. We are already often writing under duress and under less than ideal circumstances, in response to deadlines and job pressures, rather than writing at our own pace. I argue that good research project management can then help relieve some of the anxieties of writing.

I only developed a research project management system when I realized that things were getting forgotten, and I was feeling incredibly stressed out and scattered. This meant I didn't have time to *think* and hit a *flow* state—the state of effortless and focused attention (Bruya 2010)—because I was constantly trying to find things.

For example, I knew that I had a good theoretical reason for deciding to code my interview data in a particular way but could not recall it, which delayed writing my manuscript's methods section. Even worse, when the reviews came in months later I went through the process all over again when responding to a reviewer's question; I hadn't learned my lesson the first time! In another case, I found myself frantically racking my brain to figure out where I had put the models I ran with the statistical analysis with the dependent variable coded differently for a supplementary analysis. I knew I made a note somewhere, but which script file was that in? Questions like these often led to a multi-hour search through do-files across multiple poorly labeled folders (and, early on, across different USB keys and external hard drives).

Worse than wasted time, such events induced unnecessary panic and left me frazzled. Was I misremembering? Perhaps my results weren't robust? Now I have a research log that operates as a table of contents for my project and tracks such decisions, alongside codebooks. One researcher I know lost many hours of sleep not only searching for information they had misplaced but also sleepless nights worrying, in addition to the hours searching. Having a system can help. I now have an Excel sheet for timeline planning, and I have memos and notes about what I did, unexpected events, insights, and more. I have regular check-ins with collaborators. I have clearly organized metadata.

As an example, for one interview study, I can report not only that I conducted "snowball sampling" but I can also tell you how many people I contacted for interviews, and how many said yes. Even better, I know exactly where to find that information and can produce it in minutes, because it's in a sortable spreadsheet. Could I have pieced this together if everything was scattered in physical notebooks across my home and university office and possibly in a couple of notes in one of several Word documents labeled "interview notes"? Absolutely, and I have before, but at a cost to my time, other work I wanted to do, and sometimes my mood and mental health. Being able to call in this information easily and efficiently requires systematically keeping track of not only who you interviewed but who you tried to interview and could not. Or, in my case of snowball sampling, how many people were referred to you by more than one respondent? You can only report this if you kept track of referrals. While this information may never be shared and often goes in footnotes or an appendix, when it does make it to the published page, it is an important part of our research and helps make sense of our sample, with implications for validity and reliability in our research. To do this you need to know *which* information to keep track of (more on this in Chapter 4), *where*, and *how*.

My own project management system includes information on communication via email tags in Gmail, as described. For data, I have a consistent naming system that allows me to toggle between script files that clean my data, new datasets, and analysis script files. I have a spreadsheet that accounts for payments, billing, and grant spending and organizes project receipts, with folders to organize these and naming conventions for those. I have my citations, articles, and reading notes clearly sorted by project in Zotero folders. All of these specifics are part of my system, and many of them can be accomplished with a myriad of tools, which is why it is important to decide what type of information and organization you need and which tools will suit. The scaffolding of my system includes several components that I detail in the following chapters: a research log, a folder and file naming system, a Microsoft Excel sheet with metadata if I'm using qualitative data and a codebook for qualitative and quantitative data, and additional folders and spreadsheets for timelines and communication.

The next three chapters in Part II focus on executing research and developing components of your system for doing research—workflow, bookkeeping, and managing people (even if "people" is just you, the researcher!).

While administrative work is something we all need to do as researchers, it is unfortunately not something we are typically taught in graduate school. Instead, we piece together insights and often half-thought-out systems and hope we can retrace our steps. As you read the following section, remember the difference between tools, systems, and goals and that there are almost always multiple tools (many described in this chapter) that can be used to craft your system and meet your goals.

How Do I Know If My System Is Working?

One of the problems with understanding whether someone is doing research "well" or a system is "working" is our narrow focus on outputs and products: it becomes, sometimes problematically, both the output and the indicator that the system is working. However, as many of us know, we have often been seemingly productive and managing our research and time well, such as producing a published paper or report (which suggests that something is working—we have the desired product!), and yet, behind the scenes, we know how stressed out we are, how disorganized our files are, and that things may be "falling through the cracks."

It is hard to work effectively in conditions of uncertainty and disorganization. If you feel ineffective and dissatisfied in the areas you can control (e.g., not a global pandemic; no amount of research project management will forestall a pandemic, though Part III will discuss adjusting in the face of unexpected events like a pandemic), your system is not working for you. It might also just not be working as efficiently as it could be: research suggests that it takes 20 minutes to recover from an interruption (Mark, Gonzalez, and Harris 2005). Interruptions are often external, but we also interrupt and fragment our own work time with disorganization in searching for something we have not labeled well and disrupting our focus; this can be addressed by a good research management system. As always, it is essential to separate your system—which you control—from external and uncontrollable factors (for example, funding agencies rules, changes in vendors or software available via your institution, job insecurity, a global pandemic, and personal health challenges as some examples of varying scope, intensity, and difficulty to address). A sound research management system cannot fix the world. Still, I wrote this book because I do believe it can help you feel more confident and in control—so that at least you are reducing your stress and improving your organization where you can, which will, in turn, hopefully reduce errors and make your work better, easier, and less stressful.

Works Cited

Alston, Matt. 2023. "Your Project Management Software Can't Save You." *Wired*. Retrieved October 6, 2023 (www.wired.com/story/project-management-software-productivity/).

Bloomfield, Brian P., Yvonne Latham, and Theo Vurdubakis. 2010. "Bodies, Technologies and Action Possibilities: When Is an Affordance?" *Sociology* 44(3):415–33. doi: 10.1177/0038038510362469.

Bruya, Brian, ed. 2010. *Effortless Attention: A New Perspective in the Cognitive Science of Attention and Action*. Cambridge, MA: MIT Press.

Collins, Bryan. 2023. "The Pomodoro Technique Explained." *Forbes*. Retrieved August 24, 2023 (www.forbes.com/sites/bryancollinseurope/2020/03/03/the-pomodoro-technique/).

Interaction Design Foundation. 2022. "What Are Affordances?" *The Interaction Design Foundation*. Retrieved March 6, 2022 (www.interaction-design.org/litera ture/topics/affordances).

Manaher, Shawn. 2023. "System vs Tool: When and How Can You Use Each One?" Retrieved January 3, 2024 (https://thecontentauthority.com/blog/system-vs-tool).

Mark, Gloria, Victor M. Gonzalez, and Justin Harris. 2005. "No Task Left Behind? Examining the Nature of Fragmented Work." Pp. 321–30 in *Proceedings of the SIGCHI Conference on Human Factors in Computing Systems*. New York: Association for Computing Machinery. doi: 10.1145/1054972.1055017.

NCFDD. 2022. "National Center for Faculty Diversity and Development (NCFDD)." Retrieved November 6, 2022 (www.facultydiversity.org/).

Scott, James C. 1998. *Seeing Like a State: How Certain Schemes to Improve the Human Condition Have Failed*. New York: Yale University Press.

Trentman, Emma. 2021. "Systems versus Tools—Emma Trentman." Retrieved June 9, 2023 (https://emmatrentman.com/2021/05/21/systems-versus-tools/).

PART II

Execution

CHAPTER 4

Workflow

Now that you've worked on *planning* your project's scope and resources and started thinking about your system and tools in Part I of the book, it's time to talk about the *doing*: research project management in the execution stage. I cannot overstate the importance of workflow. Having a system for your research and scholarship and rendering that system legible to yourself and reliable will save you time, stress, and errors and enhance your efficiency. It is priceless. By **legible**, I mean a system that you and anyone who needs to (e.g., collaborators) can understand **reliably**, that is, not only in the moment but also weeks or years later, and ideally, it is also **efficient** so that you and they can understand it easily and quickly. Similarly, a clear workflow should allow you to bring in people for more extensive projects in a way that facilitates continuity, accountability, and clear communication. Planning, analysis, and documentation are central to research, but reading and writing are also an integral part of the research process. Ultimately, your research will yield insights, results, conclusions, reports, and/or manuscripts. Workflow is the systematic process for getting there and documenting it. This chapter provides a workflow model, but it is intended for you to adapt to your types of data and circumstances, structured around basic principles to consider.

Workflow Considerations

Principle: Accuracy and legibility should be primary.

In my own thinking about workflow, I have learned the most in five primary ways: trial and error; watching and talking to mentors and colleagues about my challenges and asking them about their workflow; working with others and negotiating the best way to do things on joint projects, which might be my way, theirs, a compromise, or an entirely new approach; reading about what other researchers are doing, whether on their websites, published pieces, presentations, or on social media; and J. Scott Long's book *Workflow of Data Analysis Using Stata* (2009).

As Scott Long (2009) notes, many criteria exist for good workflow, and the non-negotiable one is accuracy. We research, plan, and create a workflow, all in the ultimate interest of *accuracy*: we want to get our research right and avoid mistakes. He also discusses the criteria of efficiency, simplicity, standardization, automation, usability, and scalability. He is talking about a particular type of workflow related to quantitative data and tied to a specific program (Stata). Automation is sometimes possible in this type of data analysis, but many types of research do not allow automation. Indeed, the idea is antithetical to much social science, humanities, fine arts, and other types of research and scholarship. Yet his discussion of efficiency, usability, and accuracy rings true across research. Legibility is equally important: the goal of the research is accuracy, but the purpose of workflow is essentially legibility, which should enhance accuracy. Theoretically, you can be accurate in your research without a legible workflow. Workflow is about a clear record of our actions, decisions, data, and writing to facilitate the research process and so that we and others—reviewers, funders, and collaborators—can ensure we are doing the research right.

In particular, managing our data requires a system, regardless of its format (in words, images, texts, video, recordings, numbers, test tubes, or specimens). You need to find a system that works for you and others you're working with (more on collaboration in Chapter 6). In addition to the benefit of creating good research, science, and scholarship, which is the primary goal, you will be able to make things easier on yourself—hopefully with less anxiety—by not needing to double- and triple-check every step you take, nor needing to search for hours for some piece of information (and interrupting a flow state and eating up precious time), because you know you have a system. Many people can and do create good research without a clear research management system. It just takes longer and is more challenging to ensure accuracy and accountability. Without a clear research management system and workflow, you will be constantly looking for what you need, double-checking, and losing and finding things, which makes it harder to do the research you want and much more likely that you will make errors, forget about or omit data, and have a hard time accounting for your research to reviewers, grantors, and readers.

You'll need to develop a system for storing, organizing, and updating your files. These may include data, coding files, script and log files, manuscript files, or readings. It's best, of course, to have a clear and legible system. But, as we learned from James C. Scott (1998), what legibility means varies. The move toward open science is part of the push toward standardized (state-like, in Scott's sense) rather than localized legibility. If something is to be reproducible (a hallmark of reliable science and research), it must be legible to not only ourselves but also others. In terms of my stance on personal versus universal legibility in research processes, I am somewhere in the middle, I suppose, because research varies. Essential best practices do help impose order on files and projects and also enhance broader legibility. In my view, however, order is not an end but rather a means to reproducibility, analytic organization, time for thinking, and less stress, which can be accomplished with a combination of personal and universal legibility standards.

It is hard to do good research and synthesize ideas, writing, or data without knowing where things are and how to find them. I share some best practices for building your system, the principles guiding them, and some examples from my system and those of other researchers. Naturally, your system will be different than many of the examples shared: after all, your data might be in books, bacteria, or planets. Similarly, you might have different preferences or constraints. As discussed in the previous chapter, there is no one right tool or one right way, but there are wrong ways: those where you make a lot of mistakes, are stressed out, and spend hours trying to retrace a decision or track down a file. The examples may be most familiar to social scientists, but the principles are adaptable across disciplines and projects of different scopes. The system is intended to be scalable for projects small and large.

Redundancy, Storage, and Backups

Principle: Have backups, think carefully about storage (confidentiality, location), and build in some redundancy.

As discussed in Chapter 3, you should always back up your work. Too often, computers and external hard drives are lost, stolen, corrupted, or abruptly stop functioning. I create my backup in the cloud and use a program (Dropbox) that allows me to have local (on my three machines: personal laptop, work laptop, and work desktop) copies of my files along with storage in the cloud. Furthermore, I can save things only to the cloud (and download them as needed) so that my local computer storage isn't taken up by older projects that I don't need immediate access to. Having such redundancy in your system ensures that if information gets erased or lost in one place, the whole project doesn't collapse.

Redundancy may seem like the opposite of efficiency. You certainly don't want to build in too much redundancy (e.g., the same information on six external hard drives, two thumb drives, in email attachments, and four cloud servers), as that requires time, effort, space, and financial or other resources that are likely best spent elsewhere. I no longer use an external hard drive because if my computer is stolen or damaged by some external circumstance (e.g., a ceiling leak), the hard drive is in the same room. However, one can't help when computers stop working; I would certainly have an external hard drive if I didn't regularly use three separate computers (that each have the information on them locally and backed up to Dropbox) because cloud storage is also not impervious and can be hacked, lost, or corrupted. Furthermore, an external hard drive is a good idea if traveling without regular internet access. However, while I have used an external hard drive in some circumstances involving fieldwork, I always prioritize backing up my work to the cloud when I'm within internet range.

Folders and Broader Organization

Principle: Do not create too many nested folders; ideally, no more than three nested layers. Organize based on the way you work. Always include a protected raw data folder and a final folder with a replication package (if relevant) and any shareable materials.

A big revelation to many of us who are older is that current young adults—who grew up with search engines and cloud storage—may not conceive of storage and organization as hierarchical, vertical, and nested (Chin 2021). Instead, they conceive of and store their files in a horizontal capacity, all in the same place, somewhere in the cloud or on the internet. File folders and directories may be foreign ideas to many of them. However, this kind of approach is not limited to a single generation. One researcher my age had everything saved on their computer desktop, with no organization, rhyme, or reason, with layers upon layers of document icons on their desktop screen that overwhelmed them every time they sat down to work. This left them frazzled and often spending 15 minutes or more locating a single file. They have since developed a better system, guided by the advice I share below.

Your broad organizational strategy will typically depend on the scope of and how closely related your projects are. For example, and as discussed in Chapter 9 on offshoots, many of our research projects are "leaky" in that they inform one another and are in conversation with each other. However, our outcomes and products may be more discrete and self-contained (an article or report), though these too often refer to one another. Our new or developing research projects can be offshoots of existing research, and we may use the same data or draw from the same literature or theory to write different papers or reports, sometimes months or years apart. Others publish stand-alone experiments in only a single piece. How you work should help you think about the best ways to organize your files. This means that I plan my time (week, semester) in my to-do lists, but my files and folders are organized by project (or, for teaching, for example, by class) rather than semester or year. For many of us, projects may last several years, and you will want to keep everything related to it together, though how that works in practice may differ for you.

I start with a primary research project folder because the way I work is based on broader ideas for projects. I have secondary folders for each of my papers, data streams, and readings within that project. In some cases, I create folders within that folder as new projects develop. I am most likely to do this if it is a folder shared with a collaborator and in the same vein as existing projects or if I already anticipate several outputs from the same data or project. For example, when my colleague Tim and I started working together over a decade ago, we created a joint working folder. We have since published nine papers together, collected varied data, are writing several more, and applied for several grants. All of those live under that same original folder, though we have reorganized it many times since, and moved it from an institutional shared drive to Dropbox.

Another researcher I know has each data source in its own folder on the "first level" (that is, not nested within another folder) and then "calls" on that data in different folders for different products, for example, reports or articles, opting to do data analysis within discrete "product" folders that are each at the first level as well. That is a great strategy, and there is no "one right way." The examples offered here are intended to provide you with some data points and information to consider on some ways to do things, but they are not the only way, and the worksheets are intended to help guide you to building a system best suited to *you*!

You will want to consider how you work and what kinds of **files** you need to store for a project. I invite you to complete Worksheet 4.1 to think through (re)organizing either an anticipated or existing project into **folders**. The worksheet invites you to brainstorm the folders you need and what you want to include in them in broad terms. For example, you might want an IRB folder (in other countries, perhaps an ethics committee folder) that

Worksheet 4.1 Creating Folders Worksheet

CREATING FOLDERS

PROJECT: community trust

FOLDER LIST
MAKE A LIST OF THE FOLDERS (E.G., IRB) AND THEIR ANTICIPATED
CONTENTS IN BROAD TERMS (E.G., IRB PROPOSAL, IRB APPROVAL,
ETC.) THAT YOU KNOW OR THINK YOU WILL NEED FOR THE
PROJECT, BASED ON PREVIOUS EXPERIENCE OR ANTICIPATED FILES.

FOLDER	CONTENTS
IRB	Proposal, approval, certification, IRB certs for [research assistant]
Personnel	RAs being hired—work log and hours worked
Funding	Grant proposal, notice of funding, budget, spreadsheet for expenses, receipts for gift cards
Contracts	Any invoices and other contracts (survey firm, transcription, etc.)
Drafts	At this stage I envision three papers (article manuscripts): "infratrust" drawing on interviews with community leaders, on infrastructure of community trust, "neighb" drawing on the focus groups and understandings of neighborliness and community, and a full "commt" paper drawing on both sources
Interviews	Interview recordings, transcripts, notes, metadata on the sample, recruitment info, consent form, pre-interview survey
Focus groups	Focus group recordings, transcripts, focus group script, metadata on focus groups, recruitment info (note: consent here is verbal only)
Readings	Relevant readings, mostly peer-reviewed articles (note, I'll have them linked in Zotero and notes on readings will be embedded there)

includes consent forms, IRB proposals, and IRB approvals. As another example discussed in Chapters 5 and 6, you might want a communications folder where you save emails or other forms of communication, especially if you are supervising someone or working for someone.

In Part II of the book, as discussed in the Introduction, I am drawing the worksheet content from a hypothetical multi-method project about community trust that involves focus groups and interviews with American adults. This imagined project includes interviews with community leaders, including organizational personnel that work in local government, non-profits, and other services, about their respective neighborhood's needs and their views on cohesion and trust, along with focus groups with adults from a particular neighborhood about community trust and neighborliness. As a reminder, these examples are intended to help get you thinking but do not be distracted by them. Blank, downloadable versions of all worksheets are available for download at the book's companion website that you can work through.

After figuring out the types of folders you need and their contents, you will want to figure out how to organize them; I invite you to do so in Worksheet 4.2, working to figure out how you want to nest and organize your folders. Again, I recommend you do this for a specific project you are working through, as my basic or "backbone" set of folders (e.g., admin, data, IRB, readings, drafts) remains the same across nearly all my research projects. Note I am calling the project folder by the nickname "commtrust"; we'll discuss nicknames, what I call the "stub method," in the next section on naming files.

You will want to include folders for the main components of your research. Figure 4.1 provides an example. Article manuscript (or paper) folders are nested within a **"drafts" folder** within the **project folder** in my system. However, other scholars I know would nest the papers each in the overall project folder or embed them in the data stream folder (e.g., the paper drawing from interviews would live under the interviews folder). Personally, each time I submit a manuscript to a journal for publication I create a **subfolder** within that particular paper folder with a sub-folder for each revision in that same specific submission folder.

So, for example, if I were submitting the fictional paper "infratrust" to the journal SSQ (*Social Science Quarterly*), I would create a folder entitled ▢SSQ submission 2023-01-01. I have further sub-folders within that folder for R&Rs, for example, ▢SSQ R&R1 2023-08-01 and ▢SSQ R&R2 2023-12-01. Another scholar I know, however, opts to keep all the revision and files in the same main folder for that paper without creating sub-folders. Again, this is up to you! As another example, if I write a book

Worksheet 4.2 Folder Structure Worksheet

FOLDER STRUCTURE

PROJECT: *community trust*

NOW, ORGANIZE THOSE FOLDERS INTO A NESTED STRUCTURE AND GIVE THOSE FOLDERS NAMES. IN DOING SO, TRY TO REFRAIN FROM NESTING BEYOND FOUR LAYERS. THINK ABOUT HOW YOUR FILES RELATE TO EACH OTHER, AND TRY TO GROUP THEM IN THOSE WAYS. THINK ABOUT HOW YOU WORK AND HOW YOU WANT TO ORGANIZE YOUR WORK: IF YOU ARE WRITING MULTIPLE PAPERS IN A PROJECT, DO YOU WANT THOSE TO EACH HAVE THEIR OWN FOLDER? DO YOU WANT THAT NESTED UNDER A "DRAFTS" OR "PAPERS" FOLDER OR FOR EACH TO STAND ALONE?

FOLDER	FIRST LEVEL SUB-FOLDERS	SECOND LEVEL SUB-FOLDERS	THIRD LEVEL SUB-FOLDERS
commtrust	admin	IRB	
		funding	
		reports	
	readings		
	drafts	infratrust	
		neighb	
		commt	
	interviews	recordings	recordings.zip
		transcripts	
		consent forms	
	focus groups	recordings	recordings.zip
		transcripts	

I would opt to create a folder under "drafts," perhaps named "ctbook," a nickname for "community trust book."

You'll also note in Figure 4.1 I have another folder that was not listed in the previous worksheet called "pics" that contains photos I took that I want

Figure 4.1 Example of Folder Structure with Content Descriptions for a Research Project with Multiple Data Types

🗀commtrust (project nickname)	This is the overarching folder; it contains my project research log, a reliquus file for text that I did not end up using elsewhere (note you might want a reliquus file per paper) and a pensieve file; these are discussed later in this chapter
🗀admin	This is a folder that exists in all my projects and contains administrative information
🗀IRB	Contains project IRB information
🗀funding	Includes all information on funding, as well as a budgeting spreadsheet
🗀reports	Contains any kind of reporting, whether annual reporting to a funder, my institution, a partner institution, etc.
🗀pics	Contains images I have taken of neighborhood signs and other things related to the project that may inspire me, likely will not be used in write-ups or any formal capacity
🗀drafts	Contains paper drafts, nested in their folders, may have a broader document here with paper ideas
🗀infratrust	Contains outlines and drafts of Paper1: infratrust drawing on interviews with community leaders on infrastructure of community trust
🗀neighb	Contains outlines and drafts of Paper 2: neighb focusing on the focus groups and understandings of neighborliness and community
🗀commt	Contains outlines and drafts of Paper 3: commt drawing on both data sources on community trust
🗀readings	Houses all readings related to the project, I put them in Zotero at the same time I download the PDF and store it here
🗀commtrust _interviews	Folder for interviews, has recordings of interviews and transcripts, includes a spreadsheet with metadata and Atlas.TI project files
🗀Transcripts	Transcripts
🗀Recordings	Recordings
🗀Recordings.zip	Zipped folder with raw recordings
🗀Consent forms	Contains scanned, signed consent forms
🗀commtrust _ focusgroups	Folder for focus groups, contains metadata in an Excel spreadsheet, also has a document with notes about the focus groups
🗀Transcripts	Transcripts
🗀Recordings	Recordings
🗀Recordings.zip	Zipped folder with raw recordings

to store related to the project. The hope is that using the worksheets will get you a skeleton of a system, but each project has its own demands and features that might require additional folders, files, tools, and adjustments to your system, with room for you to add, subtract, or reconfigure as you work through the book.

Naming Files

Principle: Each project should have a unique abbreviated or short (stub) name (a nickname), and data files should be associated with it. File names should not be overly long or have spaces or special characters (- hyphens and _ underscores are generally acceptable). I recommend dates in the year-month-day format.

My natural inclination, if left unchecked (and it was easier to be left unchecked when I was managing only a couple of projects and data sources!), is too-long titles and lots of words. My undergraduate and early graduate school papers were all named either "First Draft" (but which class or project? Which semester? Of course, nothing was saved in a folder; everything was just in "Documents" on my computer, meaning when the computer died, everything died with it). Another researcher I know often had dozens of "final" drafts named increasingly creative things like "final final," "REALLY final," "post final," "absolutely final," and "last final." Yet another researcher I know who asked for help getting organized had lots of drafts entitled "Analysis of Corporate Social Responsibility after feedback" with various numbers and month names after it. None of these approaches are helpful; the first is not identifying enough—which is the final draft? The second has too much detail but no substance: what feedback? When and from whom? What version of the draft? Such long or repeated names make it harder to find files, may render them more easily corruptible, and are overall confusing.

File Names

The first step in our workflow is anticipating what kinds of files we will generate and where they live (lots of this happens in the planning stage, as you might remember from Chapter 2). I follow what I call the "**stub method**" (and Scott Long calls the "mnemonic method"), which is to use a stub that might be either an acronym or abbreviated name or some other short "stub" name. For this book, my stub name is "projman," for project management. However, it could have easily been "pmr" for project management for researchers or any number of abbreviations, acronyms, or nicknames. Chapter drafts are named for example "projman_ch4_v1.4" and live in a "drafts" folder. Side note: I did not create a different folder for each chapter for this book until we came to the review stage, but I did for my first book because it called in different data in particular ways. Again, your system may vary across projects and change over time! I use the project stub name for all files associated with any particular project: interview files, metadata files, ATLAS.ti project files (for qualitative analysis), data files, Stata do-files (for statistical analysis), Word documents, and more. For this book, I also use "projman" to tag emails in Gmail, for example, trying to keep everything consistent and easily searchable.

Another benefit of the stub system is that related files are searchable, which is especially important if you are navigating files for a single project that come from different countries or have different kinds of data (e.g., qualitative and quantitative). You will need to decide whether to keep the stub in all file names, even if your directory has folders. If you do not, you might end up with a cleaning_v1.1.do Stata script file that exists in several places since several projects have cleaning files. This may not be an issue since these will be nested in appropriate folders, but I usually opt to include the stub in all names. For example, I would name mine ftc_cleaning_v1.1.do (in this case, ftc stands for "For the Children," the title of a now-published article based on a research project). However, if you have a folder system that you rely on and not many projects, having a cleaning_v1.1.do in multiple folders may not bother you because they are nested and labeled.

For readings, you should keep things consistent in your **naming** approach. I always use the lastname_year convention, though there are alternative approaches that may work better for you, described below. I only list the first author's last name, but others list all authors; for example, I would name a 2019 article by Smith, Jones, and Doe as Smith_2019.pdf, another researcher I know prefers Smith_Jones_Doe_2019.pdf, while another likes Smithetal2019.pdf; the options are nearly endless. For more than one article by Smith or Smith and colleagues in 2019, I use Smith_2019a.pdf, Smith_2019b.pdf, and so forth, and have additional information and notes on readings embedded in my citation management program (in my case Zotero, as discussed in Chapter 3; for a list of other options, see Appendix B). My reading system includes keywords, summaries, additional notes, and a PDF of the reading. If you do not use a reference management program, you will need to figure out how to store your reading notes and summaries in a document or spreadsheet. You will also need to decide if you want a document for each reading with information about it, a single document with information on several or all readings, or a spreadsheet containing information on multiple readings on a project, area, or some other organizational strategy. One researcher I know has a PDF of the reading (or a physical book), and keeps a summary document for each reading separately. Then, they have a spreadsheet with a column for author(s), title, year, and a link within that spreadsheet to the summary document. Yet another researcher pastes the (sometimes long) notes and summaries into a dedicated spreadsheet column. Again, your approach should be consistent with your needs and legible and workable for *you*!

No matter how you organize your readings, you still need to name them. Some researchers like a more comprehensive naming convention, especially those who do not use a citation management program. In their naming convention, they include the author, year, and a brief description, such as "Smith 1991 LCA fitstats" so that you know the article is about fit statistics for LCA (latent class analysis) class number selection. Furthermore, you might prefer a different organizational approach. For example, some people like separate folders for readings by theme/topic or type of reading (e.g., reports versus articles) or naming their readings by subject, then author, then year (e.g., LCA_2021_Jones, LCA_2019_Smith, for readings on LCA so they can sort by topic). Each of these systems works well for the researcher that uses it; the key is to pick an approach that works for you and stick with it!

As discussed in the below section on file versions, some programs may have character limits on filenames (and variable names), so you will want to keep your filenames reasonably short. Some programs also do not allow special characters or spaces, especially when calling documents or data into other (typically analysis) programs. Therefore, I strongly recommend keeping filenames simple and without spaces or special characters (this is also true of variable names). However, again, you will know what works for you and your tools. So, for example, I will often use periods in my version names—rather than going from 01 to 02 or 01a to 01b, I prefer to move from v1.0 to v1.1. However, I only do this in programs I know will tolerate it—Microsoft Word, Stata, and so forth. If you want to be entirely consistent across all your file types with naming and are working with a new analysis, writing, or other program, do not use special characters, including periods, but go with 01, 02, or at most 01-01, 01-02 until you figure out the program's parameters and have had a chance to work with it for a while.

Versions

My other recommendation for managing your research projects is that you work by version number rather than date on drafts. Again, many people use and prefer dates, and that is fine. One scholar uses a YYYYMMDD_ name system (where YYYY is year, MM is month, and DD is day), and then they create a new copy of the file every few days so they can lose, at most, a few days of work. However, my collaborators and I may work on a draft at different times on the same day, or I may work on various drafts across my different computers or want to "start new" by accepting all tracked changes from my co-author and then editing within the same day, sometimes even more than once. Dates make that hard for me to do, but of course, you can always tack on a v1 or v2 to the date at the end. If you use dates, I recommend year-month-day, such as "ftc_draft_2021-10-21.docx"; that will allow you to sort quickly from more recent to older or vice versa more easily and intuitively than day-month-year or month-day-year.

For **version numbers**, I use decimals (e.g., 1.0) to go from 1.0 through 1.9 and then move to 2.0. However, I might move to 3.0 after 2.2 if I want to, for example, rethink the analysis entirely or accept all tracked changes before proceeding to 3.0. In that case, 3.0 represents a significant rework, which I will note in my research log, though I also know this because I know my system and what such a jump means: it is legible to me! Identifying what is different between versions might be something you want to do in a research log (described later in this chapter) or some other way, and programmers will often use Git (listed in Appendix B) for version control to track what changes across files when coding, though it could be used for any type of file, including writing. You will also need to decide when to move to a new version. For script files, this is likely with any changes on a new day (that is, not within one work session). For drafts, in my case my drafts get a new version every new day I work on them unless I'm using track changes, which for me is largely in the editing stage once I have a full draft; for others, it is when "big" changes are made (with "big" as a threshold being relative and personal!). Again, whatever works for *you*.

Worksheet 4.3 provides space to think about the types of files you will have in your project and decide on your naming convention. This will allow you to keep your naming consistent and, especially at the beginning, provide a bit of a cheat sheet on naming your files moving forward since you might need time to get used to your chosen naming system and conventions. (Note: you can also re-download this worksheet to think about types

Worksheet 4.3 Naming Files Worksheet

NAMING FILES

PROJECT STUB NAME: *commtrust*

YOU WILL FIRST WANT TO BRAINSTORM THE TYPES OF FILES YOU WILL HAVE, INCLUDING THOSE USED FOR DATA (E.G., DATASETS, DO-FILES) AND THEN INDICATE YOUR NAMING CONVENTION (E.G., STUB_ANALYSIS_V1.0.DO), DRAFTS, METADATA, AND ANY OTHER TYPES OF FILES YOU ANTICIPATE YOU WILL HAVE.

TYPE OF FILE	NAMING CONVENTION
ATLAST.ti files	by analysis for paper, e.g., intratrust_v1, neighob_v1, commt_v1
Recordings interviews	commtrust_01_int_rec. m4a, commtrust_02_ and so forth
Transcripts interview	commtrust_01_int_tr.docx, commtrust_02_ and so forth
Recordings focus groups	commtrust_01_fg_rec. m4a, 02_ and so forth (if editing to create another version of the first focus group recording 01-1_fg_rec_v1.0.m4a, 01_fg_rec_v1.1. m4a)
Transcripts focus groups	commtrust_01_fg_tr.docx, 02_ and so forth
Paper drafts	by paper, e.g., intratrust_v1.0, _v1.1 and so forth
Research log	commtrust_rl_v1.0.docx, _v1.1 and so forth
Photos	2023-01-01_location.jpg, and for each date then location, if more than one 2023-01-01_location_01, _02 and so forth
Readings	lastname_year.pdf, _yeara, _yearb and so forth (e.g., Smith_2023a, Smith_2023b), Zotero library named commtrust
Contracts	name_contract_date.pdf (e.g., Jones_Adam_contract_2024-03-12.pdf)
IRB	IRB_approval_date.pdf, and IRB_app_date.pdf, IRB_addendum_date.pdf, IRB_email_date.pdf
Funding	commtrust_spending_v1.0.xslx, grant_approval_date.pdf, name_receipt_date.pdf (e.g., ATLASti_receipt_2023-01-01.pdf)
Reports	type_report_v1.0.docx (e.g., final_report_v1.0, annual2023_report_v1.0)

of variables and naming conventions for other more specific types of information. I briefly discuss variable names in the following sections.)

Organizing Data

Principle: Have an "untouchable" version of your raw data (I recommend a zipped folder). Create new datasets as you clean data (e.g., upon adding variables, merging, or appending in new datasets). When possible (e.g., with quantitative analyses), create a replication package with data and analysis files for each final product (e.g., article, presentation, report).

You will want to figure out what works best for your data. I typically keep all of my Stata files in a single folder (cleaning, analysis). In contrast, Long recommends separate posted and work directories and a cleaning one. If I'm working with someone else we'll sometimes add initials to our naming conventions if we're both working on analysis, for example. One researcher I know in cases of collaboration creates a folder for each collaborator but still creates a singular final file when a piece is sent out for review or posted publicly that may contain bits of code from people's different files (in their case, R) that are working on the project. Again, the priorities guiding you in building your system should prioritize accuracy and lessen mistakes, whether you can find what you need quickly, and whether the system allows you to reproduce your work easily, and when appropriate share data and analyses (more on this in Chapter 9).

Raw/Source Data

It is vital to ensure you can go to the **source or raw data** in case you need to consult it for your reference, want to share it, or make mistakes in cleaning, coding, or analysis. As I teach my undergraduate survey research methods students (who are typically encountering SPSS and survey data for the first time): the source data continues to "live" on their learning management system. This, I tell them, should give them lots of confidence to play around and mess up. Suppose they've accidentally saved over and replaced their data and lost some variable or recoded a variable into a different one and deleted the original; they need not worry—the source data is always there to re-download and return to. All they need to do is exit SPSS and reopen the data to work with it again. Similarly, you want to create a source data folder for yourself in case you make a mistake. Of course, many of us do more advanced statistical analyses and work with more complex data, but you should store a copy of the original data file (whether secondary or generated by you) in a way that is impervious to tampering.

As a qualitative data example, if I am paying someone to transcribe interview files, I will typically delete the consent portion to save money on transcription and retain anonymity. Unfortunately, accidents happen and I once deleted some crucial parts of an interview before sending it for transcription. However, I knew that I had my source data folder zipped (and sometimes password-protected, depending on the sensitivity of the data and IRB requirements) with the original data and that I could re-edit the interview recording or transcribe the portion that I had accidentally deleted myself. Therefore, whatever form the raw data is in (in some cases, you can digitize physical data, such as scanning pen and paper surveys or saving images of physical specimens), I make sure I have a foolproof version (mainly from myself)—that is, protected from a hasty "Yes" click when I am asked if I want to save over the original file after having made amendments and changes.

My way of doing this is to maintain a zipped version of that data in a folder—whether it is an Excel sheet or Stata dataset exported from Qualtrics or downloaded from a website for secondary data or interview recordings—in my project folder. I know one researcher with a single folder containing only zipped versions of raw data across all their projects so that all their "raw" data is in one place. I find this more confusing than not, and my system relies on a research log and a central location where everything related to a single project is housed (my project folder), including this zipped version of the raw data, but whatever works for you.

Zipped files have three benefits: primarily, and most importantly, they are virtually impervious to tampering; you cannot save and replace them with what you are currently working on. That is, the zipped file or folder will remain protected. Second, they compress the data and, therefore, take up less room than just saving the files as they are. Third, they are bundled and more straightforward to transfer or share without losing components. Some researchers have shared with me that they upload their raw data somewhere else, for example, to their website, sometimes sharing it immediately; otherwise, they use their website as a holding spot without publishing it. Others rely on email or the collection platform (e.g., Qualtrics) to store a raw version of their data. I find each of these a little riskier because your website access may expire or be hacked, as may your institutional subscription to a platform.

Data Cleaning

Principle: Prize efficiency and parsimony. Document your decisions.

In cleaning your data once it is digitized, whether qualitative or quantitative—for example, images, transcripts, variables—you will want to be familiar with the program's limitations for naming (space, name length) and work within those parameters. Again, you may have additional things to label—test tubes, boxes, and artifacts—that will require you to develop a system that works for you. For example, one researcher who works with test tubes needed to revise their naming system because they needed to start labeling at the top and color coding to reduce errors and increase efficiency in sorting by lab workers. Previously they had labeled the test tubes at the side all in the same color, which meant tubes needed to be picked up and removed to be identified. In short, we encounter different things to label and organize, but each requires a system.

If I clean a quantitative dataset, I have separate script files—do-files in Stata—for cleaning and analysis. Each one follows its sequential numbering and code and matches the stub name I have assigned to the data (if a project only has one data source, it will be the same stub for the project, paper drafts, and data). For example, I may have STUB_clean_v1.0.do (.do is the extension of a Stata script file) and STUB_clean_v1.1.do, which each clean the data and generate unique datasets (STUB_v1.0.dta and STUB_v1.1.dta; .dta is an extension of Stata datasets). For analyses, I will have STUB_analysis_v1.0.do, STUB_analysis_v1.1.do, and so on, where both the first and second analysis do-files may call on the same data file (STUB_v1.0.dta), created by the first cleaning file (STUB_clean_v1.0.do). Figure 4.2 shows this process. I do not repeatedly alter the same do-file; once I decide I am "done" with it—which may be within a day or an hour or a week—it remains as is. I create a new one if I need to make additional cleaning decisions (e.g., create new variables to deal with missing data differently).

Other researchers find this less helpful than a hard and fast rule about when a do-file can/should be edited, though this system has worked for me thus far. However, if you are concerned about this, Long (2009) recommends separate directories or folders for Stata, including working and posted directories. Once something is "posted," you can no longer edit it. Similarly, you may opt for greater detail and make different decisions about when you are "done" with an analysis document or a paper draft. That is, you could have separate folders for "drafty" work when you are still tinkering and "posted" or "complete" for when you are finished. Another option

Figure 4.2 Example of Relationship between Data, Cleaning, Analysis, and Output Files

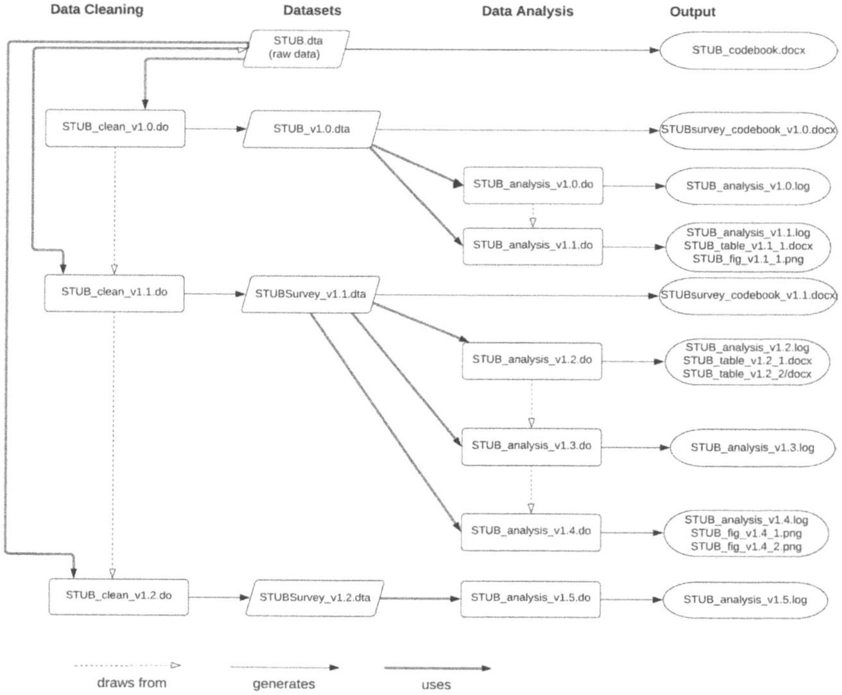

would be to distinguish between STUB_analysis_v1.0.do, which you can still edit, and STUB_analysis_final_v1.do, which you save when you decide you will no longer edit it. This would then roll you over to a STUB_analysis_v2.0.do, and you could create a final each for v1 and v2. Finally, as mentioned earlier, you can have a working and final or posted directory, which Scott Long recommends.

Figure 4.2 also includes examples of data analysis outputs: a log file that I ask Stata to generate for each script file and any tables or figures I've generated, exported, or pasted into a Word document. The numbers on the cleaning files correspond to the numbers on the datasets, but in my system, the analysis files' version names do not correspond to the cleaning of data file version. One researcher I know likes to start with a new number every time the data changes, which happens in the cleaning file. So, all corresponding components (cleaning, data, analysis, log file) match in version number, which changes for all each time. Both naming conventions are acceptable as long as they work for you and can be accommodated by your chosen tools (in this case, software).

My cleaning files contain all my cleaning functions and new variables created. This means that if I decide mid-analysis that I need a new variable, I always embed this in a new cleaning file, which generates a new dataset, rather than in the analysis file. I then call that dataset into the analysis file. So, for example, if I had a variable "age" measured in years (18–89) and I created a dichotomous variable with one category for those younger than 65 and another for those 65 and older, I would not do this in the analysis do-file where this idea occurred to me. Instead, I would build a new cleaning file that creates a dataset with this variable and then open that data in the analysis file to use the variable. This prevents my having to sift through dozens of analysis files to figure out where I generated the desired variable and where I generated the data in any single analysis file.

Furthermore, although some do, I do not "stack" analysis or cleaning script files. So any variables I created in STUB_clean_v1.0.do, if I still need them, will also be created in STUB_clean_v.1.1.do with additional variables or corrections, rather than running several cleaning files to clean a single dataset. The same is true for analysis files; each stands alone so I will have one cleaning file and one analysis file for any paper or set of analyses. This may not be your preference, especially if the cleaning is extensive and you need to copy hundreds of lines of code. In that case, you might want to call a previous script file into a current one (that is, have one script file that runs a variety of others to "stack" them), but this will depend on your needs and what program you are using.

Other data, including much social scientific qualitative data, is not amenable to automation or scripting (including coding loops and so forth, not discussed in this book but an important part of a quantitative data analysis workflow), so the research log and memos become important for documenting decisions. Similarly, some researchers opt to create a codebook for qualitative data analysis, detailing what is in the data and what edits have been made. While codebooks, research logs, and memos are not script files, that is, they don't do the editing, they do walk me through my analysis decisions and document them. For audio or interview transcripts, for example, I will also use versions: if I have STUB_01_int_rec.m4a and want to delete some background noise from before we began, I would rename the original STUB_01_int_rec_v1.0.m4a and iterate to STUB_01_int_rec_v1.1.m4a and so on.

You, on the other hand, might want not want to include the sub-name for these types of files because they will be nested in folders; this means you might have a 01_int_rec.m4a in several places across different interview projects and folders, but since they will be nested in a labeled folder you might be fine with this! Again, you'll note I use 01 and 02 rather than dates, and I do the same for field notes, with information about dates and other details contained in my metadata file, but you may want to use dates for some kinds of files. This book does not preach a one-size-fits-all workflow or management system but is instead intended to help you organize your research in a way that works for you. I'm providing general ideas, systems, and examples to think about organizing your research more broadly. Still, there may be dedicated resources and courses where these issues are addressed in ways specific to different types of data.

Naming Variables and Cleaning Quantitative Data

The same general guidelines in naming files also apply to variable names: you will want to stick to shorter names because many programs have character limits. Furthermore, seeing longer names on a screen or a side window is harder. For quantitative data, the best practice is not to modify the original variable but instead to clone or copy the existing variable into a new variable based on the original one so I can always check it against the original.

Personally, if I have a series of survey questions that generate separate variables I use a shared stub. For example, I might have a question: "To what extent do you agree with the following statements? Politicians and government officials are good models of kindness for me," followed by "Members of my family are good models of kindness for me," and so forth. I would label these variables "kindpol" and "kindfam," using "kind" followed by the actor "pol" for politicians, "fam" for family to label these variables. These names are more informative than numbers to me, and in general, I recommend that if you are dealing with a list of questions (a "matrixed question," as it is sometimes known), that they share the same prefix (such as "kind") to which are added different suffixes, such as kindpol and kindfam, rather than naming these variables kind01 and kind02. However, one researcher I know uses and likes numbers for variable names in such questions, has an organized codebook, and labels all the variables in a script file they can refer back to, so they continue to label different variables using numbers. Hence, as before, do what works for *you*!

When you recode variables, you must decide how to do so. When recoding a Likert-scale variable into a binary variable, I will create a new variable and label it kindpola (recoded where 1 is agree and 0 is disagree or neither) or kindpold (recoded where 1 is disagree and 0 is agree or neither). One researcher I know opts to attach a new number to each recoded variable, such as kindpol01 for the newly created binary variable where 1 is agree and kindpol02 for the newly created binary variable where 1 is disagree; as long as you label the variables in the program and add them to an updated codebook, either should work. You might run into issues when numbering variables this way is if you are running repeated experiments or collecting repeated cross-sectional waves (or sets) of data and have more kindness questions. Personally, I save numbers for sequential (in time) repeated variables and instead use letters, for instance "a" as I did for "agree" on such "list" or "matrixed" questions.

It is also essential to identify both the variable and its values in ways you understand. You will likely develop your own shorthand; if I have a Likert-scale variable (strongly agree, somewhat agree, neither agree nor disagree, disagree, strongly disagree), I label the values SA, A, N, D, and SD to see the entire label when examining frequencies or making charts because "strongly agree" may get cut off whereas "SA" will not.

I keep any original codebook and questionnaire for quantitative data zipped with the original data. That is the codebook that comes with the data in my case: this includes secondary data, data I gathered via Qualtrics, and so forth. I can then create a "live" codebook that I edit and add to as I create new variables.

Analyzing Qualitative Data and Themes

The analysis of qualitative data is not, in my experience, more or less complex or challenging than quantitative data. Still, in my experience there are more possible ways to code and analyze and less disciplinary consensus on this than is the case for some standard quantitative approaches, for example regression models. Just as I do not run my statistical models without software (my tool), I also rely on qualitative analysis software, though many people code entirely manually. For example, one researcher I know prints out and physically cuts up their transcripts, spreads them out, and moves them around on the floor. Another prints them out and uses color-coded highlighters as their coding tool, while another highlights themes in Microsoft Word by changing the text rather than highlighting color. If you code on paper, I recommend you take photos and put them in your research log. I use ATLAS.ti. However, most qualitative data analysis software works similarly (albeit with varying features), allowing you to code images, videos, and texts and build on your coding scheme. I maintain a codebook for my larger qualitative projects and use my software to pass through and create preliminary codes for topics of interest (e.g., religion or government). Depending on the type of data and goals, you can start with specifics and build up—that is, you might code "god" or "heaven" or "prayer" and then aggregate up (into a "code family") to "religion" or opt to start in the opposite direction, coding any religion-related content as "religion" and then parsing it out into sub-topics or themes.

How you approach and analyze your data is discipline-specific; there are many different philosophies and approaches. As those of you who use this kind of data know, many books, manuals, courses, methodologies, and techniques exist for coding qualitative data, often varying by discipline or sub-field. As discussed in the Introduction, this book will not tell you how to code your data. But this book does advise that, especially given so many valuable and valid ways to approach coding and analyzing qualitative data, keeping good notes documenting your decisions is essential for when it comes time to write-up and share your research. I do so in my research log— what I code and the ATLAS.ti project it is in. I document my rationale and thinking using the memo feature in ATLAS.ti. However, you might want to document your rationale in your research log, as part of your codebook, or elsewhere.

Metadata

Principle: Metadata should contain a description of your data that allows you to understand its contents and include *relevant* information about it.

The most common metadata format that quantitative social science researchers are familiar with is a codebook. It contains information on variables and their values and typically also introductory information about the sampling frame, missing data, and more. For quantitative data, you should keep a "live" codebook that you update as you add to your data, including new variables. Ideally, that codebook should be legible to others, especially if you plan on sharing the data. However, it differs from a research log; it contains information about the data. The research log (see below) should summarize what each script file contains in terms of analysis, not just the data. My codebooks are usually in a Word document, but the variable information is in tables that detail the values and frequency of variables within that document.

For qualitative data, storing metadata in a spreadsheet allows for easy sorting (again, you can use a document, but as discussed in Chapter 3, the great benefit of spreadsheets is that they are easily sortable) and easy calculation of averages or sums for numeric information (e.g., interview length). Based on the type of data but also the discipline and intended outlet, what might be considered essential or relevant metadata varies. Most people will agree that the date is important: when a photograph was taken, an interview or focus group was conducted, or a document or article one is analyzing was published, written, or accessed. Beyond that, disciplines differ in what metadata may be necessary; as I mentioned before, if using snowball sampling for interviews or focus groups, I will keep track of who referred a respondent and who a respondent referred, as one example. Another researcher I know keeps track of the time of day of the interview in addition to date.

Your decision on what metadata to collect and document has two related considerations: first, what you need to know about the file and, second, what you might need when writing up your results and answering questions about the data. For example, for interviews, I recommend including the name of the transcript file, the name of the audio file, the time when consent was given (if recorded; if not, the name and the link to the scanned consent form that is saved as a PDF), the pseudonym of the respondent if relevant, and in, another column, the name of the participant (you might want to keep this only in one document and password-protect that one depending on IRB rules and your confidentiality concerns). I also like to include interview length in minutes to figure out an average quickly and information on gift card (as compensation for respondents' time) codes and dates sent, which I often need to reconcile spending (see Chapter 5).

Other types of data might require different types of information or additional spreadsheets. For metadata on focus groups, for example, I create a workbook with a spreadsheet with a row for each participant with a column for which focus group they attended and the date, length, and other information I want to keep track of. These will be the same for all participants in any one focus group. Still, I want to have the information about each participant but also be able to provide descriptive information on each focus group, which I can quickly gather from the workbook. Suppose you have over a dozen focus groups. In that case, I create a separate spreadsheet in the same workbook where the information is organized by focus group (rather than participant) as the unit of analysis to have that additional information on hand and provide a description of key aspects of the dozen focus groups.

Figure 4.3 Example of Interview Metadata Spreadsheet

	A	B	C	D	E	F	G	H	I
	intID	name	psuedonym	do they want me to share results?	consent time	audio	zoom transcript	professional transcript	interview length
1									
2	1	Tim	Henry		2:14	STUB_01_audio	STUB_01_transcript_zoom	STUB_01_transcript	90
3	2	Amy	Vivian		1:32	STUB_02_audio	STUB_02_transcript_zoom	STUB_02_transcript	56
4	3	Dana	Patricia		3:45	STUB_03_audio	STUB_03_transcript_zoom	STUB_03_transcript	62
5	4	Loretta	Ann		1:20	STUB_04_audio	STUB_04_transcript_zoom	STUB_04_transcript	59
6	5	Brenda	Joanna		4:12	STUB_05_audio	STUB_05_transcript_zoom	STUB_05_transcript	64
7	6	Caitlin	Monica		3:22	STUB_06_audio	STUB_06_transcript_zoom	STUB_06_transcript	50
8	7	Rachel	Sara		2:50	STUB_07_audio	STUB_07_transcript_zoom	STUB_07_transcript	67
9	8	Jenn	Erica	1	2:01	STUB_08_audio	STUB_08_transcript_zoom	STUB_08_transcript	58
10	9	Bridgette	Jessica		2:35	STUB_09_audio	STUB_09_transcript_zoom	STUB_09_transcript	62
11	10	Allen	Barry	1	1:58	STUB_10_audio	STUB_10_transcript_zoom	STUB_10_transcript	49

J	K	L	M	N	O	P	Q	R
email	phone	state	interview date	contacted via	gift card code	gift card email date	transcription firm	transcription price
Tim@email.com	614-567-8309	Ohio	3/9/2021	email	Claim Code	3/9/2021	TD	225
	307-567-8310	Wyoming	3/9/2021	email	Claim Code	3/9/2021	rev	84
	812-567-8311	Indiana	3/10/2021	email	Claim Code	3/10/2021	rev	93
	614-567-8312	Ohio	3/10/2021	phone	Claim Code	3/10/2021	rev	88.5
Brenda@email.com		New York	3/11/2021	email	Claim Code	3/12/2021	rev	128
	502-567-8314	Kentucky	3/12/2021	email	Claim Code	3/12/2021	rev	75
	312-567-8315	Illinois	3/13/2021	phone	Claim Code	3/15/2021	rev	100.5
Jenn@email.com	415-567-8316	California	3/15/2021	email	Claim Code	3/15/2021	rev	87
	202-567-8317	DC	3/16/2021	email	Claim Code	3/16/2021	rev	93
Allen@email.com		New Jersey	3/16/2021	phone	Claim Code	3/16/2021	rev	73.5

You will likely want to include other information depending on the type of data: perhaps the size of images, some basic descriptors about where they were taken or their contents in keywords, how many participants were in a focus group, whether a document has been translated, which archive a document is from, and so forth. Ideally, it would be best to do this as you collect data rather than save it for the end or mid-way through the process to reduce reliance on memory and the probability that you will get overwhelmed. This will also allow you to identify and hopefully fill in gaps or missing information in real time.

I invite you to use Worksheet 4.4, on **metadata**, to brainstorm the type of metadata you know you will need, based on your experience, or that you anticipate you might want to record. If you are using a new type of data, you can browse published articles to see what kind of information they report or refer to, especially if there is a dedicated data and methods section or chapter of the manuscript, and of course, you can ask peers or mentors what type of metadata they think is necessary to collect.

Worksheet 4.4 *Metadata Worksheet*

METADATA

PROJECT STUB NAME: commtrust

TRY TO ANTICIPATE THE TYPE OF INFORMATION YOU WILL NEED ABOUT YOUR DATA (E.G., INTERVIEW LENGTH) BASED ON YOUR PREVIOUS EXPERIENCE WITH REPORTING AND PUBLISHING RESULTS, ARTICLES YOU'VE READ, AND SO FORTH. YOU MAY WANT TO DO THIS SEPARATELY FOR DIFFERENT TYPES OF DATA. YOU CAN THEN INCLUDE THIS IN YOUR METADATA SPREADSHEET (OR DOCUMENT IF YOU WISH).

1. participant name
2. participant pseudonym
3. length of interview in minutes
4. length of focus group in minutes
5. transcript name
6. date
7. emails of participants
8. how participants were recruited
9. note if they requested follow up
10. recording name
11. transcript name
12. gender of respondent
13. neighborhood where respondent lives for interviews
14. organization of employment for focus groups
15. consent form name for interviews
16. verbal consent time in original recording
17. number of participants in focus groups

To-Do Lists

Principle: Leave yourself a note, in either a to-do list or the document you're working on, about what you want to do next, ideas, and plans. Whenever possible, end a work session with an action item embedded in the thing you are working on—including, for example, a script file, word document, or reading summary.

This advice has been given about writing: you always want to leave yourself a note and ideas about where to start when you next open the file so you're not staring at white space and a blinking cursor. I find opening a draft I'm writing or a dataset I'm analyzing somewhat overwhelming if I'm mid-project without a clear next step. Given our many demands, it may be some hours, days, or weeks (heck, months or years) until you can return to some of your research.

If you are actively working on things, there are a couple of ways to address continuity: leave yourself a note in the document or script file or put it on your to-do list. I recommend you do both. As discussed in planning (Chapter 2) my general approach to to-do lists in my everyday life is not so much project-specific as it is time-specific. Because my time structure is in semesters (though yours may be in quarters, 12 months, or any other period), I create a strategic plan (as recommended by the NCFDD) at the beginning of each semester (NCFDD 2022). Mine is divided by week and contains not only my research goals in one column but also a column for teaching (while my teaching planning is primarily in my syllabi, I note "heavy grading" or other specific teaching-related tasks that require a lot of time in the week), service, and personal goals. If I am traveling or on vacation, the research column might read "travel, [name] conference." Then, each Friday afternoon, I plan out my following week by consulting my strategic plan's goal for that week and create a to-do list for each day by the week. I then put those tasks in my Google Calendar, though of course if you prefer a paper planner that works great. I find that a to-do list that is a never-ending list, which never seems to get shorter because you constantly need to add things to it, stresses me out and makes me feel like I'm never getting enough done. By giving each task a specific timeslot in your calendar or giving each time slot a job, as it were, the to-do list gets reset each week and feels less overwhelming to me.

One researcher I know has a separate column for each project in their strategic plan. So, for example, your strategic plan might have columns for project1 and project2 rather than an overarching research column. This may be especially important for team projects and projects where you supervise people to ensure you check in regularly (see Chapter 6). You could include information on delegation, checking up on things, or anything else you might need to do. In short, it depends on your projects' complexity: how many moving parts there are, how many people are involved, and how much you can and do delegate.

Research Log

Principle: Give yourself information about where you can find what you need, whether files, decisions, or other information. The research log should operate as a map and table of contents for your project; it will not have all the information you need, but it should tell you where it can be found.

However your research project management system comes together, you should prioritize keeping organized in a way that allows you to find everything quickly and in a way that can accommodate additions and changes. Within my research project log file, if I collect and clean various data streams, each gets its own section. I am a big fan of using the headings feature in Microsoft Word (my word processor of choice and that of most academics, it seems). This is because you can see a nifty "table of contents" with the (handily indented) headings on the left side of the document if you choose (under the "View" tab on the top of the Word ribbon); see Figure 4.4.

Figure 4.4 Example of Word Document Navigation Pane Using Headers for Excerpt of a Research Log

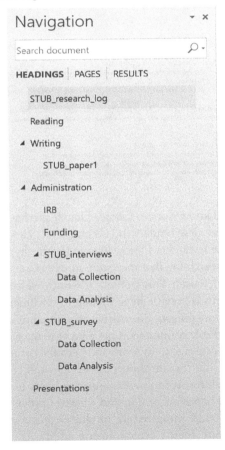

Figure 4.5a Example of Excerpt of a Research Log

STUB_research_log

Reading
Dropbox/STUB/readings
2020-12-05: putting PDFs into while the references are also logged in Zotero, library Zotero/mylibrary/STUB

Writing
Note: there is a [funder] Style Guide that I need to consult for all papers and presentations to acknowledge funding
Dropbox/STUB/admin/funding/[funder] Style Guide.pdf

STUB_paper1
Dropbox/STUB_survey/STUB_paper1
2022-05-11: asked [name for comments], comments received back 2022-05-21, named STUB_paper1_v1.7_[initials].docx
2021-12-10: up to pok_v1.4, split up section on topic1 and topic2
2021-10-30: Dropbox/STUB/interviews/STUB_paper1.altproj has paper1 code, started writing
2021-06-30: started writing, lit review, STUB_paper1_v1.0.docx

Administration
Dropbox/STUB/admin

IRB
Dropbox/STUB/admin/IRB
2022-10-31: requested addendum for follow-up interviews
2022-10-31: IRB approved for follow-up STUB interviews, approval in folder
2021-07-27: IRB Approval for STUB interviews, pdf in folder

Funding
Dropbox/STUB/admin/funding
All expenses saved in spreadsheet STUB_spending.xslx – each grant has its own tab, points to PDFs of receipts

Expenses saved in spreadsheet [name] tab in STUB_spending_v1.2.xslx
2021-09-09: heard from [name] they need the information in pounds not dollars, edited and sent Noy_Shiri_Final Seed Funding Reporting Form_2021-09-09.docx sent to [email address]
2021-06-28: completed final funding report for [funder], Noy_Shiri_Final Seed Funding Reporting Form_2021-06-28.docx sent to [email address]
2021-03-10: Noy_Shiri_Interim Seed Funding Reporting Form_2021-03-10.docx sent to [email address]
2021-02-15: created separate [name] sheet in xslx for gift cards for interviewees called giftcard with just R# and code, STUB_spending_v1.2.xslx
2021-02-02: receipt from Qualtrics
2021-01-28: quote from Qualtrics, Qualtrics Quote RS - 2021-01-28
2021-01-24: phone call with [name] from Qualtrics, discussed needs, they will send a quote
2021-01-20: invoice Grant - Denison Invoice 2020-12.pdf completed, signed
2021-02-15: created separate [name] sheet in xslx for survey data, STUB_spending_v1.0.xslx

Other researchers I know work in Google Doc. It also has a feature to create a table of contents and view headers (by clicking the "View" menu and then "Show Outline"). One researcher I know likes to include hyperlinks to materials in their Google research log that they store in their Google Drive (e.g., the files of folders they reference). This would not work well for me, but it works perfectly for them. This is because hyperlinking to documents does not work well if you primarily work on your documents on your computer rather than on a browser and use multiple computers. This is because the path to the resource may differ; that is the case across my work and personal computers: the path to Dropbox differs, and I don't control the path in my work computers. Overall, the principles of what information to document and how to organize it should hold whether you can hyperlink or not, and whatever program you do it in.

Some people can find things easily in clutter, but a cluttered location (room, folder, desktop) doesn't accommodate additions, subtractions, and changes easily or quickly nor does it accommodate others clearly seeing the

Figure 4.5b Example of Excerpt of a Research Log (Continued)

spreadsheet with metadata: Dropbox/STUBSTUB/STUBinterviews/STUB_interview_log1.8.xlsx with information on Rs from survey
who agreed to be interviewed, begin recruitment and do interviews
2022-10-31: IRB granted permission for follow-up interviews, filed in IRB folder
2022-10-31: emailed IRB, requested permission to conduct follow-up interviews
2021-06-15: transcriptions placed in STUB_interviews and zipped to preserve – STUB_interviews.zip
2021-06-01: made sure all interview transcript are anonymized
2021-05-02: interviews sent for transcription
2021-04-01: finished interviews, all dates in spreadsheet, all recordings and transcripts in
2021-03-19: added a column for whether they want me to send them products of the research after respondent 07 asked
STUB_interview_log1.1.xlsx update as I go
2021-03-01: begin interviews, STUB_interview_log1.0.xlsx

Data Analysis
Dropbox/STUBSTUB/STUBinterviews/STUB.atlproj: imported all data to AtlasTI, 53 transcripts
Dropbox/STUBSTUB/STUBinterviews/STUB_pok.altproj: has codes for pok
2021-11-16: looking at tolerance, code: tolerance, see memo pok-code2
2021-10-30: moving back up, looking at structural v individual mentions of [topic] as related to politics, codes: struct, indiv, see
memo [paper1]-code1, STUB_paper1.altproj
2021-09-01: decided to go in and code specifically for politics, coding all mentions of politics, code: politics, see analytic memo
politics-code
2021-08-15: finished first round open coding, generated 190 specifics codes, before aggregating up I want to think through what
parts of the results to write up

STUB_survey
Dropbox/STUB/STUB_survey/
Data Collection
2021-02-25: codebook, STUB_survey_codebook_v1.0.docx
2021-02-11: exported data to Stata, STUB_survey.dta
2021-02-10: raw data from Qualtrics, zipped into STUB_survey
2021-01-10: survey wording exported from Qualtrics STUB_survey_asgiven.docx

Data Analysis
- STUB_survey_clean_v1.1: recoded dignity variables (dig*) into binary, agree v other, generates data generates data:
  STUB_survey_v1.1.dta 2021-02-11 Updated codebook, codebook_v1.1.docx
- STUB_survey_analysis_v1.1.do: uses data STUB_survey_v1.0.dta, trying factor analysis with social media variables, generating a
  table of factor loadings STUB_table_v1.1_1.docx. I, and a bar graph STUB_fig_v1.1_1.png 2021-03-29
- STUB_survey_analysis_v1.0.do: uses data STUBsurvey_v1.0.dta, running some cross-tabs, taking a look at the social media
  variables 2021-03-29
- STUB_survey_clean_v1.0.do generates STUBsurvey_v1.0.dta, labels all variables, checks all missing in the correct format

Presentations
Note: there is an [funder]Style Guide that I need to consult for all papers and presentations to acknowledge funding in
Dropbox/STUB/admin/funding/[funder] Style Guide.pdf

Noy_[name]_conf_2021-07-06.pptx: presentation in location, [name] Conference 2021– discussing STUB interview data
Noy_location_2021-06-29.pptx: presentation to senior center location, mostly theoretical, no data presented

contents of the location. Having a "home" and clear labels for everything reduces anxiety and helps avoid wasting time finding things and can facilitate collaboration, sharing, and reproducibility. If the system is intuitive enough to you (and with enough practice), you might not have to consult your research log very often, but it should remain updated.

My research log takes the form of a Word document. I use level 1 headers for the name of the document/project and second-level folders—the main components of research projects. I typically have at least the following headers: data collection, data analysis, reading, writing, administration, and presentations. In this example research log, I have several types of data, and the excerpt includes two types of data from one component of the project, an interview and survey, so I have level 2 headers for each of these. I allocate two second-level headings for interviews and survey data in the research log.

Figures 4.5a and 4.5b include excerpts from a research log file with several data streams and funding sources. I could have organized each subcomponent as a separate "project." However, I recommend organizing your research log according to how you work. For me, the project all came together as the result of a single idea and roughly simultaneously, meaning the subcomponents share brainstorming and readings, so they share an overall folder and research log. But many projects will be more straightforward and smaller scale (e.g., one survey and a single article, or a single experiment and report). I chose this example because the more components there are, the more carefully you'll have to think about organization, and it is easier, in my experience, to scale down than to scale up. Therefore, you'll note that I have data analysis and data collection nested under broader data streams (as described in the folder structure, in this case, interview and survey data).

Similarly, for data analysis, I will point myself (or anyone working on the project) to another file—in my case, these are typically ATLAS.ti project files or Stata do-files. I will highlight the folder location and metadata documents (whether about spending further described in Chapter 5, or interview metadata, an example of which is shown in Figure 4.3) in yellow to easily find them. Under the research log headings, you'll note that the most recent entry is at the top when I indicate a date, so I can go back in history while scrolling down. My research log allows me to quickly search any given document name to determine its contents and when I've done what to it.

My research log doesn't catalog each paper draft, and each script file does not list all the specifics of whatever I've done. It is more of a table of contents for essential decisions and actions than an index. Because I create a new version nearly every time I open and work on a paper draft, I do not update each version but note the latest version. You do not want to over-document (or under-document) your decisions. Deciding where to draw the line will likely be the result of some trial and error and will vary by project and researcher. I typically document important decisions about data analysis and sometimes about framing. In my research log, I also note mistakes and the reasoning or impetus for particular decisions about data analysis. That points me to the files and places where I can find what I need rather than replicating the level of detail of the files themselves (remember, there's a reason maps are not to scale). I organize the contents via headers and locations of project pieces (including writing and data analysis), rather than, like a book index, pointing to all mentions of an idea but with no context.

Again, how you organize your research log may vary. One researcher I know has their research log in the form of a spreadsheet and catalogs every single file, including documents, drafts, and images in their project folder, each file's (nested) location in a second column, a brief explanation of contents in a third column (though sometimes this is blank or short, e.g., "edited document" for a report draft), a fourth column for author or originator of the file, and a final column for any extraneous information. In their case, their research log is structured more like a table of contents than a log. For myself, I want to use my research log to catalog not just files but also ideas and reasoning, though you can add columns for this. The worksheets will prompt you to think about what you need from your research log and should help you figure out the best form and format for it.

Worksheet 4.5 provides space to think through the type of information that you might want to include in your log file. In addition to basics like decision-making about naming variables, try to think about the last time

---

Worksheet 4.5 *Research Log Worksheet*

RESEARCH LOG

PROJECT STUB NAME: commtrust

WHAT INFORMATION TO INCLUDE
BELOW, LIST THE TYPE OF INFORMATION YOU WANT TO RECORD IN YOUR RESEARCH LOG. THESE SHOULD PROBABLY INCLUDE IMPORTANT ANALYSIS DECISIONS (E.G., ADDITIONAL MODELS) AND WHERE TO FIND INFORMATION (E.G., CODEBOOKS OR RECEIPTS).

1. information on ATLAS.ti files with particular codes
2. location of a codebook and updates on its content
3. location of receipts and contracts, which will be kept in a spreadsheet in the admin folder
4. list of reports by dates
5. information on where photos are kept
6. decisions about codes related to reading/theory
7. articles sent out for review—date, venue
8. information on recruitment for interviews and focus groups
9. RAs names, work

you went searching for something that took you some time to find (a date, a name, an idea)—how might you incorporate its location into your research log or system so that you can more easily find it in the future? What kinds of things do you find yourself looking for repeatedly? Might there be a way to include their location in your research log so that you can easily find them in the future?

After thinking through *what* you might want to include in your research log, you'll want to think through *how* to organize that information. Worksheet 4.6 should help you think through how to organize the information. Figures 4.4 and 4.5a and 4.5b provide you with a research log example, with its own headers, but of course you can use a spreadsheet and columns. The important part of the exercise is to think through how to group and organize your research based on your needs. It may be that there are some things that you list that will end up in a different location, for example, keywords for readings, that do not end up in your research log but rather as part of your reading and citation system. That is OK; this process is to help you figure out what information you need to keep track of, but also where to put it, which as you move through the book and worksheets will likely need to be revisited.

Odds and Ends

Principle: Try to anticipate what other information you will need to store and create a "home" for it. Are there things (files, decisions, ideas) you find yourself looking for and can't find? Do they belong in one of your existing folders, can you point to them in your research log, or might they belong in another place (file, folder) that you should create and systematize?

In my experience, there are two other important things I will want to keep track of in any given research project: discarded text from my writing, which I call "reliquus," ("reliquus" is Latin for remaining or left behind) and a brainstorming "pensieve" file that holds future ideas and random thoughts. I will also sometimes have a "random stuff" folder that might have tweets or images that remind me of the research project. You can also store these in Zotero, but I like a computer folder because I often browse it for inspiration rather than as a reference—if it inspires me, I put the idea in my brainstorming document.

For my projects, I have a file called STUB_reliquus.docx. This file is where I keep swathes of text that didn't quite make it into a write-up of some kind but may be useful to me anyway—perhaps for grant proposals, other

Worksheet 4.6 Research Log Organization Worksheet

RESEARCH LOG ORGANIZATION

PROJECT STUB NAME: commtrust

NOW THAT YOU HAVE THOUGHT ABOUT WHAT INFORMATION YOU WANT TO RECORD, YOU WILL WANT TO THINK ABOUT HOW YOU WANT TO ORGANIZE IT. BELOW, GROUP THE INFORMATION YOU HAVE DECIDED TO INCLUDE INTO HEADERS AND SUBHEADERS AS WELL AS THE INFORMATION INCLUDED.

HEADER	SUB-HEADER	INFORMATION
admin	Funding	Points to spending, receipts, communications
	Personnel	RA (research assistant) work information, hours
	Contracts	Contract information
	IRB	Points to information on IRB application, approval, amendments
	Reports	Tells me where reports are, and what time period they cover
focus groups	Recruitment	Information on recruitment
	Data	Information on data, points to where metadata are, as well as consent forms, transcripts
	Analysis	Points to ATLAS.ti files, analysis decisions, and codes
interviews	Recruitment	Information on recruitment
	Data	Information on data, points to where metadata are, as well as consent forms, transcripts
	Analysis	Points to ATLAS.ti files, analysis decisions, and codes
writing	infratrust	Points to drafts and decisions made, as well as which analysis files they draw from above
	neighb	Points to drafts and decisions made, as well as which analysis files they draw from above
	commt	Points to drafts and decisions made, as well as which analysis files they draw from above

papers, or footnotes. I find that it often helps me practically when I need to find or want to reuse something I had to cut, but I primarily appreciate the psychological permission it provides. I find cutting words I've taken time to craft, edit, and recraft particularly painful, but this way I know they are safe and sound in a document of their own, where they seem less lonely, and it feels less painful than deleting them wholesale.

I also have a "pensieve" file for many projects. This file is inspired by the Harry Potter Pensieve (harrypotter.fandom.com 2022), where recollections are stored and accessible as they happened, with all their vivid detail from the moment to avoid the fallibility of memory, where one can peruse them at their leisure. Indeed, a big part of the reason I stay so organized is precisely because I have the working memory of a raisin. Therefore, my system relieves my anxiety and the cognitive burden of worrying about forgetting. I typically use pen and paper for mind-mapping (and photograph this and sometimes add it to the pensieve or otherwise index it) to keep track of ideas and insights, but sometimes I do this on Scrapple or LucidChart (see Appendix B) and/or in a Microsoft Word document. This allows me to have a place where I jot down "random" insights and ideas. This is especially important to have as a bird's-eye view, connecting multiple papers, ideas, options, or data streams.

I refer to my project pensieve most intensively at watershed moments in a project: at the beginning and end or when I'm trying to figure out the following paper to write or an idea to dig into. So, for example, in one project I am writing papers, collecting several data streams, and conceptualizing a book. I'm constantly thinking and developing insights that connect my data and thoughts, which might not fit neatly in a particular paper or presentation but may be necessary for the next article or book-to-be. I like having this file in a brainstorm (rather than document) format, as I find it inspiring to go back to it and often find some long-forgotten or neglected insight that sparks more ideas and directions in my research. I call it STUB_pensieve, and it lives in the overall project folder.

While it doesn't work for me, you might want a "holding pen" for some documents or some of your work; I do not recommend these because it is so easy just to put everything there and never return to it. Sadly, this kind of "waypoint" folder often becomes a place where things go to be forgotten (or ideas go to die, as the saying goes). So, for example, some folks will opt to have a "to read" folder (and I used to as well!), but somehow, I never went back to read the hundreds of papers that accumulated there (across projects but also about teaching and other interests). Instead, I save the document in readings corresponding to the project or topic and enter it in Zotero and my to-do list. As a reminder, Zotero is just what I use; you can do this in other citation management systems or in a document or spreadsheet where you keep information on your references. If I need to read something in a pressing way, it goes into my to-do list for the next day or week. Similarly, others will have a "hold" folder. If I have time to download a paper, I usually have time to rename it according to my system (authorlastname_year) and put it in the readings folder and Zotero. If I don't have time, I make a note on my to-do list for the next day/next time I have to work on it to download the paper and import it and its citation into Zotero, but as always, you want to structure your system, your actions and organization, and your tools in ways that work for *you*. The next chapter focuses on bookkeeping, that is, the keeping of administrative data, as compared to our focus until now, which has been the research information we need to organize.

Works Cited

Chin, Monica. 2021. "Kids Who Grew up with Search Engines Could Change STEM Education Forever—The Verge." *The Verge*. Retrieved October 12, 2022 (www.theverge.com/22684730/students-file-folder-directory-structure-educa tion-gen-z).

harrypotter.fandom.com. 2022. "Pensieve | Harry Potter Wiki | Fandom." Retrieved November 6, 2022 (https://harrypotter.fandom.com/wiki/Pensieve).

Long, J. Scott. 2009. *The Workflow of Data Analysis Using Stata*. College Station, TX: Stata Press.

NCFDD. 2022. "National Center for Faculty Diversity and Development (NCFDD)." Retrieved November 6, 2022 (www.facultydiversity.org/).

Scott, James C. 1998. *Seeing Like a State: How Certain Schemes to Improve the Human Condition Have Failed*. New York, NY: Yale University Press.

CHAPTER 5

Bookkeeping

Research project management requires crucial professional and disciplinary skills for making decisions about your research, including data and analysis. However, that is the part we typically receive training for, and so much of that depends on our discipline, projects, and interests. Research project management, however, includes research project administration, which we typically don't get guidance on and help with. In this book, I argue that this gap is to the detriment of ourselves, the research, and our stakeholders (see the Introduction). Documentation is critically important in service of the outputs and outcomes (Chapter 1) we wish to gain from our research, including data, results, reports, and publications. In that way, documentation and administration are not the goal, but they work in the service of your research goals. They help get you to the goal smoothly and efficiently and allow for accountability to the research, yourself, and stakeholders.

Internal and External Administrative Data: Recording and Reporting

I find it helpful to think about the data you need or want to keep track of in terms of internal and external data. Workflow (Chapter 4) is mainly concerned with information internal to the research and important to you as the researcher and research project manager. As we've discussed, you might be called upon to report metadata and other information (e.g., the length of interviews), but that information is related to the research data. There is also administrative data that is external to the research in that it is about the research but not part of it and is often required to be shared externally. You'll want to think, then, about the difference between **recording** for internal use and how this recorded information will be used for **reporting** for external use.

Bookkeeping should be a part of your workflow but requires additional dedicated attention. I find it particularly important to keep administrative documents organized and easily accessible. This is especially critical if you are collaborating across organizations or if you've moved institutions and are working with different granting agencies, partners, and more in the face of change at your own place of employment. Especially if you are an academic and leading your research, using your email as a repository for things works to a certain extent, but access is contingent on institutional affiliation. If you change positions, you lose that communication and information. This underscores the importance of having a well-defined, backed-up, accessible, and organized bookkeeping system.

Researchers with some control over their research, especially academics, often have more freedom to create their bookkeeping systems and don't always have access to dedicated software. In contrast, accounts payable and human resources offices typically have mandated software and filing systems. As researchers, we often have to create our own organizational system in ways that can accommodate other offices and actors that we need to rely on (e.g., accounts payable or timesheets). The benefit is the autonomy we have, allowing us to customize it to our needs and circumstances. Still, it also requires we think carefully about crafting it and requires significant energy—very little is built in for us, yet we face myriad external reporting demands, not to mention their own processes, rules, and regulations.

Types of Administrative Data

An administrative folder (in my case, titled "admin") for each project is a recommended practice (as discussed in the context of our research log in Chapter 4). Information and administrative data that are particularly important and need to "live" in that folder may include contracts, ethics/IRB approval, financial and money transfer information, hiring or personnel paperwork, and annual (or quarterly or any other time interval) reporting. You may want an additional layer of protection in the form of a password for this folder since it will often contain sensitive, personal information.

An aside: I also have a more extensive, overarching "admin" folder for my administrative work that is not specific to any research project or research in general that is not nested in any single project folder. This "overall" admin folder includes work-related items (e.g., my work contracts teaching courses in the summer sub-folder, an honorarium sub-folder, a sub-folder for recommendation letters I write) and personal items (e.g., a tax sub-folder, a home sub-folder, and so on). However, I nest administrative information about any one project within that project's research folder (see Chapter 4).

Within my larger (that is, not project-specific) overall "admin" folder I keep a separate Excel workbook for all my research expenditures by account that is not nested in any particular project folder, and I create a new spreadsheet at the beginning of each fiscal year (which is how most of my spending is structured). I decided to create this spreadsheet after relying on my institution's online system led to some confusion because of how transfer and funding were coded in the institutional system. This led to some uncertainty about how much money I had left after an annual rollover and in which accounts. I found that I could piece together my spending from my separate research project expenses spreadsheets but that I wanted to keep my own concurrent record of expenditures across my research accounts in this way as a "bird's-eye" view of my research monies.

An example of such a "research accounts workbook" is included in Figure 5.1, and you can see that I am organizing it by research account. You could also add a column for type of expense (e.g., travel, equipment) within each account, which might be important for grant or institutional reporting purposes. I can then sort each account number by the stub name to see what is being spent overall on each project or by date. You may instead opt to have one long list of expenditures across all accounts and a column for what account it came out of, which would make for easier overall sorting by stub name, but I prefer to see my accounts this way visually. You could also have a separate spreadsheet for each account in the same Excel workbook. I typically keep a separate expenses workbook for each project that involves funding; this duplicates some of the information in this "research accounts" workbook but allows me to track my expenses by and across accounts (Figure 5.1) but also by project (described below).

Depending on the size of the project, some scholars I know opt to organize their administrative information by year (e.g., for a multi-year project). I find this less intuitive and often keep most files in overall "admin" project folder. However, this may be sub-optimal under some circumstances; for example, in the case of a multi-country study where data are collected in other countries and different languages, you would may want a folder per country, which has been my approach in such cases. This way, information, including receipt and personnel, is organized within the country, with overall approvals (for example, for IRB) in the overall project admin folder.

At this stage, as we've done before, I invite you to use Worksheet 5.1 (as always, blank downloadable copies are available on the book's companion

Figure 5.1 Example of Accounts Spreadsheet

	B	C	D	E	F	G	H	I	J	K
	startup spending, account#	date	stub name	summary	receipt name/link	grant1 spending, account#	date	stub name	summary	receipt name/link
1										
2	$10,000.00	2023-07-01		starting amount; needs to be spent by 2028-06-30, started 2022-07-01		$154.47	2023-07-01		starting amount, needs to be spent by 2025-06-30, started 2022-04-01	
3	-$1,423.31	2023-08-20	stubname123	computer	website_receipt_2024-05-21.pdf					
4	-$125.96	2023-09-05		part of hotel for conference [name], total hotel fee was $560, rest is coming out of college travel grant account	hotel_receipt_2023-09-05.pdf					
5	-$230.27	2024-04-05	stubname123	flight to [name] conference	airline_receipt_2024-05-20-destination.pdf					
6										
7										
8										
9										
10										
11										
12										
13										
14										
15	$8,220.46					$154.47				

L	M	N	O	P	Q	R	S	T	U
grant2 spending, account#	date	stub name	summary	receipt name/link	college travel grant, account#	date	stub name	summary	receipt name/link
$150,000.00	2023-07-01		starting amount; needs to be spent by 2027-05-30, started 2023-07-01		$500.00	2023-07-01		starting amount; needs to be spent by 2023-12-30	
-$42,000.00	2024-01-15	stubname90	survey fielding by [name] firm	firmname_receipt_2024-01-15.pdf	-$230.27	2023-09-01	stub123	rental car to conference [name]	rentalcarcompany_receipt_2023-09-01
					-$269.73	2023-09-05	stub123	part of hotel for conference [name], total hotel fee was $560, rest is coming out of startup account	hotel_receipt_2023-09-05.pdf
$108,000.00					$0.00				

website) to brainstorm the information you will want to keep track of for a particular project (as a reminder, for the examples in this second part of the book, we're using a hypothetical qualitative study on community trust, stub name commtrust). In your brainstorming, you'll want to think about the type of information you find yourself consulting during and after the completion of research projects. This might be information you would like to double-check (e.g., how long ago did I submit that grant), information you need for reporting purposes (e.g., when did I spend that money), or

---

Worksheet 5.1 Administrative Data Brainstorming Worksheet

ADMINISTRATIVE DATA

PROJECT STUB NAME: *commtrust*

TRY TO ANTICIPATE THE TYPE OF ADMINISTRATIVE INFORMATION YOU WILL NEED AND WANT TO KEEP TRACK OF, FOR EXAMPLE, ACCOUNT NUMBERS, SPENDING, AND SO ON.

1. *ATLAS.ti license/upgrades*
2. *RA (research assistant) contracts*
3. *Transcription receipts*
4. *Account numbers (overall research for ATLAS, grant for RAs)*
5. *Dates and information on presentations (will need for reports, reviews)*
6. *Hours spent by RAs*
7. *RA payment*

---

information that might need to be accounted for officially (e.g., RAs worked such and such hours in Fall semester). Focus on **external administrative data**; if you find a new piece of information you want to keep track of that is centrally related to the research (rather than "administrative"), you should integrate it more fully into your metadata and research log (Chapter 4) rather than storing it in the "admin" folder.

After doing the above, try to see if you can group the types of information you need to keep track of together. In the following, I cover several significant categories of administrative data that often (but not always) arise in research project management: equipment, people, approvals and contracts, expenditures, and communication. Given what you brainstormed earlier, there may be more, or you may only need some of these categories; it depends on your project and its scope and type.

Equipment

Under equipment, I consider hardware (e.g., laptop or microscope) and software (e.g., data analysis programs) and other tools I use to do my research. Importantly, these may be project-specific or span across your research (and even teaching or other work tasks, e.g., laptop). Previous chapters have discussed how to think about the resources you have and those you need (Chapter 2) as well as tool selection (Chapter 3). However, you also need to keep track of resources and tools purchased, used, and so on. In general, you should keep track of anything relating to the version or particulars of equipment that needs reporting in publications or other outputs. That may be accomplished by keeping enough detail in an expenditures worksheet related to the project. One of the issues researchers commonly run into and have shared with me is "double-counting." So, for example, I may purchase and upgrade my software program (for example, data analysis software) to a new version or purchase a new laptop. That program is one that I may (typically do) use for multiple projects. I note the version in my script files so that the code is reproducible and so that I can note it in subsequent publications. But where to store such information about these kinds of equipment, tools, or purchases? I like to keep my information on equipment in a general spreadsheet that is not project-specific, but rather specific to me as the researcher. If the funding comes from a project-specific grant, I will also include it in my bookkeeping of project-specific expenditures because it is from the grant. Otherwise, this information will be stored in my overall equipment spreadsheet and also in my overall research accounts spreadsheet (e.g., Figure 5.1). I also track where funding came from (for example, a specific grant or professional development account) in that "equipment" spreadsheet. If you have project-specific equipment, you will want a centralized place to catalog it; for me this is in my project "admin" folder. I keep a spreadsheet that includes information on any project-specific equipment and any associated documents (for example, receipts or manuals), which I scan electronically and save in that same folder and indicate that file name in the spreadsheet.

People

Keeping track of human effort and resources is another common type of information you will need to "bookkeep." This information is not about participants (that is, part of your workflow; Chapter 4) but about people in researcher or researcher-support roles. Once again, figuring out what information you need and want to store, as well as how to store it, is essential. You may wish to document detailed information about your own effort on the project, which may be helpful for your time management or self-reflection. This information can also answer the increased push toward the quantification of research via metrics, scores, and standardized evaluations that we sometimes have to report administratively, for example, you can account for time spent on data analysis for a particular grant (Pardo-Guerra 2022). You can keep track of a variety of work, for example, writing time; other scholars I know keep track of teaching, course prep, data collection versus data analysis time, and so on.

In general, if you are working with others you will want to keep track of people's hiring and contract dates and hours worked, how much they have been paid when they worked, and what they did. This information is essential from an external or accountability approach and helps you manage the project. As discussed in the following chapters, it will help you figure out who is working when and getting what done. In terms of organization, I prefer to keep this information in a spreadsheet for easy sorting because I enter it by date but often like to look at it by person or task (each of whom gets a dedicated column). I always include a column for the task since I often like to figure out which tasks require what types of external support and how much that is, which helps when budgeting on subsequent projects.

Approvals and Contracts

Research often requires layers of approvals from different actors, depending on the type and context of research. You will generally need some ethics committee approval (in the United States, IRB) if you do research with human subjects. You may have a supervisor if you're working in a research institute; in some departments, you might need approval from a department chair or from a set of supervisors or clients if you work for a corporation. Approvals might also be necessary for particular types of project expenditures, such as contracts and travel to present research. For anything requiring approval, there is sometimes a system or form set up, but even if not, I always try to get approvals in writing, and if I get them via email, I generate a PDF copy of that email and save it in the project's admin folder. I usually name these with the date they were signed (rather than my research naming convention of version v1.0 and so forth). So, if I'm getting approval for money for travel, for example to the American Sociological Association meetings in 2024, I will save it in the admin folder of that project (in this case "stubname738") as "ASA2024_approval_ProvostOffice_2024-05-01.pdf," which indicates that this will have my approval and attendant information for travel to

Figure 5.2 Example of "Admin" Folder Indexing Spreadsheet for a Specific Project

	A	B	C	D	E	F	G
	project stub	type of document	date	signatory	approver	contact	number (e.g. of invoice, receipt, contract)
2	stubname738	approval	3/5/2022	IRB	Jane Books	irb@college.edu	SP23-131
3		contract	3/12/2023	Adam Jones	-	adamjones@gmail.edu	6704
4		approval	5/1/2024	Joe Smith	Joe Smith	jsmith@gmail.com	-
5		receipt	5/16/2024	-	-	-	1234

H	I	J	K
amount	event/info	source of funding	document link
-	IRB approval for stubname1	-	stub738_IRB_approval_2022-03-05.pdf
$2,000	RA for commtrust hourly work, transcription, approximately 3 hours	PD accont, account #1267	Jones_Adam_contract_2023-03-12.pdf
$1000 for travel	ASA 2024, Montreal August 9-13,2024	Provost office, up to $1000	ASA2024_approval_ProvostOffice_2024-05-01,pdf
$470.04	flight to ASA	Provost office, see approval 2024-04-24	ASA2024_receipt_flight_2024-05-16.pdf

that conference. You may want to index these documents in a spreadsheet (including perhaps equipment receipts and manuals if project-specific)— see for example Figure 5.2—or you may opt to include some or all of this information in your research log or divide it into multiple spreadsheets within a single workbook, for example, one for just personnel, another for IRB, and so forth. How you organize and keep track of the contents of your admin folder really depends on the volume and scope of your project and administrative needs. While there are many different ways to do this (spreadsheets, documents), you should first commit to keeping track of the administrative information that is important for record keeping and reporting, and second organize it in a way that is legible to you. Whether you need separate folders (and different indexing spreadsheets) for different approvals is up to you. For the most part, I opt to create an "admin" folder for each project and point to documents saved there in my spreadsheet, but for large projects that span over years, with a large set of approvals or contracts, you might want to store it by year or by firm if you have many contracts with many different people or firms. You will, as always, want to plan your naming and organizational system (name, date, or other information) for these files.

As a reminder, project management should help you do your research in a way that enhances the research and reduces stress. I keep track of this data, filing it diligently in ways where I can easily access it because I don't want to panic when the time comes to report when IRB approved my project when writing an article or how much such and such person was paid and when to my accounting office or an external funding agency.

As you'll note, I build in some redundancy: a PDF of a receipt will only be saved in one place but will be indexed in several places, for example, a project-specific admin spreadsheet, my research accounts spreadsheet, which accounts for all research spending, and if it is a laptop, for example, an equipment spreadsheet as well. While it does take a little bit of time to enter this information, my system means I no longer have to root through my email (and of course if it's a previous institutional email, then I can't even search for it!), trying to figure out what keyword would be most straightforward to search for that information (somehow, it never works the first time and often not the second or third time either!) and cross my fingers that I didn't accidentally delete the relevant email, if and when I can find it.

The information I store for approvals in my spreadsheet includes the date, approver, name, approval number if there is one, and the name of the PDF document containing the approval stored in the same folder. Similarly, I will detail contracts in the same spreadsheet with, at minimum, information about the date, signatory name, contact information, a brief description, and contract number. Again, you may opt to include more or different information and create different spreadsheets for contracts as compared with approvals; it depends on what works best for you!

Expenditures

You will want to keep track of spending for research projects that have them. Effective bookkeeping lets you see where effort, hours, and dollars are spent. Having this information organized systematically can yield important insights about your rhythm, the needs of your research, and the resource-intensive tasks and, ideally, will allow you to more accurately plan for future projects based on the data you now have (Chapter 2). Keeping careful records may also be particularly important if you are, for example, as one scholar shared with me, working on two separate grant-funded projects related to a broad topic. Your day-to-day work and life are deeply intertwined, but you likely still need to adhere to clear rules about allocating funding to research assistants or travel from each grant. For example, if you are traveling to a conference and presenting work from both projects across two panels in that same conference, you will need to decide how to divide and record the expenditures and so forth (this is part of the reason I keep records by account number as well as by project; see Figure 5.1). Keeping clear records is especially important in cases like these.

Communication

The final area that researchers may want to bookkeep is communication. Whether you need an additional spreadsheet or tab in a spreadsheet or folder to keep track of communication is entirely up to you. However, you will want to keep communication stored somewhere you will retain access to, for example in a professional email account, that is not tied to your current institutional affiliation (Chapters 3 and 11). However, you may also want to track particular types of communication and associated information. For example, saving not only contracts and estimates but also emails that may have administrative details, deadlines, and beyond as PDFs and cataloging them in a spreadsheet. For my part, I will sometimes paste in or note the name of emails I save as PDFs about division of labor, for example into a research log or meeting notes, or authorship order on a manuscript in my research log (Chapter 4) that is "of the research," rather than keep this in the "admin" folder where I keep things that are "about the research." However, you may want to have a separate "comm" or communication spreadsheet with this kind of information rather than or in addition to noting it in the research log!

The "Admin" Folder

Altogether, I recommend you create an "admin" folder for each project—that way, you know that all administrative information is in a single folder and should have all of the "wrap around" information you need. Depending on your decided naming conventions and the project scope, you may want to create a standalone "table of contents" spreadsheet or a contents log for your admin folder. You can think about this as a kind of research log for administration. Figure 5.2 provides an imagined example of an index spreadsheet where everything is in one place. However, for some bigger projects I will have a workbook with multiple spreadsheets (e.g., a separate one for approvals, expenditures, and so forth). Whether or not you have a spreadsheet or more than one for a research project depends on how much administrative data you store. One scholar I know working on a multi-million, multi-year grant has a dedicated project administrator (who supervises two others) creating multiple folders in their admin folder (and their personnel folder has sub-folders for each person working as a researcher since the project involves doctoral students, hourly undergraduate students, and post-doctoral students), and each of those had their own workbook in that sub-folder to index the documents there, which acts as a table of contents.

Another question you will want to ask yourself, as we discussed for your research flow, is how *you* work. That is, I do not typically divide my "admin" folders for projects by year (though my accounts workbook has spreadsheets by fiscal year; Figure 5.1) because my naming system for admin files accounts for dates, as does a dedicated column in admin spreadsheets, and I do not find years or semesters the best way to organize my administrative research information. Instead, I group by project, and then type and substance (e.g., equipment, personnel). However, if you find that organizing your projects by year, whether fiscal, academic, or Gregorian, would be helpful, especially for the "external" administrative demands such as annual reports to funding agencies, your own institution, and beyond, do so! Do this in a way that first serves the research in that it promotes accuracy and reduces stress, and second, do it in a way that helps you meet those external demands.

Worksheet 5.2 invites you to think about how you want to organize your **"admin" folder**: what types of sub-folders you want (if any at all; you can also just place everything in the admin folder) to include and their contents. You will want to consider whether you would be best served by having a spreadsheet or document to keep track of information in this folder, and if so, what types of information. You can refer back to Worksheet 5.1 to see

Worksheet 5.2 The "Admin" Folder Organization Brainstorming Worksheet

THE "ADMIN" FOLDER

PROJECT STUB NAME: commtrust

USE THE SPACE BELOW TO DECIDE ON YOUR FOLDERS, THEIR FILES, AND WHETHER YOU NEED AN INDEXING WORKBOOK/ SPREADSHEET(S) OR OTHER WAY TO KEEP TRACK OF CONTENTS, AND IF SO, WHAT KIND. IF YOU DECIDE YOU NEED THIS, FOR EXAMPLE, A SPREADSHEET FOR EXPENDITURES IN ADDITION TO RECEIPTS, LIST THIS UNDER THE RELEVANT SUB-FOLDER.

NAMES OF SUB-FOLDERS IN THE "ADMIN FOLDER"	CONTENTS
IRB	Proposal, approval, certification, IRB certs for [research assistant]
Personnel	RAs being hired—work log and hours worked, includes communication about hours (will save emails and index them in research log)
Funding	Grant proposal, notice of funding, budget, spreadsheet for expenses, receipts for gift cards, information about which account money is coming from
Contracts	Any invoices and other contracts (survey firm, transcription, etc.).

NEXT, CONSIDER HOW YOU WILL WANT TO INDEX THIS FOLDER: A SPREADSHEET, DOCUMENT, SECTION IN YOUR RESEARCH LOG? WHAT KINDS OF INFORMATION WILL YOU WANT TO DOCUMENT ABOUT YOUR "ADMIN" DATA IN THIS FOLDER?

My plan is to index the "admin" folder contents in a single spreadsheet but in the same workbook/Excel file I will have another expenses spreadsheet for this specific project. Separately, I will have a spreadsheet that is shared with the RAs where they can track their hours every week that will be in this folder. I will also include IRB information and progress on work tasks in the research log while gift card information will also be in my metadata spreadsheet, but the PDF receipts will be kept in the admin folder. Some of the funding will also be kept in my accounts spreadsheet.

what information you want to keep track of and make sure it fits in your organizational system. As always, you might need to adjust this across different projects or as your needs, tools, or systems change over time.

Works Cited

Pardo-Guerra, Juan Pablo. 2022. *The Quantified Scholar: How Research Evaluations Transformed the British Social Sciences.* New York: Columbia University Press.

CHAPTER 6

Collaboration and People Management

To paraphrase the famous astrophysicist and public figure Neil DeGrasse Tyson in a popular tweet: human behavior is complex, and when it enters the equation, things go "nonlinear" (Neil deGrasse Tyson [@neiltyson] 2016; he continues to remark that this is why physics is easy and sociology is hard, so you can imagine that sociologists loved this sentiment). Even if you are working on a project where you are the only researcher, this requires managing yourself. Indeed, some of the biggest obstacles for people planning, executing, and disseminating their research are imposter feelings (Parkman 2016), perfectionism (Ocampo et al. 2020), and anxiety (Einbinder 2014), all of which manifest in the researcher, which is not to minimize or ignore the significant structural and contextual contributors and roots or causes to these issues.

When working with others, challenges often compound exponentially rather than linearly. Indeed, people often find the "human element"— themselves and others—to be the most complex piece of the research enterprise to organize and manage. When I use the word "manage," I do not mean this in a top-down, dictatorial sense or in the sense of complete control, but rather in terms of organizing, administering, and handling. Managing suggests manipulation, but again, I mean this not in the supervillain sense but rather, like we discussed in previous chapters with workflow, bookkeeping, and project scope and planning—manipulating, or using gentler words, organizing, or systematizing to facilitate research.

We need to manage our motivations, efforts, time, and emotions. For many of us conducting research, and perhaps especially acutely for those within academia, our lives are a series of rejections and failures. Grant funding and publication rates often hover between 5% and 10% and are usually lower, and academia can become all-consuming (cf. Allen, Donoghue, and

Pahlevansharif 2020). For many people doing research, we are socialized to believe that our work is not just work but a vocation. We spent years training for it, and many have noted the cult-like tendencies of graduate training. While racism, sexism, underfunding, inequality, rejection, and other pervasive challenges are not unique to our profession, for many of us, graduate school and perhaps academia itself may be cult-like in several meaningful sociological ways, for example, information withholding and emotional control (Benton 2004). This makes it particularly important not to neglect people, including ourselves, collaborators, and participants, in our research management process. The urge and incentives to do so are often intense as we scurry to get things done and focus on the data and other aspects of research.

The "people management" issues of work–life balance and imposter feelings have each spawned dozens of books and deserve dedicated attention. There are specialized resources if these are issues you confront since this book cannot give them the attention they clearly deserve. In this chapter, we focus on your values surrounding work, people management, and leadership to inform the types of relationships that typically characterize research.

While this chapter and attention to managing people might seem a bit of a digression, I argue it's quite the opposite. People management is integral to effective project management and can help unlock some of our resistance surrounding managing ourselves. Many of us believe (or used to, which was the case for me) that research and writing are at the whim of the muses and that our intellectual work is beyond any orderly kind of "management." In this way, our resistance to thinking carefully about managing ourselves in our role as researchers echoes our resistance to managing our research: it's too unpredictable, too creative, and so forth (see the Introduction). This book seeks to provide you with resources, ideas, and tools to construct a system that helps you not only *do* your research better but also *feel* better while doing it, with less stress and more confidence that things are accounted for. This is good for you, the research, and the organizations and institutions you work in and for. Managing people in ways that align with your values, priorities, and circumstances is critical.

Control and Process

A fundamental challenge to "people management" is the issue of control. We feel that people are in many ways beyond control in meaningful ways, by which we mean beyond our ability to make them do what we want the way we want it. And indeed, complete control is nearly impossible. It would be best to think of ourselves as coaches or facilitators when managing people—including ourselves (Gilley and Gilley 2007). This suggests we need to ask more questions rather than only give directives. Much like anything else, our research projects would benefit from systems that facilitate accountability and transparency in our roles. As discussed in previous chapters, workflow and bookkeeping are essential for myriad reasons, not the least of which is that organization is vital in research. That is, we should be able to explain our steps (and missteps) when reporting our research, accounting for the decisions and the rationales undergirding those decisions. This chapter focuses more on people (rather than data or "stuff," e.g., money, equipment) management.

Control, however, is sometimes illusory. The "illusion of control" in management studies refers to overestimating decision-makers' influence on chance events (Meissner and Wulf 2016). Beyond chance, however, many components of research project management, if not research itself (e.g., we cannot control our results), are in the researcher's control. Indeed, good research project management helps you adjust to the curveballs and unexpected events that you confront in your research! While we tend to think of problems as "people" issues, they are often "process" issues that we can work to manage and avoid. This chapter seeks to help you control, systematize, and organize what you can. In addition to arguing that you can control your management system, I believe doing so will position you to best deal with change and other challenges you *cannot* control (Part III of this book is dedicated to adjustment in the face of challenges).

Desirable Attributes of a Research Manager

A **good people manager** looks different for each of us, and we respond differently to the same behavior. For example, some of us prefer a relational approach; others prefer a more unemotional and directive style. Personally, a key **attribute** that I value and try to enact, and is particularly important to me among people I work with (whether they be peers, those who have more authority than me, or those I have authority over) is that they are accountable. For me, the **behaviors** I associate with that attribute are sharing progress and setbacks, having mechanisms for reporting issues or errors, taking responsibility for decisions, and apologizing when mistakes are made. Accountability, however, might mean something different to you or may be lower down your list of priorities. As another example, one researcher I know prizes independence. They do not want to work with people they need to micro-manage, nor do they want to be micro-managed. The behaviors they associate with this trait are problem-solving, taking initiative, and concise communication. This differs from another scholar who prioritizes warmth as an essential trait. They associate this with engaging in dialogue and conversation, focusing on relationships rather than outcomes, and frequent communication. All of these are positive and important traits. As you read this, I hope you find yourself thinking, "That is something I care a lot about," or "I actually think I value such and such." I invite you to complete Worksheet 6.1 (as a reminder, blank versions are available on the book's companion website) to think through the attributes that you value, thinking specifically about your research, and brainstorm their associated behaviors.

Worksheet 6.1 Desirable Attributes of a Research Manager

DESIRABLE ATTRIBUTES IN A RESEARCH MANAGER

BELOW YOU LIST THE ATTRIBUTES YOU FIND VALUABLE IN A MANAGER. THEN THE BEHAVIORS YOU ASSOCIATE WITH THOSE ATTRIBUTES.

ATTRIBUTE	ASSOCIATED BEHAVIORS
Accountability	sharing progress and setbacks, having mechanisms for reporting issues or errors, taking responsibility for decisions and work, and apologizing when mistakes are made
Clarity	clear and regular communication, task lists, instructions about where/when/how
Openness	openness to questions and an ability to incorporate new information, adaptiveness and willingness to change course and pivot as necessary
Decisiveness	ability to make decisions in a timely manner and related to accountability, the ability to explain those decisions
Organization	organized and stays on top of communication, new information, and requests

By brainstorming the attributes you value in a research manager, I hope you can start thinking about your behaviors and relationships and how to apply your values and priorities to your research management system. For example, if I value accountability, I can build that into relationships and expectations vis-à-vis others I work with in my research and include that in my milestones and timelines. Identifying the attributes of a good manager to you will allow you to integrate the associated behaviors into your system in a focused way, just in the same way that deciding what information is essential to keep track of allows you to build it into the metadata (Chapter 4) you collect and your bookkeeping system (Chapter 5), for example.

Next, following the above example, you'll need to consider the **practical, measurable, behavioral** ways these attributes can be integrated into your project management system for a particular project. That is, you need to concretize and further operationalize these behaviors for your research project. So, what does accountability mean if we use the SMART goal framework described in Chapter 1? If one of the behaviors associated with accountability is having mechanisms for reporting issues or errors, how can you integrate this into your project management system? In my own case, I incorporate this into my workflow via my research log and have draft naming and file version conventions that allow me to document and move beyond errors rather than pretending they never happened, forgetting them, or repeating them. I schedule regular check-ins if I'm working with others, as discussed in Chapter 7. Changing attitudes, values, and ideas may be more complicated than changing behavior, at least in the short term (Olson and Stone 2005). In this way, by making behavioral expectations particularly clear (to yourself and others), you can follow up on more tangible outcomes. In Worksheet 6.2, I invite you to use the behaviors you brainstormed in Worksheet 6.1 associated with particular attributes as a starting point and then, using the SMART framework (Chapter 1), identify ways to implement and incorporate these behaviors into your project management in specific, measurable, attainable, relevant, and time-bound ways.

Supervision versus Collaboration

Our relationships with people are complex and, in many ways, unequal and asymmetrical. How we relate to people is political, and we want to stick to our values in our treatment of our data, including participants who generate that data (if our research is of that variety), archival material, and beyond. I argue that it is also essential to be clear in our values and priorities

Worksheet 6.2 Operationalizing Desired Behavior

OPERATIONALIZING DESIRED BEHAVIOR

PROJECT STUB NAME: *commtrust*

THINKING MORE CONCRETELY ABOUT HOW TO OPERATIONALIZE
THE BEHAVIORS YOU BRAINSTORMED IN THE PREVIOUS
WORKSHEET, USE THE SMART FRAMEWORK FROM CHAPTER 1,
TRYING TO BE AS SPECIFIC AS POSSIBLE ABOUT HOW TO
IMPLEMENT THIS BEHAVIOR IN YOUR PROJECT MANAGEMENT
SYSTEM.

BEHAVIOR	OPERATIONALIZATION
Sharing progress and setbacks, having mechanisms for reporting issues or errors, Taking responsibility for decisions, and apologizing when mistakes are made	• weekly check-ins that involve conversations about errors • discussion of how to prevent errors in the future • project check-in with RA (research assistant) s each semester
Clear and regular communication, task lists, instructions about where/when/how	• regular check-ins—every other week with RAs • a document that has instructions for each week of work and check-ins
Openness to questions and an ability to incorporate new information, adaptiveness and willingness to change course and pivot as necessary	• asking for ideas from RAs • weekly reflection and check-in about recruitment and data analysis strategy
Ability to make decisions and, related to accountability, the ability to explain those decisions	• working within the timeline • clear, articulated rationale for changes in research plan, in the research log
Organized and stays on top of communication, new information, and requests	• research log that is updated regularly • spreadsheet of expenditures • alerts for new literature with relevant keywords including "community trust"

when interacting with people who work for or with us as part of research management.

It's vital in project management to understand inherent power dynamics. You may be the kindest, most self-deprecating, and most informal advisor there is, but you still have power if you are an advisor or supervisor. It's important to remember that this patterns the relationship and affects how others behave toward you. For example, in graduate school, I knew many people who had baby/dog/cat/house-sat for their PhD advisors. I think this is generally a mistake even though most advisors do this with the best intentions: students can earn some extra money, and the advisor hires someone they trust who is accountable to them. However, there are power dynamics inherently at play. Once a student says yes, they often feel obligated to keep saying yes: even if it's inconvenient and they have to cancel other plans to do so. Personally, I think staying in an empty house may be different than babysitting children in that there is less pressure, more freedom, and more perks, but the situation may vary. The issue is that the advisor may never know the student is uncomfortable or inconvenienced, but that is part and parcel of the problem.

My general practice is to steer clear of entangling the personal and professional, especially in cases of power and role asymmetries; there are enough people in the world, and students can often recommend friends or roommates, especially once you explain that the reason you're not asking them is about boundaries between personal and professional. But this book is not about imposing my opinions or practices. These examples throughout the book are intended to get you thinking about *your* priorities, roles, and relationships. I raise the above issue as a single example of power dynamics and roles you may want to consider carefully.

Your values and situation may differ; people are adaptable and diverse, and reality is context-specific. As a counterpoint, why not offer an opportunity to your graduate student, whom you trust and who would benefit from extra income? There is no hard and fast rule, but only things for you to consider to arrive at your own decisions. When managing research projects, there are situations in which things are more collaborative (e.g., between co-PIs) than supervisory (e.g., hiring a lab manager or a student to conduct some interviews). The difference often comes down to who has ultimate authority, and therein power, and what responsibilities such authority requires and connotes. In both situations, the bottom line advice is to *set clear expectations* and *communicate*, which have consistently been found to be important in project management (Kerzner 2002). This gives everyone a foundation and touchstone from which to evaluate and communicate. It is especially essential when you might have to adjust (discussed in Part III) as new obstacles and challenges arise in your project (and be assured, they always will).

Supervision

For supervision, you must remain aware of power differentials. This is important because, as a supervisor, you might expect those who work for you/under you/with you to be able to voice any issues or challenges that arise and ask questions. But there are a variety of reasons why supervisees don't or won't. And when they don't, it is often read as a lack of interest or a poor work ethic. This underscores the importance of communication. Therefore, in a supervisory role, you want to invite questions and have regular check-ins to avoid miscommunication.

As a supervisor and/or principal investigator, you set the tone and culture of that particular project and work environment. It's important to communicate clearly, promptly, and often. For example, if someone you are supervising/have hired doesn't hear back from you about a question they had over email, their inclination might be not to ask next time, lest they be viewed as bothering you, needy, or troublesome. This is particularly pernicious if the supervisor is oblivious that this may be the reason. The dreaded "Well, why didn't you ask me?" is met with silence because of power inequalities even as the person being supervised wants to respond, "Because you didn't get back to me last time!" With supervision, in particular, there are sometimes long-lasting and significant consequences of even a single poor experience, which may repeat themselves and escalate. This is why it's crucial to articulate your values and desired attributes; this allows you to discuss them with a supervisee/supervisor and explain why you operate how you do to reduce miscommunication.

Collaboration with a Peer

While the above relates to people you might supervise or employ, where the relationship is hierarchical, there are also many good reasons to think carefully about people management when you collaborate with peers. You may run into like-interested individuals at conferences, graduate school, online, or your institution who might be interested in collaborating. Or, the reverse: you might be a fan of someone's work and interested in collaborating with them! This is exciting, but I think it is essential to walk into it carefully. Collaborating with people who have similar goals may help avoid frustration. For example, if you're both up for tenure, this often adds an element of time pressure to research and publication that might not affect someone early in their graduate school training or someone much more advanced. Of course, this is not always the case, but it is something to consider.

In my experience, it is frustrating to invite or be invited to collaborate with a clear and set timeline in mind, only to be thwarted and delayed, or rushed, by a collaborator. Again, I think communication and clarity are key, alongside deep attention to power disparities. For example, early in my career, I was incredibly excited to guest edit a special issue of a journal. Unfortunately, no one told me, and I didn't realize, that I might have to reject publications from senior colleagues, who might one day be called upon to write tenure letters or otherwise weigh in on my career. This had never occurred to me; this goes beyond research project management per se but has implications for our research and professional lives.

In the case of equal peer collaboration, it's essential to set expectations and have a personal exit strategy. My approach to collaboration (and many things) is that I try not to come from a scarcity mindset (Ren et al. 2023)—a belief that resources are limited and any opportunity should be taken. In many ways, graduate school sets you up to take every offer: of collaboration, of work, of free food (I still get excited about free pizza at events), and so on. In this way, we are primed to say yes and feel lucky to get *any* opportunity. In my experience, that's a difficult but important habit to break. This is not to say that you shouldn't approach your work (and life) with an attitude of "yes" but that this yes should be thought out. For most of us, there are fewer hours in the day than things to do, and you need to trust your ability to develop new ideas and projects. I know they are in you! This means that you don't have to nor can or should you say yes to everything.

Co-authorship

Just as citations are political (Mott and Cockayne 2017)—who you cite signals your values in many ways and has important professional and field-level implications at a broad level—co-authorship is also political and should be considered carefully. When co-authoring, whether there is a power or position differential or not, I strongly recommend sketching out responsibilities clearly, in advance and, ideally, in writing. The latter cannot be overstated. This doesn't mean the discussion cannot begin in person or on the phone, as a conversation. Still, I make it a habit to follow up in writing, whether via email or in a shared document with co-authors, by writing authorship orders on draft outlines or paper drafts. This is because I find this minimizes misinterpretation or misremembering. Most often, or at least I like to think so, this is not typically willful, but we are limited creatures with limited cognitive abilities, including memory. Further, our relationships change, and this may affect the way we remember agreements, as well as the ways we think arrangements should be changed. Beyond supervision, collaboration and co-authorship are among the most common relationships that characterize research. Of course, collaboration may be with a supervisor, but others are more horizontal. In these relationships, communication is also crucial, and there may be more room for negotiation regarding the content of projects and their management and workflow, for example, deciding on a shared naming convention for files.

First, I recommend you meet and talk to potential co-authors. If you are running a lab or a larger research team, you may not have specifics before the data is collected (e.g., this is a three-year study covering many sites or countries). But you can talk to them about what they might expect, that is, will you invite them to co-author, or are they being paid for their work as a research assistant? This also varies by discipline; in some fields, if you pay a student to do hourly work, for example, the pay is the remuneration, and co-authorship is not implied; in others, if they work on an experiment, they will typically be listed as a co-author. You will want to consider what types of contribution merit co-authorship in your outputs (Nature Geoscience 2017). Figure 6.1 includes a template for a post-meeting discussion about collaboration and co-authorship on a project with a student worker. I would send this type of email to a student I do not know well.

An email to a longtime student worker or peer collaborator would likely be much shorter and more informal. I have included some sample language in Figure 6.2. You might want to create co-authorship contracts, but I find those to be too rigid and transactional for my purposes. However, contracts can be broader and more informational and may be particularly helpful for large data collaborations (e.g., Primack, Cigliano, and Parsons 2019). However, the stringency and specificity of your communication surrounding projects, funding, collaboration, and beyond and whether you want to do this solely in person (or over the phone), by email, or with a signed contract is entirely up to you.

As the above examples suggest, you should also indicate a timeline inasmuch as you can. That is, when do you expect to start working on

Figure 6.1 Example Co-authorship Email to a New Student Worker on a Research Project in Its Early Stages

---

Subject: Manuscript Plan: SUB-TOPIC

Dear NAME,

I wanted to follow up on our conversation today and outline plans for manuscripts coming out of project on TOPIC.

As you know, I am planning to write a series of papers. You will be acknowledged on each for all the work you are doing with data collection and cleaning. However, as I also mentioned, I would like to create an opportunity for you to collaborate on a peer-reviewed paper. Particularly, I anticipate this paper will focus on SUB-TOPIC. You would be second author, I would be first, and it is possible we will bring on another co-author, as I also mentioned. As such, I will do the majority of the writing of the manuscript and the submission of the manuscript, as well as correspondence with editors, though I hope that this will be a truly collaborative experience, as I value your voice and input.

I anticipate starting work on this manuscript on MONTH-YEAR, and would schedule a meeting with you to sketch out an outline and decide on how to distribute responsibilities. I anticipate that we would send it out or review around MONTH-YEAR.

I want to reiterate that working on this manuscript this is not required as part of your position, and you can choose not to work on any papers related to the project. While I don't anticipate issues, I do want to note, for the sake of transparency, that ultimately I retain the rights to the data and anything written, and you can also recuse yourself from the paper. However, I anticipate working collaboratively and resolving any issues we might have. Further, if at any point you think our work together merits reconsideration of the author order please do let me know—this will be part of our ongoing conversations.

Best,

Shiri

---

manuscripts? In particular, if you are working with someone who might be time-limited (that is, someone who is managing a lab or project on a fixed contract, an undergraduate or graduate student who will graduate and may not take a position that includes time for research), it would be helpful to note if they would be invited to collaborate or listed as a co-author even if their time on the project had ended before, for example, you publish outputs. Further, you'll want to consider whether and how that will be decided. Will it be determined depending on whether they had a substantial hand in data collection, analysis, or writing?

It's important to note that there are different perspectives on this. Some researchers believe that if you are being paid for your work (e.g., to conduct

Figure 6.2 Example Project Collaboration Email to a Long-Time Collaborator on a Research Project Where Data Is in the Analysis Stage

Subject: Manuscript Plans: TOPIC

Dear NAME,

I wanted to follow up on our conversation today and outline plans for manuscripts coming out of project on TOPIC. As we discussed, I think we see three manuscripts coming out of this project as we analyze the data, the first on SUB-TOPIC1, the second on SUB-TOPIC2, and the third on SUB-TOPIC3.

As we discussed, I think it makes the most sense for the following authorship order and timeline, but as we know from working together things change, and we can revisit any facet of this as we continue our work and planning.

SUB-TOPIC1—this paper will draw on DATA (e.g., VARIABLES, THEMES, EXPERIMENTS,) and we'll start it in MONTH-YEAR. You will be first author, I'll be second author, and we'll aim to send to JOURNAL on MONTH-YEAR. You'll get started with the data analysis when we start, and I'll begin working on an outline. We discussed possibly sending to one of the following two JOURNALS.

SUB-TOPIC2—this paper will draw on DATA (e.g., VARIABLES, THEMES, EXPERIMENTS,) and we'll start it in MONTH-YEAR. I'll be first author, GRADUATE STUDENT will be second author, and you will be third. GRADUATE STUDENT will clean the data and begin analyses, I will work on the outline and literature review, and we'll send you a rough draft around MONTH-YEAR. We'll aim to send to JOURNAL on MONTH-YEAR and present it at CONFERENCE in YEAR.

SUB-TOPIC3—This paper is the least fleshed out that this point, but we will draw on DATA (e.g., VARIABLES, THEMES, EXPERIMENTS) and we'll start it in MONTH-YEAR. I will be first author, you'll be second author, and potentially we would invite PERSON NAME to join us as third author, after sketching out the preliminary outline, which I will do. We'll aim to send to JOURNAL on MONTH-YEAR.

Best,

Shiri

interviews for a project), there is no requirement or obligation to invite the person to co-author. Typically, in academia, this person would be a student, which perhaps changes the calculus somewhat. As a project lead/principal investigator/supervisor, we are often interested in providing (and sometimes expected to provide) career support and mentorship, even when we hire students and pay them for their work. Further, there are debates about whether payment alone is ethical or, on the other hand, whether expectations of co-authorship are sufficient. Different disciplines have different norms, including, for example, about the weight of first versus last authorship. In my field, sociology, things are less clear in determining co-authorship order, whereas, in many natural sciences, the last author often connotes the principal investigator whose lab it is.

Communicating clearly is essential, as norms vary by discipline (Dance 2012; Pain 2021). Further, your institution may have rules or guidelines for co-authorship—so be sure to check by talking to relevant folks, including perhaps your research office, supervisor, or colleagues. Credit can also be given in acknowledgments, and outputs can include reports or posted data; the CRediT system (Contributor Roles Taxonomy) provides information on categorizing contributor roles in research outputs, e.g., conceptualization, methodology, validation (National Information Standards Organization (NISO) 2022).

I try to always side with maximum equity with particular attention to power differentials. So, if I'm leading the project, I work to get students working on it paid and will discuss co-authorship and who can use the data and how upfront. However, suppose I am hiring outside people or a firm (e.g., for translation or transcription)—the same rules don't apply. Partly, the question is one of who you are collaborating with, what the nature of the relationship is, and what is the goal of the collaboration beyond the dataset/paper/book/report/publication? (Co-authorship might be appropriate for some outputs but not others from a single project!) What is your role (e.g., mentor, mentee, supervisor), and does that affect how you think about co-authorship (and authorship order)?

Notably, there are many resources and guidelines for this, and journals sometimes ask authors to specify what each author contributed specifically. Broadly, many note a requirement of "substantial" rather than tangential contributions to merit authorship status. As one example, the Proceedings for the National Academy of Sciences (PNAS) requests authors note their contribution with the following guidelines:

Authors must indicate their specific contributions to the published work, which will be published as a footnote to the paper. Published contributions are taken from the submission system, not from the manuscript file. Examples of designations include:

- Designed research
- Performed research
- Contributed new reagents or analytic tools
- Analyzed data
- Wrote the paper

An author may list more than one contribution, and more than one author may have contributed to the same aspect of the work.

(PNAS 2023)

The International Committee of Medical Journal Editors (ICMJE) Guidelines for authorship have been broadly used and adapted and may help guide your thinking (ICMJE 2023). As some examples, they note that someone who has helped acquire funding for research merits acknowledgment but not co-authorship. Similarly, general administrative support does not merit **authorship**, nor does "writing assistance" in a technical sense (e.g., copyediting). I invite you to use Worksheet 6.3 to think about co-authorship. Even if you have co-authored a lot, take this opportunity to (re)think your threshold and conventions around co-authorship to ascertain that you are comfortable with your approach, which may have been implicit until now.

Worksheet 6.3 Co-authorship Brainstorming Worksheet

CO-AUTHORSHIP WORKSHEET

LIST THE KINDS OF WORK ON A RESEARCH MANUSCRIPT (WHETHER ARTICLE, REPORT, ETC.) THAT YOU BELIEVE WOULD MERIT AUTHORSHIP.

1. data analysis
2. writing manuscript
3. significant data collection

ADD ANY RELEVANT QUALIFIERS OR IDEAS ABOUT THE ABOVE (E.G., ARE THERE ANY CIRCUMSTANCES UNDER WHICH WHAT YOU LISTED ABOUT WOULD NOT MERIT CO-AUTHORSHIP). TAKE ANY NOTES BELOW OF THINGS YOU MIGHT WANT TO THINK FURTHER ABOUT OR DISCUSS WITH OTHERS (MENTORS, PEERS, COLLEAGUES) IN THINKING ABOUT CO-AUTHORSHIP.

When I say significant data collection, I imagine this being somewhere more than 30% or so; it is fine if both the data analysis and collection were paid (research assistants, RAs) in part or in full but it would still have to be some significant data analysis and collaboration in writing.

Worksheet 6.3 first invites you to list the kinds of work you believe merit co-authorship—perhaps that is data analysis, data collection, writing, or some combination. Then, it asks you to add qualifiers. So, for example, co-writing the manuscript might be something you consider to merit co-authorship, but if they only edited it or wrote only one section, which you heavily edit and ends up very different than the original and it was part of paid work, does that change your views on whether that merits co-authorship? What about if they collected and shared the data with you, but you only use a few variables in your analysis? Does that warrant co-authorship or instead only citation and acknowledgment in the manuscript? As a reminder, you can also view different types of research work as identified by the CRediT taxonomy, which outlines 14 different types of contributions (National Information Standards Organization (NISO) 2022).

While I have provided examples of inviting someone to collaborate on a manuscript (Figure 6.1 and 6.2), if you are working with someone for the first time, and they are working for pay, you might want to protect yourself from commitment to co-authorship before you figure out whether they are reliable and if their work style is consistent with yours. One researcher shared with me that they had, in retrospect mistakenly, offered co-authorship to a graduate student in their program they had hired on an hourly basis to help them conduct interviews. The graduate student turned out to be unreliable (more on adjustment in the next chapters!) and ended up conducting only five out of 100 interviews on a project. All other graduate students working on the project had conducted over 20 interviews, including the researcher/principal investigator on this project. Therefore, you might want to lay out the terms of hiring and collaboration very carefully in advance. In Worksheet 6.3, you brainstormed the terms of co-authorship for yourself, and again, I would recommend you be as clear about this with new collaborators and potential co-authors at the outset of any potential collaboration.

If you do this, you avoid misunderstandings in the future, awkward emails uninviting folks from co-authorship, or even ultimatums. As one researcher shared with me, they had to email an unresponsive senior collaborator an ultimatum: respond or be taken off the paper, after trying to reach them for over a month before sending a completed paper out for review. This paper was important for the researcher's graduate student, who was on the job market and wanted to have the piece under review to increase their chances of getting an interview and position. The senior collaborator had been part of the grant and helped with data collection and analysis alongside the researcher and the graduate student. The researcher and graduate student wrote the manuscript including this senior collaborator as a co-author.

Figure 6.3 Example of Co-authorship Guidelines for a Research Project in Its Early Stages

Subject: Project SUB-TOPIC, credit for work

Dear NAME,

I wanted to follow up on our conversation today on our project. I am thrilled you will be working on this. As part of that, as I discussed, you will be acknowledged for assisting with data collection in all publications that come out of the project.

As you know, I am planning to write a series of papers. In general, my expectations for co-authorship on any manuscripts is assistance with 20% or more of the data collection, significant participation in data cleaning and analysis, and an active role in writing (not just editing) of any manuscripts. We can discuss potential collaboration on manuscripts once the data has been collected and analyzed.

Best,

Shiri

The researcher needed the senior collaborator's OK for any edits before sending the manuscript out for review since they were included as a co-author, but could not get them to respond. Ultimately, they emailed them with a two-week deadline (after already trying to reach them for a month), indicating they would take them off the manuscript and instead list them in the acknowledgments if they did not hear from them before that deadline. Thankfully the senior collaborator finally emailed back and approved sending it out, and the manuscript has since been published.

Next, I invite you to focus on a specific project to think about what co-authorship might look like in the particular project you have been working through so far in the book's worksheets. Each project is different in scope and they may also vary in methods and involvement of collaborators, students, and beyond. Therefore, you may have different ideas and expectations for what merits co-authorship across projects. In Chapter 1, you thought about outcomes and outputs for a particular project and brainstormed them in Worksheet 1.2. In Worksheet 6.4, I invite you to re-list your outputs and consider what the **threshold for co-authorship might be for planned outputs** as well as, if you have them in mind, potential or possible co-authors. As a reminder, we are following the fictional community trust project in Part II of the book. Potential co-authors you are thinking of may be people in the role, for example, John Smith, my lab manager of two years, or a more general co-author, for example, a "lab manager" you haven't hired yet.

This chapter has invited you to think through what you want supervision, collaboration, and co-authorship to look like and the desirable attributes of

Worksheet 6.4 Co-authorship Worksheet for a Specific Project

PROJECT SPECIFIC CO-AUTHORSHIP WORKSHEET

PROJECT STUB NAME: commtrust

WHAT ARE THE OUTPUTS FOR YOUR PROJECT? RE-LIST THEM HERE (AND EDIT OR UPDATED THEM IF NEEDED).

THEN, WITH AN EYE TO THE SPECIFIC COMPONENTS AND NEEDS FOR EACH OUTPUT, LIST ANY POSSIBLE CO-AUTHORS THAT YOU ANTICIPATE MIGHT BE INTERESTED IN BEING INCLUDED.

THEN, IN THE THIRD COLUMN, INDICATE WHAT TYPE AND QUANTITY OF WORK YOU WOULD EXPECT FOR CO-AUTHORS ON THAT OUTPUT.

OUTPUT	POTENTIAL/ KNOWN CO-AUTHORS	WORK EXPECTATION OF CO-AUTHOR
infratrust	RA1 (research assistant 1)	RA1 is helping with interviews, and with recruitment in a substantial way (about 30%) if they are interested in collaborating with me on the paper I would want them to work on data analysis, in addition to some collaboration in writing. Because they are such a big part of the data collection, even though this portion is paid, as long as they follow through with analysis and writing co-authorship should be reasonable.
neighb	RA2	RA2 is helping with focus groups but in a secondary capacity (taking notes while I facilitate). If they are interested in co-authorship they would have to contribute substantially to writing the manuscript, particularly results and conclusion.
commt	RA1 and RA2	RAs would need to work on data analysis and contribute substantially to the joint analysis, as well as the theoretical frame of the paper.

a project manager. Further, I've asked you to consider the kinds of contributions you believe merit co-authorship and given you some examples for how to communicate about co-authorship. More broadly, I hope that chapter has helped you think about your priorities and values related to working with and managing people involved in research, including yourself (more on this in Chapters 10 and 11). As always, this may vary by project or over time; no two research projects are the same, and there may be different considerations for each!

Works Cited

Allen, Kelly-Ann, Gregory M. Donoghue, and Saeed Pahlevansharif. 2020. "Addressing Academic Rejection: Recommendations for Reform." *Journal of University Teaching & Learning Practice* 17(5):1–10.

Benton, Thomas H. 2004. "Is Graduate School a Cult?" *The Chronicle of Higher Education Online*. Retrieved May 5, 2023 (www.chronicle.com/article/is-graduate-school-a-cult/).

Dance, Amber. 2012. "Authorship: Who's on First?" *Nature* 489(7417):591–93.

Einbinder, Susan Dana. 2014. "Reducing Research Anxiety among MSW Students." *Journal of Teaching in Social Work* 34(1):2–16.

Gilley, Jerry W., and Ann Maycunich Gilley. 2007. "The Manager as Coach." *Harvard Business Review* 97(6):110–19.

ICMJE. 2023. "ICMJE | Recommendations | Defining the Role of Authors and Contributors." Retrieved August 10, 2023 (www.icmje.org/recommendations/browse/roles-and-responsibilities/defining-the-role-of-authors-and-contributors.html).

Kerzner, Harold. 2002. *Strategic Planning for Project Management Using a Project Management Maturity Model*. New York: John Wiley & Sons.

Meissner, Philip, and Torsten Wulf. 2016. "Debiasing Illusion of Control in Individual Judgment: The Role of Internal and External Advice Seeking." *Review of Managerial Science* 10(2):245–63. doi: 10.1007/s11846-014-0144-6.

Mott, Carrie, and Daniel Cockayne. 2017. "Citation Matters: Mobilizing the Politics of Citation toward a Practice of 'Conscientious Engagement.'" *Gender, Place & Culture* 24(7):954–73. doi: 10.1080/0966369X.2017.1339022.

Nature Geoscience. 2S017. "Editorial: Where Credit Is Due." *Nature Geoscience* 10(5):323. doi: 10.1038/ngeo2949.

National Information Standards Organization (NISO). 2022. "ANSI/NISO Z39.104-2022, CRediT, Contributor Roles Taxonomy." NISO. doi: 10.3789/ansi.niso.z39.104-2022.

Ocampo, Anna Carmella G., Lu Wang, Kohyar Kiazad, Simon Lloyd D. Restubog, and Neal M. Ashkanasy. 2020. "The Relentless Pursuit of Perfectionism: A Review of Perfectionism in the Workplace and an Agenda for Future Research." *Journal of Organizational Behavior* 41(2):144–68.

Olson, James M., and Jeff Stone. 2005. "The Influence of Behavior on Attitudes." Pp. 223–71 in *The Handbook of Attitudes*, edited by Dolores Albarracin, Blair T. Johnson, and Mark P. Zanna. Mahwah, NJ: Lawrence Erlbaum Associates Publishers.

Pain, Elisabeth. 2021. "How to Navigate Authorship of Scientific Manuscripts." *Science*. doi: 10.1126/science.caredit.abj3459.

Parkman, Anna. 2016. "The Imposter Phenomenon in Higher Education: Incidence and Impact." *Journal of Higher Education Theory & Practice* 16(1):51–60.

PNAS. 2023. "Editorial and Journal Policies." *PNAS*. Retrieved August 10, 2023 (www.pnas.org/author-center/editorial-and-journal-policies).

Primack, Richard B., John A. Cigliano, and Parsons, Chris. 2019. "Co-Authors Gone Bad—How to Avoid Publishing Conflicts." *Elsevier Connect*. Retrieved June 7, 2023 (www.elsevier.com/connect/co-authors-gone-bad-how-to-avoid-publishing-conflicts).

Ren, Menghao, Shengqi Zou, Siying Zhu, Mengjie Shi, Weiwei Li, and Daoqun Ding. 2023. "The Effects of Scarcity Mindset on Envy: The Mediating Role of the Sense of Control." *Current Psychology* 43: 7612–27.

Tyson, Neil deGrasse [@neiltyson]. 2016. "In Science, When Human Behavior Enters the Equation, Things Go Nonlinear. That's Why Physics Is Easy and Sociology Is Hard." *Twitter*. Retrieved May 29, 2023 (https://twitter.com/neiltyson/status/695759776752496640).

PART III

Adjustment

CHAPTER 7

Communication and Diagnosis

Managing and organizing our research projects includes planning, execution, and adjustment. In this book, I argue that each of these components is equally important to your research management process and system. While planning is vital, and having a system in place for managing and organizing your research should contribute to enhancing your research and reducing your stress, building mechanisms for adjustment is also essential. As we know, research often requires adjustment (or the favored word of the COVID-19 pandemic: pivoting), sometimes minor and other times significant. I know researchers who have had to modify the planned socio-demographics of their samples slightly, a comparatively minor adjustment, but also researchers who have had to select an entirely different country as a research site because of emergent access or safety issues, a big change. We cannot plan for everything, but I argue that by building in mechanisms for communication and accountability (again, both with others involved in our research and ourselves, whether we are working on a solo project or a collaborative one), we can create better conditions for adjustment and success of our research projects.

How Do I Know Things Need Adjusting?

Sometimes, it is evident that something needs to change. For example, no progress is being made, you haven't hit planned milestones, or something prevents you from doing the work you need to do. Again, there are countless examples I can think of from my own experience and that of colleagues and other researchers: the software you use is no longer supported, data is lost without a backup, there's a global pandemic, someone quits mid-project, you can't gain access to your research site because a gatekeeper is barring your way—the examples go on and on. Some of these issues can be solved by planning; for example, as discussed in Chapter 2 and Part I, building in pilot data collection can ensure you can gain access. Others can be solved by good workflow; for example, as Chapter 4 and Part II discussed, having an effective workflow means having backups for your data. Other challenges, however, cannot be solved or prevented by either planning or good work-flow, like a global pandemic or someone quitting. However, having mechanisms built in for adjustment can help in many cases, though sometimes this adjustment requires putting a particular project on hold or changing it so extensively that you'll need to (re)start at the planning stage.

At the heart of this book is a focus on what you do and how you *feel* doing it. Broadly, there are two ways that I know things need adjusting in my research. First, something is wrong with the *doing*, that is, the work. Things aren't getting done, I'm off my timeline, I am making lots of mistakes that I should have had checks for, or I lose data or my jotting of ideas or directions. Or, second, something is wrong with the way I *feel*. I feel stressed, anxious, and disorganized in my research.

Remember, *feelings aren't facts* (Goldsmith 2013).

As we know from imposter phenomenon and perfectionism, common among academics (Parkman 2016), just because you feel something doesn't mean it's true or based in reality. That doesn't make feelings trivial or unimportant. Those feelings, I argue, still need to be addressed. Either "talked down" and dismissed or dealt with whether individually or with the help of a professional such as a therapist or coach, friends, or other resources. While good research project management will not solve perfectionism, it can help reduce the stress that stems from disorganization. For me and many researchers I know, we typically *feel* disorganized because things *are* disorganized. So, *while feelings are separate from reality, I believe a problem in each requires attention and adjustment.*

In this chapter, we focus on three primary factors that facilitate adjustment: first, **clarity**, particularly in communication; second, regular and comprehensive **check-ins**; and third, **diagnosis**. We'll continue the discussion from Chapter 6, where you worked to align your values with how you manage yourselves and others, whether in supervisory or collaborative relationships. We'll focus on how to incorporate feedback mechanisms for your research work—whether it be data, people, or writing, how to figure out when things aren't working, and how to diagnose your challenges. In the following chapter (Chapter 8), we'll focus on some ways to address these issues and how to adjust (or "pivot") when things get off track.

Clarity

As discussed in the previous chapter, **clarity** is critical in goals, organization, systems, workflow, and communication, whether collaborating, supervising, or working alone in your research. The people component might be the most challenging (Chapter 6) but is particularly important for research, where people come from not only different professional, cultural, or other backgrounds but also various epistemological and ethical commitments and levels of research experience. Clear communication will pay dividends and let everyone know where they're going and their goals. Again, this clarity in goals, outputs, outcomes, bookkeeping, and administration that we've worked on in previous chapters (Parts I and II) should reduce stress and allow you to recognize if things are off track and take steps to fix them. It will also be welcomed by the institutions and organizations you work in and for, allowing for clarification of what is getting done, how resource-intensive it is, and where growth opportunities lie. Clarity in workflow and communication means legibility (Part I), whether to you or others, depending on who is involved in the research. Your approach to clarity depends on goals and to whom things need to be clear. However, this also means that meetings should have agendas, and emails should have relevant subject lines. This helps you keep organized and reduces unease, often unintended, plaguing others who wonder, "Why did they call me into this meeting?"

Communication

The best way to avoid misunderstandings in working with others, in which people "learn" from past interactions, sometimes with unintended consequences (e.g., that email may have accidentally been deleted or slipped your mind, but now the person thinks you are ignoring their concern!), is to create clear and regular mechanisms for communication. That is, clear times and communication channels: whether weekly meetings or emails, a shared to-do list on a Google Doc or whatever you find works for you.

As we discussed in the context of workflow and bookkeeping (Chapters 4 and 5), you must build a way to keep track of information. Worksheet 7.1 invites you to brainstorm the **types of communication** you need in your research project vis-à-vis whom and to anticipate the modality (e.g., email, meeting) and the frequency. Determining the frequency of communication is up to you; I would err on the side of more often, at least early on (e.g., even every couple of weeks or monthly at the start), and then if appropriate,

> ### Worksheet 7.1 Anticipated Communication Modality and Frequency Worksheet
>
> > **COMMUNICATION FREQUENCY AND MODALITY**
> >
> > **PROJECT STUB NAME:** medtour
> >
> > **FIRST, FOR THIS PROJECT LIST THE PEOPLE YOU ALREADY KNOW WILL BE WORKING ON IT, AND ANTICIPATE ANY ADDITIONAL PEOPLE YOU PLAN OR WOULD LIKE TO INCLUDE. START WITH YOURSELF, THEN INDICATE THE FREQUENCY AND MODALITY OF EXPECTED COMMUNICATION.**
> >
> > | PERSON/ROLE | MODALITY | FREQUENCY |
> > |---|---|---|
> > | Self | | weekly, part of Friday afternoon weekly planning |
> > | Co-PI | Zoom/phone | weekly or twice a week during planning and data collection, bimonthly thereafter |
> > | Survey firm contact | Zoom | daily for the first three days while survey data is being collected, thereafter weekly until the quota is reached, sum-up meeting after that with co-PI in attendance |

transitioning to twice a year or once a semester or quarter, or whatever time period you are working on. Further, some weeks, months, or periods might require intensive communication, others less frequent check-ins. However, you might want a daily update email or a shared document, Slack channel, or shared task sheet or area in a project management software (Appendix B) if you use one where people check in, perhaps even more than once daily. As described in Chapter 6, people management is challenging, and you'll want to be clear about expectations; there is a fine line between micro-managing and being an absent manager, and you'll need to find the middle ground that works for you and those you are working with.

In the chapters in the book's third part, as described in the Introduction, I draw on a hypothetical mixed methods (discourse analysis of newspaper articles and survey) project on medical tourism, stub "medtour." As always, these examples give you another data point; do not be distracted by them, and you can go straight to work on your own worksheets, downloadable on the book's companion website. As you fill out the worksheet, **your first row should be yourself** (and that might be it for a project for which you are the only one conducting the research without funding in an academic setting, though even then, you might want to include mentors or the department chair)—how often do you expect needing or wanting to check in on your research project? For me, for most projects, this is weekly. I do this when I plan out my following week (see Chapters 4 and 6), and once I begin work on a project, I try to work on it every week, even if briefly, unless I'm at the stage where the paper is out for review or a paper draft is with a co-author, for example. I find it important to keep things consistent in my mind, but the rhythms and demands of your life might differ, as may the types, number, and scope of the projects you work on and how many people are involved. As discussed in Chapter 3 in the context of tools, depending on the frequency and type of communication a dedicated group communication platform may work better than email or in-person meetings.

The Importance of Check-Ins, Even If Only with Yourself

Regular check-ins are essential when managing a project. Compared to general communication, check-ins are where you *systematically* reflect on project progress. This is useful for various reasons, for example, for use in annual assessments and reports or yearly updates to granting agencies. However, they are even more critical to ensure that the project is on track and to make corrections. Again, there is a lot of latitude and variation in what people find effective, and much of it depends on your timeline and the rhythm and scope of the research project(s) you are managing. As we discussed with workflow (Chapter 4), if you work on a semester system, it might make sense to check in once a month and then do a more thorough check-in at the beginning and end of the semester, primarily if you work with a team where people scatter at certain times; if you're on a quarter system, or a fiscal year system, or another time system, you may want to follow that rhythm. It's a good idea to have a general check-in at the quarter, halfway, and three-quarters point of any project at least as a starting point, relying on your timeline (Chapter 2). Again, however, you might have deadlines for your grant, institution, or project that require different or additional intervals. As we discussed in bookkeeping (Chapter 5), it is also essential to understand the timing of other partners and stakeholders in your research. For example, many funding agencies and universities operate on a fiscal year schedule ending June 30, which may be a more appropriate "end of the year" marker than the end of December.

Check-ins allow you to figure out what's going well, what needs to be improved, and what is failing, and to consider exciting opportunities or valuable ways to adjust. For example, suppose there's an opening to collect additional or new data that arises mid-project. In that case, you can ask yourself whether and how this contributes to the project goals and your desired outputs and outcomes to ensure you do this intentionally rather than experiencing sneaky scope creep (Chapters 1 and 2) and keeping in mind the context of your career and research goals and possible broader organizational goals). Further, check-ins allow you to redistribute work and perhaps reallocate particular tasks based on skills and strengths (or weaknesses) that have emerged in the context of the research project. Sometimes, this involves difficult decisions and conversations (e.g., finding new collaborators or people to do paid work), but it is an integral part of the project. Further, regular and candid appraisals of progress and check-ins allow a more honest, less stressful, and more realistic approach and ensure your project is not derailed beyond repair. Importantly, they are also a way to build trust and enhance your research relationships.

Check-ins should be an opportunity to examine progress and then transition to providing mutual feedback: that is, it should be more of a dialogue and conversation than a lecture (again, even if only with yourself). If working with others, you should ask for feedback on your behavior (or management, in the case of supervision), and then ask for the other person to reflect on their behavior: for each noting an accomplishment and a challenge of progress so far, which allows for self-reflection and, as needed, course correction. One of the most valuable functions of check-ins is seeking a different perspective, understanding where the issues lie, and formulating a plan for moving forward, whether that involves resources, a restructured timeline, goal adjustment, or any other issues.

Reflection is a critical component of effective project management and is particularly important to diagnose any issues. Some issues are apparent (e.g., work is not getting done), while others may be hidden (e.g., someone is stressed or insulted but has not shared this concern). Like some larger companies, some labs and organizations have manuals or handbooks outlining expectations for behavior and appropriate conduct. While this is less common for fine arts, humanities, or social science projects since people are not typically working in a "lab," it may be a good idea to create a centralized document or manual if you are running a research group. Even lab manuals may provide more technical information about equipment and data than behavioral or communication expectations. A project handbook might be useful for your project, mainly if the project "staff" is of a size to warrant this. However, you might also be able to rely on existing handbooks at your organization or a more formal human resources department or unit. There are few mechanisms to formally assess people's work for many smaller-scale research projects, even those that employ student workers or research assistants. This makes it particularly important that you build in these mechanisms for communication.

Worksheet 7.2 invites you to expand on the list you made in Worksheet 7.1 by adding information about the check-in's contents. In particular, you may want to include more than one kind of check-in with any given person or role, perhaps with a different frequency or modality than the ones you identified in the previous worksheet. So, rather than thinking only about the person/role as the unit of analysis when thinking about the **frequency and modality of check-ins**, think about the **goal of the check-in**. So, for example, I mentioned that I check in weekly with myself to track progress on my research projects. I also check in with myself at the beginning and end of every semester to figure out how things are progressing in a "big picture" way and reflect on how each project fits into the other demands of my semester. I also need a check-in at the end of the fiscal year (which I sometimes fold into my end-of-spring semester check-in since they coincide) to examine my expenses and determine if I need to request an extension from a funding agency if the project is externally funded.

Similarly, I like to schedule weekly or bimonthly check-ins with research assistants, depending on how many hours they work on the project each week. I also schedule meetings at the end of each semester to do a general check-in. The former is always in person or over Zoom, but the latter is sometimes over the phone and, in some cases, over email. I urge you to think about scheduling check-ins frequently enough that you can figure out if anything is amiss and then work to adjust it but not so frequently that they are a waste of time, though at the beginning this might require trial and error, and may vary across projects. The example in the worksheets in Part III of the book is from the imagined "medtour" example, which includes a co-PI and personnel from a research firm but no assistants or other people involved.

We can categorize check-ins in myriad ways, but I think of them as falling into two broad categories: formal and informal. **Informal** check-ins are more regular/ongoing check-ins concerned with continuing work. In contrast, **formal**/larger check-ins mark critical periods passing, deadlines, or correspond to particular outputs or outcomes. Again, check-ins can occur vis-à-vis other people, but as discussed in the worksheets in this chapter, you should also have check-ins with yourself. The proposed agendas and discussion points should be undertaken even if you only check in with yourself!

Worksheet 7.2 Check-in Worksheet

CHECK-INS

PROJECT STUB NAME: medtour

EXPANDING ON THE ABOVE WORKSHEET, NOW CONSIDER THE AGENDA OF CHECK-INS, AND NOTE THAT YOU MIGHT NEED MORE THAN ONE CHECK-IN IN TERMS OF FREQUENCY OR GOAL FOR A SINGLE PERSON OR ROLE.

PERSON/ ROLE	FREQUENCY	AGENDA
Self	weekly	• check -in on progress • make weekly to do list • enter tasks in calendar
Self	beginning of the semester	• semester plan by week • review timeline, spending (start new sheet in research accounts workbook)
Co-PI	weekly or twice a week during planning and data collection, bimonthly thereafter	• check-in on data collection • discuss and allocate duties for data analysis, writing across both data sources
Survey firm contact	daily for the first three days while survey data is being collected, thereafter weekly until the quota is reached, sum-up meeting after that with co-PI in attendance	• discuss data quality and collection progress • finalize data delivery, codebook

Agendas and Minutes for Meetings

For more informal/regular/ongoing check-ins, I recommend you go through at least the following:

1. Revisit the goals you had set for the period (e.g., week or month)
2. Check in on progress:
   a. Accomplishments/achievements

    b. Decisions to be made
    c. Challenges and brainstorming discussion of possible changes
3. Set goals for the period before the next check-in

I urge you to send an agenda before any meeting, including a check-in meeting, and you can fill in particular specifics for any single meeting (e.g., check on progress for interviews).

For more formal check-ins, you should undertake additional preparation and ask your counterparts (if any; remember check-ins can be just for you on any given project!) to do the same. I recommend you do the following:

1. Specify the task/period under review
2. Note/discuss anything that needs to be done, particularly as related to goals and administration, for example reports or budgets, and agree on a timeline for drafting, feedback, editing, and completion
3. Ask yourself and (if relevant) your collaborator (e.g., colleague, employee, student) to reflect on their progress and critical updates
    • For someone you supervise, before the check-in, you can ask them to think about one challenge, an area of improvement, and one accomplishment
        • Start by acknowledging and thanking them for their work

Figure 7.2 Sample Meeting Agenda

Discuss progress on writing STUBpaper1 draft since meeting in October

    - Review tasks set at previous check-in:

        o Finish literature review

        o Flesh out concept X in introduction

        o Coding documents for focus on [topic]

        o Rough draft of results

    - Decisions:

        o Should we still target journal A?

        o Should we split the paper out into two papers?

    - Any challenges? Adjustments needed?

Set goals for next meeting

When discussing the challenge and area for improvement, you want to be sure of the following:

- Make sure to revisit the overall goal of the project and any particular goals of the time period/even under discussion
- Get the person's perspective on what they think the following steps/adjustments should be
- Offer whatever support you can (the best way to approach this is to ask them what would make them feel more supported and help them accomplish their tasks)
  - If it is a collaborator, you might do this differently, having more of a conversation surrounding these issues, but you should still discuss accomplishments, challenges, progress, and critical updates

For most meetings, you should have an agenda and minutes. That is, you want to take notes on what was discussed and, as relevant, share this with the person post-meeting to make sure that anything that may have been misunderstood or unclear can be corrected, discussed, or anything that requires follow-up can happen.

Building Your Schedule

One of the most challenging parts of project management is fitting it all in. We often underestimate the amount of time a given task will take, which can set everything off track. The more we do particular kinds of tasks (e.g., reading and summarizing articles, writing, data analysis), the more we improve not only in the quality of our work (practice, practice, practice) but we can often complete the tasks faster (to a point). Perhaps of even broader utility, we become better at estimating how long tasks take. When confronting your schedule, you will want to think about your obligations and events related to your research in terms of their priority to you (Chapter 2).

The Eisenhower matrix is a tool to think about tasks you encounter and how you should prioritize them. It distinguishes tasks along the **criteria of important/not important and urgent/not urgent**. The idea is that we want to avoid getting bogged down by things that are not urgent and unimportant, for example, distractions, and instead focus on the things that are important to you. Ideally, tasks that are urgent and important get priority. Worksheet 7.3 invites you to populate your own Eisenhower

---

Worksheet 7.3 Priority Checklist: Urgent/Important

PRIORITIES WORKSHEET

PROJECT STUB NAME: *medtour*

USE THE BELOW TEMPLATE OF THE EISENHOWER MATRIX TO CATEGORIZE VARIOUS RESEARCH TASKS.

	URGENT	NOT URGENT
IMPORTANT	*Pay survey research firm* *Gather and clean data* *Update research log regularly* *Data analysis*	*Brainstorming target journals for publication* *Theorizing inductively*
NOT IMPORTANT	*Answering some emails* *Interruptions* *Meetings with no apparent purpose*	*Worrying about things that have not yet happened and that I cannot control*

---

matrix with your project tasks (you can refer back to your worksheet in Chapter 2).

For urgent but unimportant tasks, you should figure out whether these can be delegated, while for those that are not urgent and not important, it would be ideal to eliminate those if at all possible! You will need to be especially careful to schedule time for those tasks that are important but not urgent, as these can often fall by the wayside. Some things are urgent or, worse, seem urgent but are ultimately less important. For example, photocopies that need to be made. Ideally, you can delegate these tasks or put aside dedicated time for them in the planning state, for example (see also Chapter 11). Preferably, we can eliminate tasks that are not urgent and not important, as they are a drain on our time and resources—but only *you* can decide what is important!

However, you also need to consider your commitments in terms of **fixed** as compared with **variable** obligations and events, and those that are within and outside of your **control**. As a non-research example, dropping off kids at school is a fixed commitment that you do not control the timing of, in that you cannot change the time that kids need to be at school (though you might be able to change how they get there, e.g., bus, carpooling, having another household member drive or walk them). On the other hand, you may have some control over your teaching schedule if you are a faculty member, but once it is set for the semester, it becomes fixed. If you're a faculty member, when you schedule your writing time or data analysis is flexible, potentially variable, and within your control on a more rolling basis (that is, you can change it from afternoons one week to mornings the next or even from day to day). However, it may be important for you to "fix" this writing time in your schedule consistently, so that it does not drop by the wayside. Finally, some things are outside your control and variable in that they are not fixed at a regular, known in advance time. For example, a meeting you are summoned to by someone in a position of authority over you (e.g., supervisor, Dean). You do not control the time, but neither is it fixed in advance in your schedule. Thinking through your scheduling excludes emergencies, as these are not under your control (more on how to adjust to these in Chapter 8).

Many researchers find that their research challenges arise from not adequately budgeting time for these important but not urgent tasks, which you can and should incorporate into your system. I urge you to think about finding a scheduling tool (Chapter 4) to manage one of your most prized resources, time—whether a calendar on paper or online, or project management software. Scheduling check-ins and time for important tasks relieves much stress and the cognitive and mental burden of worrying about if and when things will get done.

Research is often only part of our jobs, and even if you are a full-time researcher or research scientist, fellow, or on a research fellowship, you may be juggling between research projects and certainly across tasks (e.g., data cleaning, analysis, meetings). When building your monthly/weekly/daily schedule, you will want to determine if there are fixed commitments you have or want to establish, for example, regular research group meetings. Suppose you are selecting times for particular tasks or events. In that case, you may need to schedule them around other fixed demands on your time that are outside your control (personal or professional). Importantly, events or tasks that are variable and in your control might be the ones that seem easiest to put off, but they are often the most important.

With this in mind, I invite you to use Worksheet 7.4 to **schedule any research project tasks that you want to "fix" in your schedule**—at least for the time being—and allot time to do so. Try eliminating items in your above-populated Eisenhower matrix's "not urgent/not important" quadrant if at all possible. For your variable tasks, are there some that you want to fix

Worksheet 7.4 *Scheduling Tasks Worksheet*

SCHEUDLING WORKSHEET

PROJECT STUB NAME: medtour

REVIEW YOUR POPULATED EISENHOWER MATRIX AND DECIDE
WHICH TASKS YOU WANT TO "FIX" IN YOUR SCHEDULE AND WHICH
YOU MIGHT WANT TO KEEP VARIABLE. LIST THE TASK, FREQUENCY,
AND SCHEDULE—IDEALLY AN ACTUAL DAY AND TIME.

TASK	FREQUENCY	SCHEDULED FIXED TIME
Pay survey research firm	Twice	October 15 for first tranche, December 1 for last payment
Gather and clean data	Weekly for 4 months	October–December for survey—cleaning happens in December, budget 8 hours/week for 4 weeks (split among co-PIs), probably Tuesdays and Thursdays August–November for newspaper articles, budget 6 hours/week for 12 weeks (split among co-PIs), probably Tuesdays and Fridays
Data analysis	Bi-monthly for 3 months	November–February, initial meeting on November 10 to divvy up data analysis plan with co-PI, then every other week, can be coupled with data cleaning meeting for first few weeks on articles as we're cleaning survey data
Update research log regularly	Daily/weekly	After each activity, but at the least each Friday afternoon when making weekly plan
Brainstorming target journals for publication	Once or twice	November 12, once data cleaning is mostly underway as analysis begin, create an overall list of journals for each paper, with ranking of order of submission in case of rejection. Revisit as data analysis finalizes before sending papers out for review (target date for first is January)
Theorizing inductively	Set aside at least one 2-hour block/month	Maybe last Wednesday of each month?

NEXT, CONSULT YOUR SCHEDULE WHEREVER YOU KEEP IT (PLANNER, DESKTOP CALENDAR, ONLINE, ETC.) AND FOR THE NEXT WEEK/MONTH/YEAR, DEPENDING ON FREQUENCY, ENTER THESE TASKS AS WELL AS THE CHECK-INS YOU DECIDED ON IN THIS CHAPTER INTO YOUR CALENDAR TO "PROTECT" THAT TIME FOR THAT PURPOSE. IF THERE'S A TASK YOU WANT TO SCHEDULE AND "FIX" WEEKLY, YOU MIGHT WANT TO TRY IT AT A PARTICULAR DAY/ TIME FOR A MONTH AND REVISIT AFTER THE FIRST MONTH TO SEE IF THAT TIME WORKS. IF THAT IS THE CASE, JUST NOTE THAT YOU WILL REVISIT THE TIME/DATE AT THE END OF THE MONTH IN YOUR CALENDAR.

a regular time for? If so, when? Try to enter those into your calendar for the following week/month/year now so that this time, in particular for those tasks that are important/not urgent, is protected in your calendar. This is because urgent tasks usually get done whether or not you schedule them, often because there are immediate incentives and accountability to complete them (e.g., people will come by and interrupt me if I don't email them back).

Works Cited

Goldsmith, Barton. 2013. "Feelings Aren't Facts." *Psychology Today.* Retrieved June 11, 2023 (www.psychologytoday.com/us/blog/emotional-fitness/201310/feel ings-aren-t-facts).

Parkman, Anna. 2016. "The Imposter Phenomenon in Higher Education: Incidence and Impact." *Journal of Higher Education Theory & Practice* 16(1):51–60.

CHAPTER 8

Troubleshooting When Things Get Off Track

Now that you have examined the urgency and level of importance of your tasks, and considered the frequency, modality, and goal of check-ins, we will tackle how to diagnose issues that arise in those check-ins and in other ways throughout your research project. In this chapter, we'll talk about how to adjust our research, systems, workflow, plan, behavior, tools, and beyond to address the issues and challenges we encounter. We will discuss moving from diagnosis to adjustment for some common research challenges. Following diagnosis, you will want to brainstorm possible courses of action first. Second, you will want to pick an approach and action (or more than one concurrently) to address and implement as a response.

Diagnosis

One of the biggest problems with adjusting is diagnosing the issues and challenges arising in our research and their causes. People often fear a diagnosis because it confirms that something is wrong (e.g., for medical diagnosis see Dawson, Savitsky, and Dunning 2006). Labeling the problem can sometimes "make it real." However, labeling a problem is also the first step to addressing or fixing it.

Sometimes, we are aware of the symptoms of the problem but don't quite understand the problem itself, while other times, the problem is painfully apparent. Diagnosis and assessment are essential whether you are managing a solo six-month research project or a three-year project with four co-leads and 20 employees. Of course, larger scales bring their own challenges. Still, ideally, you can avoid some problems before they arise at the planning stage (Part I) and while the work is happening in the execution phase (Part II) by clearly articulating and aligning goals, expectations, workflow, and communication. This ensures that everyone is starting from a similar foundation, and again, the more precise and transparent you can be at the planning and execution stage about what's expected of each of the project leaders (e.g., the researcher, co-investigators) and then, in turn, what is expected of people who are working on the research (e.g., people contracted to help whether for pay, credit, whether students or subcontractors), the better.

Diagnosis requires, first and foremost, an awareness and opportunity to figure out that something is amiss. This can be accomplished, I have argued, by scheduling regular check-ins and clear communication (Chapter 7). Once we identify a problem, we need to figure out what the cause(s) is, including the root of the problem. When other people are involved in your research project, this sometimes requires difficult conversations. Whether these are conversations with yourself or others, understanding what is preventing progress and how the issue can be addressed is required.

Worksheet 8.1 follows the imagined mixed methods project on medical tourism as an example and invites you to think about issues in your own research project (again, blank worksheets are available at the book's companion website). Later in this chapter, we'll think about possible solutions, but the first step is figuring out whether there is a problem or issue, which you can do with regular check-ins, good planning, timelines, and so forth. The next step is trying to figure out the root of the problem. If the issue involves someone else (in any capacity—supervised, supervising, collaborating), you will likely want to include them in the conversation. For example, a task you scheduled with a particular due date may not have been completed on time. The cause might be that the person assigned to the task, such as a research assistant assigned to complete an annotated bibliography, did not. You know this because you had a clear timeline (Chapter 2) and regular check-ins with yourself and them to assess progress (Chapter 7). At this stage, it's crucial to have a conversation and figure out the root cause: perhaps the timeline expectation was unreasonable, which should be adjusted and has implications for the rest of the timeline on this project or future projects. It could be an issue of access to articles or unclear instructions, which can be fixed and help you be more explicit and figure out permissions and access in the future. It could be that the research assistant is not performing the task for other personal reasons or that they did not understand the importance of the deadline. Again, each of these has its own solutions, so diagnosing an issue accurately is essential for finding the most appropriate solution and has implications

Worksheet 8.1 Diagnosis Worksheet

DIAGNOSIS WORKSHEET

PROJECT STUB NAME: medtour

IDENTIFY PROBLEMS OR ISSUES THAT YOU HAVE ENCOUNTERED IN YOUR PROJECT. THEN IDENTIFY THE CAUSES, AND REMEMBER THAT THIS MAY REQUIRE CONVERSATIONS WITH OTHERS WORKING ON THE PROJECT.

PROBLEM/ISSUE	CAUSE(S)
Delays	pandemic, personal issues
Data cleaning is not consistent and not being documented	difficulty with coordination across co-PIs

REFLECTION

Co-PI and I will need to meet and adjust our planned timeline based on delays and develop a reliable, joint workflow for data cleaning. We did not coordinate file names for the newspapers gathered and we're not updating the research log in consistent ways, which has resulted in confusion surrounding the data. This is an important lesson for when we work together next, and for my future projects with collaborators.

for making changes to your system including your tools (Chapter 3) or workflow (Chapter 4).

Another example: it may be that as you sit down to write your annual report, you have lost some vital documentation, for example, a receipt or an invoice. The cause might simply be that people make mistakes, and sometimes, no deeper cause can be identified—mistakes and accidents sometimes happen! However, having a clear bookkeeping system would have identified this earlier, helping you avoid leaving administrative tasks for months later when the missing receipt will likely be harder or perhaps impossible to recover. Similarly, you may want to adjust your workflow to ensure you work through your bookkeeping more regularly. Identifying the root cause is particularly important because it helps you determine how to make adjustments not just in your current project, but to your system in general.

We do not want to think of "blame" but instead of causes even though issues can often be traced to being someone's "fault." Assigning blame is less important than identifying the cause for two purposes: first, figuring out a solution to the particular issue. While accountability is important, blame and even an apology cannot typically fix the research issue. (Nonetheless, as discussed in Chapter 1 in the context of ethical commitments and again in Chapter 6 in the context of good research management, one of my core commitments is to accountability, so I do think taking responsibility is critically important for its own sake). Second, figuring out the cause of an issue or mistake can facilitate adjustments that might help prevent the same or similar issues from arising in the future. Once these are listed in Worksheet 8.1, I invite you to reflect in the space allocated on the worksheet on any trends you might be able to spot: is there anything shared among the types of issues or challenges you identified? Do they group in some meaningful way? Keep this in mind as we move toward adjustment!

Brainstorming Adjustments and Approaches

The next step is to brainstorm potential solutions or approaches to address the issue(s) you've identified, which may require single-time adjustments or more systematic changes. For example, suppose you encounter an external reality you cannot control, such as illness or a pandemic. In that case, you will likely need to work around it, possibly altering the timeline or reducing the work you do in that time period. On the other hand, personal or people issues (including, for example, the imposter phenomenon) require additional and sustained work rather than a one-time adjustment.

Let's walk through three recent real-life examples. As always, these are meant to be illustrative, not prescriptive. They are examples, not exemplars, that should give you some more data points rather than mandating a particular solution. Your circumstances may differ, or you might have an identical problem but have different solutions that are better suited to your circumstances, ethical commitments and values, and preferences.

A first example: a researcher who regularly does fieldwork abroad is confronted with the COVID-19 pandemic. This is an external reality over which the researcher has no control. The cause is a global pandemic, and their specific problem/issue is that the pandemic is preventing travel to their field site, which prevents progress on data collection. Further, there was little information in the early pandemic about how long this might last and when travel to this location would be possible again. Indeed, travel was not possible for over two years in this case, either because of restrictions on entry into the location by the local government or by the researcher's institution. Possible solutions in this case are several: first, the researcher can ask for an extension from a funding agency or on their tenure clock if they're an academic. Second, the researcher can hire a local research assistant or seek a local collaborator to collect data. Third, the researcher can change field sites, finding one that is accessible. Fourth, the researcher can change the nature of the data they are examining on their research topic, for example, shifting from ethnographic research to online surveys.

A second example: a researcher hired a student research assistant to transcribe interviews. They had set up a clear schedule and a deadline and agreed on payment and terms. The deadline came for the first transcript, which had yet to be deposited in the folder. The researcher emailed the student to check-in, and the student responded after a few days. There are several possible solutions, but in this case, given the nature of the relationship, their supervisor offered to take them out for coffee and helped them figure out what was creating the stressors and offering some advice, in addition to referring them to several resources at their institution. Some possible solutions include granting the student an extension, hiring someone else already working on the project, turning to an external, professional transcription service (which in this case would require additional IRB approval), seeing if another research assistant already working on the project could complete the transcription, or having the researcher/principal investigator complete the transcription themselves.

In another example related to software, a colleague was working with a data analysis program they had been using for years. They updated their software and found two problems: first, there was a feature that was gone in the update; second, if they saved their project in this software version, their collaborators/research assistants could not open it in the previous version, which they had access to. Possible solutions included: searching online to see if others had this issue, contacting the software company, investigating if there was a way to revert to the previous version, checking if there was money that could be found in the budget to update collaborators' version, figuring out workarounds or alternatives for the feature that was missing— for example, a user-written add-on or a combination of other functions, or changing software programs.

Worksheet 8.2 invites you to take the issues you identified in previous worksheets and brainstorm solutions. Recognizing and categorizing the cause might help you think about more structured solutions. At this stage, **brainstorm three to five solutions**, whether or not they seem particularly

Worksheet 8.2 Brainstorming Adjustments

BRAINSTORMING ADJUSTMENT

PROJECT STUB NAME: medtour

PROBLEM/ ISSUE	POTENTIAL BRAINSTORMING PARTNERS	POSSIBLE ADJUSTMENT
Delays	co-PI, maybe talk to [name] about my own time management during pandemic	1. adjust timeline 2. work on time management 3. reduce workload—smaller sample? Different analysis? 4. bring in additional people, RAs (research assistant)?
Data cleaning is not consistent	co-PI	1. discuss convention with co-PI 2. have each person in charge of one data source (survey v news articles) 3. check in more regularly on each other's data cleaning and reconcile differences 4. hire RA for data cleaning (with supervision)
Data cleaning is not being documented	co-PI	1. decide on an update schedule 2. set reminders for update 3. check up on each other's work 4. hire RA for data cleaning (with supervision)

easy or feasible as you write them; just write what comes to mind and think expansively.

Importantly, I often like to brainstorm solutions to issues with other people. This may be required in a collaborative project, but even in my solo research projects, I find this invaluable. This is because our vistas limit us and we have personal "universes of the possible." Others can offer different perspectives and possible ideas for troubleshooting, not to mention their own experiences. For external realities, for example a pandemic or sudden illness, the issue/event is often overwhelming logistically and emotionally. This means I find that I need to draw on additional help to think clearly and holistically about how to approach the problem. Therefore, I also invite you to identify a person or two you might want to discuss these issues with: mentors, peers, colleagues, an institutional research office, IRB, or beyond. We'll work to select an appropriate approach from this list later; at this point, you're just brainstorming in the below sheet.

Adjusting and Troubleshooting

Now, you will want to determine which solution(s) to pursue.

Suppose we were filling out this worksheet based on the three examples discussed earlier; again, for illustrative purposes let's work through some of the possible solutions for each. For the researcher whose research assistant was not completing work by the deadline: a pro of issuing an extension, for example, is that you are giving the student another chance and you do not have to train and onboard someone new to do the work or change the budget. A con is that the core cause may be unresolved, and it's unclear if the work can be done by the deadline. Another solution was to use an external transcription service rather than a student assistant. A pro is that the result would be done quickly and efficiently. Still, the cons are that spending the money will require additional budgetary resources and approval. It would require an IRB amendment and entering the transcription firm into the researcher's institution's fairly complex purchasing system.

Returning to the example of the researcher whose travel and fieldwork were derailed by COVID-19. Some possible pros of finding a local collaborator are that the researcher is investing in that location's economy and employing a local researcher, creating new or strengthening existing connections, and relying on previous experience and research on the context. Some possible cons involve a lack of control over how data is collected and the risk of incompatible work styles, the need for additional approval to use the funding differently, and an IRB amendment. In this example, transitioning from ethnographic research to a survey was simply a non-starter; the researcher's discipline, training, and epistemological commitments are to ethnographic and qualitative research. In that case, they didn't even bother listing the pros and cons of that option; it was simply a no for them! Again, the benefit of initially brainstorming expansively is that you can have many solutions or approaches that are theoretically possible. Still, in practice, it's perfectly fine if you're unable or unwilling to do some of them.

For the example of a researcher with a problem caused by a software update, each possible solution has some potential pros and cons. The pros of changing the analysis software program are that it would have the needed features, and the versions have both backward and forward compatibility. The cons would be the cost for both the researcher and the assistants to purchase licenses and the learning curve of learning the software and "translating" or redoing some previous work that had already been completed on the current software to the new software.

These examples should give you a jumpstart to thinking about the **pros and cons of the different solutions** you brainstormed for your issues or problems in Worksheet 8.2. In Worksheet 8.3, I invite you to list the pros and cons of the solutions you brainstormed to help you select the best solution(s).

Importantly, as we discussed in Chapter 2 in the context of scope and mission creep, and in the context of abduction in Chapter 1, you may want to adjust mid-project because of some exciting or new developments and new directions, not only because of problems. The below worksheet should allow you to consider the pros and cons of any adjustment, not just one concerning a problem! However, adjustment always requires change, and there are often trade-offs and opportunity costs of your time, resources, and beyond with any adjustment. The goal is to adjust with as much information and thoughtfulness as possible.

The Fallacy of Sunk Costs

Notably, the last solution of our illustrative examples, changing the data analysis software (your tool; Chapter 3) mid-project, is costly—it requires learning and buying a new software program. However, such changes can sometimes be the best possible course of action. Recognizing and remembering the fallacy of sunk costs has served me well personally and professionally. The idea of the **fallacy of sunk costs** is that once we invest (time, resources, money, effort) in something, we believe that we're already "in too deep" to backtrack or make a change (Jarmolowicz et al. 2016), but that change may be the best course of action. For example, if you're waiting in a check-out line at a grocery store with multiple check-out lanes, and you've been waiting in that line for ten minutes, if another line seems to be moving faster, you're hesitant to move into the other line. After all, you've invested so much of your time in "your" line.

Worksheet 8.3 Adjustment Pros and Cons Worksheet

ADJUSTMENT PROS AND CONS

PROJECT STUB NAME: medtour

PROBLEM/ISSUE: delays

POSSIBLE ADJUSTMENT 1: adjust timeline

PROS is more realistic, gives us more room to work also reducing mental load

CONS we had other things planned after this, co-PI has a review coming up and having papers submitted to journals would help their case

POSSIBLE ADJUSTMENT 2: work on time management

PROS can help me think about my priorities, may help me brainstorm ways to be more efficient, can include delegation

CONS I am already feeling at capacity, I have other projects that require attention

POSSIBLE ADJUSTMENT 3: reduce workload—smaller sample? Different analysis?

PROS more feasible, would reduce time commitment

CONS not sure if sample will be sufficient, especially of newspaper articles, analysis was carefully planned

POSSIBLE ADJUSTMENT 4: bring in additional people, RAs?

PROS would help with timeline, helps with work, trains a junior scholar

CONS requires training which too requires time, brings in another person with particular needs, requires funding

SELECTED ADJUSTMENT(S): after conversation with co-PI we decided to adjust the timeline (adjustment 1) and I will think through time management (adjustment 2) for my own workday/tasks. We will revisit in one month, in the meantime both co-PI and I will see whether we can divert any funding or apply for institutional funding to hire a RA (research assistant, adjustment 4) since both of us think that might be an exciting idea but currently not feasible within our budget. We both decided that the project was carefully and well planned and at this stage we don't want to change the scope (adjustment 3) but we might revisit this in our meeting in a month.

However, moving to the other line makes the best sense if your goal is to get checked out of the store and leave as soon as possible. However, since we've devoted time to "our" line, we often opt to stay there even though the benefits no longer outweigh the costs. I want to remind you that it's OK and sometimes preferable to change course and amend your approach, even if you've invested time or other resources in your chosen path. Remember, the goal is to get your research done accurately, ethically, and in a timely and effective way, and sometimes that requires abandoning your original strategies or reorienting your approach. However, it is essential to figure out what the costs and benefits are, or in other words, pros and cons, to avoid falling into the fallacy of sunk costs as you move toward selecting an approach or solution to any issue or problem.

Selecting an Approach

To follow up on the previous examples, for the researcher whose student research assistant was not completing work, they scheduled a meeting so the researcher could connect with the student. Together, during the meeting, they decided it would make the most sense for the researcher to find someone else to complete the transcription, with an open invitation for the student to contact them when they were ready to complete work that the researcher could allocate if there was additional work to be done. In this case, another research assistant already covered by IRB and familiar with the project was able to complete the transcription.

The researcher who could not access their field site ultimately decided on a combination approach: they re-oriented to collect some data from online sources. Also, they hired a research assistant to collect local information, including interviews and photographs. This required additional IRB approvals and approval to use the previously authorized travel budget to hire a research assistant, but this was the most productive approach.

In the case of the software issue, the researcher found that the feature was indeed gone, and while there was a workaround (that is, a way to cobble together what that feature did in other ways), it would require more time and turned out to be quite convoluted. Further, the budget was already tight, and there would not be a way to update the version of everyone collaborating on the project. After contacting the software company, the researcher found they could revert to the previous version, which they did for that project. Notably, given this, following the completion of that project the researcher opted to transition to an entirely new data analysis program with stellar reviews, better backward and forward compatibility across versions, and a reasonably priced group license for future projects. While this required significant adjustment, with everyone learning a new program, this decision ultimately enhanced their work long-term. This is an example of how this issue was resolved in the short term for this project (reverting to a previous version) and a tool change in the longer term (changing software programs).

Worksheet 8.4 invites you to list possible solution(s) and the **steps necessary to implement your preferred solution** for the issues you identified in Worksheet 8.3. You will want to fill this out for each issue you have and

---

Worksheet 8.4 Adjustment Implementation Worksheet

ADJUSTMENT IMPLEMENTATION

PROJECT STUB NAME: medtour

PROBLEM/ISSUE: delays

SELECTED ADJUSTMENT(S): adjust timeline, in my own schedule: work on time management

STEPS TO ADJUSTMENT IMPLEMENTATION

We had originally hoped to complete data collection by August, but we are pushing this back to October. We have adjusted our timeline, and will continue work in June; at the end of June we plan to meet again to see whether we need to further adjust our timeline. We have also decided that we will each consult our research budgets and any possible internal sources of funding that might allow us to hire a research assistant to help with the article data collection and some of the survey data cleaning as well. But this adjustment is contingent on budget. For now, we have each reduced the planned work for this month, and re-charted our timeline through October.

TIMELINE

We've adjusted our Gantt chart and timeline from data collection ending in August to October. We will meet at the end of June to revisit progress and check in on how our progress is going in terms of delays and the new timeline. At the same time, I am going to devote two hours this week to my own time management, track where my time is going, and see whether I want to pull back on some other projects, and maybe adjust some of my work schedule in the next month.

its decided solution. I also invite you to consider a timeline for dealing with this issue: for example, if the answer is to change field sites because of the pandemic, what are the necessary steps needed to do so, and what is your timeline for researching additional field sites, talking to IRB and any relevant stakeholders?

Further, you will want to determine if anything systemic in your project management may benefit from adjustment or change. This means an issue that occurs repeatedly within a project and/or across research projects. For example, a repeated issue with meeting deadlines you identified for the project in the planning phase can be solved by adjusting your timeline, workflow, communication frequency, or modality with collaborators or assistants (Parts I and II). You may be finding that you are constantly behind on everything; this may, again, require adjusting your timeline and plans and recreating your timelines and Gantt charts (Chapter 2) to allot more time for particular tasks. You may find that you are not saving crucial administrative information, for example, timesheets, in your admin folder because you have relied on your organization's system or office. However, it may be that their records are only available for the last 12 months, and you have found that you sometimes want or need to access older records; you may need to consider your bookkeeping system and download and save those records as part of your own bookkeeping (Chapter 5). Or you may want to explore a different tool, whether a software program or something else. If you do choose to use a different data analysis or writing program, for example, this might be something that you want to change across your research projects if you are engaged in more than one. If you are considering a new or different tool, you can revisit Chapter 3 and the worksheets on tool selection. Worksheet 8.5 invites you to keep a running list of **systematic issues and corresponding adjustments** you want to make; again, this can be relevant to the project you are working on or changes to your research project management system that extend beyond any single project so that you can adapt and improve your research project management system more broadly.

Worksheet 8.5 *System-Level Adjustments*

SYSTEM-LEVEL ADJUSTMENTS

PROBLEM/ISSUE	SYSTEM-LEVEL ADJUSTMENT
Delays	budget more wiggle room in timeline
Data cleaning is not consistent	clearer decisions and written directions, which we didn't think were necessary because we were long-time co-PIs, but this is a new project and articles for media analysis are a new form of data for us
Data cleaning is not being documented	again, more communication of expectations with co-PI or future collaborators at the beginning, and a clear understanding of what information nears to be cataloged in the research log and in what way to make it legible to us both

Works Cited

Dawson, Erica, Kenneth Savitsky, and David Dunning. 2006. "'Don't Tell Me, I Don't Want to Know': Understanding People's Reluctance to Obtain Medical Diagnostic Information." *Journal of Applied Social Psychology* 36(3):751–68.

Jarmolowicz, David P., Warren K. Bickel, Michael J. Sofis, Laura E. Hatz, and E. Terry Mueller. 2016. "Sunk Costs, Psychological Symptomology, and Help Seeking." *SpringerPlus* 5(1699):1–7. doi: 10.1186/s40064-016-3402-z.

CHAPTER 9

Project Completion, Dissemination, Reproducibility, Replication, and New Offshoots

Our research projects are dynamic, and sometimes, mid-project or nearing completion, we will come up with offshoots to that research. Sometimes, that is a new paper (what may be considered an output as discussed in Chapter 1 on planning) from the same data, but sometimes it is a "side" project—a true offshoot, branch, or extension of an existing project. In this chapter, we'll first tackle wrapping up a project, with a specific focus on reproducibility, replication packages, and organizing your data, metadata, and other information in a way that will be legible externally (for reproducibility and replication as necessary) and internally in case you return to your data, a year, five years, or even ten or more years later. We all know the trepidation with which we approach a project or data that we have not "touched" in a while, trying to understand where things are and when and why we made the decisions we did. Much of that can be tacked by having a good workflow and research log (Chapter 4) and a comprehensive book-keeping system (Chapter 5). There is a benefit to having a tidy replication package for reproducibility if possible, which is sometimes required and noted at the project planning and funding stage in the form of data management plans. Further, conducting a post-project reflection allow you to first return to past research projects as needed (e.g., you may one day write a review article about your research referring to many projects across your professional life course), and second, to use to improve your system for future research projects.

Data Sharing

In Chapter 2, you worked on a data management plan, thinking about how your data will be collected, analyzed, stored, and shared. Researchers have felt a push toward increased accountability and transparency with their data. The National Science Foundation (NSF) started requiring a DMP with all proposals beginning in 2011 (NSF 2023a). In 2020, the NIH released an updated policy for "Data Management and Sharing (DMS)," effective 2023 (NIH 2023b). These agencies and many others, as well as for IRB approval for research involving human subjects and ethics committees, require clear information on how and where the data will be shared. This includes the data and related tools and codes, the provision of metadata (e.g., codebooks and other data documentation), and information about how compliance will be managed, which may last well beyond the project (NIH 2023c). The NIH has a list of repositories (NIH 2023a), and all researchers can upload data to the ICPSR repository (ICPSR 2023b) and use openICPSR for downloading data for replication and reproducibility purposes (ICPSR 2023a). There are many more options, including GitHub (a repository; while separate from Git it hosts Git repositories; Git is listed in project management tools in Appendix B), and some NSF directorates provide a list of repositories, for example, in the Division of Earth Sciences Data Policy Appendix from 2017 and 2018 (NSF 2023b). In general, it is preferable to share data on a website that is less subject to change and expiration, such as an institutional (e.g., your university's) webpage over a personal one, or the ones mentioned above, because of the stability and longevity of access. Many of us have run into the frustration of looking up replication or reproducibility code that should have been available only to find that the person had moved institutions, their personal website had changed, or the link was broken.

You will want to think about what and how you share data and what kind of metadata you share. In general, to ensure that your data are being used correctly (an issue that is important not only for the quality of your research or "good science" but an ethical issue as well, I argue), you will want to include some metadata, perhaps a codebook or some additional information about sampling. As always, you will need to refer to disciplinary conventions by reviewing some of the resources listed above, and you will likely want to revisit the resources in Chapter 2 about sharing data in the context of data management plans.

Replication, Reproducibility, and Transparency

Reproducibility and replicability have sometimes been used interchangeably, but at other times **reproducibility** is used to denote obtaining the same results with the same data and analysis codes while **replication** is generating consistent results across studies in response to the same research question with different data, while in some cases the meanings have been inverted (National Academies of Sciences 2019). In this chapter, we focus on ensuring reproducibility (though confusingly this results in what many in the social sciences call a "replication package" that contains data and code to generate the results presented) but of course clear organization and cataloging of data collection, analysis, and other research steps are also important for replication and sharing of approaches to the broader research community (not just in science or social science). For each quantitative publication (and possibly data, depending on the circumstances), you should create a replication package and, as always, back it up (Chapter 3). Replication packages (which really refer to reproducing published or shared results) for quantitative data analysis should contain the raw (source) data and the script or code that generates the results presented in any publication (paper, report, public post, possibly a presentation). I create these packages even if I do not post my code and data and doing so may not be possible because of IRB or other restrictions or is otherwise inadvisable. But you will still want to make sure you have a start-to-finish file and a clean copy of the data that gets you to the results you have published or otherwise publicly shared. Like with my source data, I zip this file to avoid inadvertently editing it after the fact. I store this within my data folder (and typically call it STUB_replication.zip or STUB_toshare.zip).

The questions for other forms of data are more complex: images, documents, interviews, and other qualitative data. Generally, best practices for many situations in which data come from and involve human subjects are fully de-identifying the data (and de-identification is also important for much quantitative data), including names, place names, zip codes, and voice recordings. Regarding summary statistics and data collection about people, the Census has recommended that it be divulged only if it comprises 600,000 or more people (using the least populous state, Wyoming, as the rule of thumb). For other characteristics, the recommendation is that any cell contains at least 100,000 weighted cases. So, for example, you may want to combine information about the county of residence or another characteristic until it is large enough to have over 100,000 people (Pascale et al. 2020).

There are benefits to sharing qualitative data, but there are also risks, not just of identification but also of lack of context. Some argue that qualitative data can only be understood in context and that sharing it renders it only partially useful and challenges its integrity, while others have argued against such claims (Alexander et al. 2020; van den Berg 2008; Feldman and Shaw 2019). A more significant concern is the changing context in which the shared data exists (rather than the context for the data itself). Some behaviors, issues, and attitudes viewed as normal or acceptable may be subsequently criminalized or decriminalized. These are issues that the researcher cannot always anticipate at the time of data collection (for example, seeking an abortion or using marijuana, to cite only a couple of examples, may become criminalized from one day to the next depending on the place and time period), which necessitates extreme care.

In deciding whether and how to share your data, you should consult the best practices within your discipline and a burgeoning literature on the costs, benefits, and risks of sharing data. While you may not always be able or choose not to share data, transparency about analysis methods is always advisable, and you should be able to defend your analyses and answer questions about them—to peer reviewers, committee members, and any other interested parties. This requires a clear workflow and organization strategy that can support confidence in your analyses and the ability to go back to your data in an organized way. This may not culminate in a replication package for reproducibility or even a shared codebook or detailed discussion of process, but remember; research project management is about accuracy, reliability, organization, and legibility, and the most important person to whom your research, data, results, and process should be legible to is you—current you but also future you. You should be able to double-check the accuracy of your analyses even after some time has passed. The best way to do this is to ensure your organizational system is legible and clear to you so that you can retrace your steps and explain them to someone else, even if you do not provide a replication package.

When Is a Project Over?

As we defined in Chapter 1, a project is generally a set of related tasks with a common goal and seeking specific results. A project also has a start and end date. However, research projects are often very susceptible to change and research is deeply emergent and dynamic. As we know, good research raises at least as many questions as it answers. Occasionally, we have external constraints that may create bounds for a research project: a fixed budget, time, or a mandate given by an employer or someone else. However, sometimes it is for us to decide. As we have discussed in Part III of this book, adjustment is a critical component of research and, indeed, of any project.

It is sometimes hard to decide when a research project is over and treat research projects as discrete things, especially given offshoots, changes, and extensions. That is, your research about a topic may have raised another closely related question about the same broad topic. Is this part of the same research project, an extension, or a new one? Unlike a bridge, which is complete when built, research projects' completion can be more amorphous. In many ways, it depends on the outcomes and outputs you identified at the planning stage, in Chapter 1. However, research projects involve within-project discoveries and extensions, which can sometimes make their boundaries more porous or "leaky."

Research projects can be considered bound and "completed" in several ways: a research question is answered, a particular set of data is collected, or a paper or research project is published but can also be considered complete when the time allocated to it has passed, a deadline reached, or budget is spent. Which of these strategies you follow is up to you, and indeed, my research projects are "over" based on different criteria. For example, the dissertation was done when it was filed. It was then that I moved on to other stub names as I significantly reworked and collected additional data to publish different articles and my first book. The research project was not over, though the dissertation research and dissertation were complete. However, for some who worked on a three-paper dissertation model, there may have been three stub names and folders (for each paper) all along with a separate folder for dissertation that drew on each of these and added an introduction and conclusion (and indeed, in some disciplines a three-paper dissertation model means some papers must or should be published when the dissertation is defended or filed). When moving to publication, they may have continued with the same stub and in the same folder. Sometimes, on the other hand, a project is about data collected or in the context of a grant. In that case, offshoots involving other data may also have their own folders, but as discussed in Chapters 3 and 4, they can be nested in the overall project folder.

Worksheet 9.1 invites you to brainstorm when your project is complete across several dimensions that may or may not be relevant for any given project. (As a reminder, we're following through with our hypothetical "medtour" project in this chapter). As with most worksheets in this project, focus on one project; you can repeat the process with additional research projects as you see. So, what are the **criteria for the project being completed** based on outputs/products (e.g., reports, articles, datasets), time (e.g., a specific date), and budget/funding (e.g., when such and such amount is spent, when such and such grant runs out)? I also encourage you to think about whether any of these are **necessary as compared with sufficient conditions** for project completion: that is, is a published article both necessary and sufficient for you to declare the project as complete? Or perhaps it depends on a grant and the final report or monies spent are a necessary but not sufficient condition. In the below example, project completion is contingent on outputs/products whereas the budget and timeline are secondary.

Worksheet 9.1 Project Completion Worksheet

PROJECT COMPLETION WORKSHEET

PROJECT STUB NAME: medtour

WHEN IS YOUR PROJECT COMPLETE BASED ON THE BELOW DIMENSIONS? ARE ANY OF THESE NECESSARY AND/OR SUFFICIENT FOR PROJECT COMPLETION?

OUTPUTS/PRODUCTS

Dataset—posting of survey data and codebook
Two published articles
Two national conference presentations
One short public-facing piece

TIMELINE

Originally survey data was to be posted by September, now we are aiming for November after adjustment
Articles ideally will be sent out for review by May, with presentations of the work in progress in conference1 in March and conference2 in April
Public-facing piece out by April

BUDGET

$15,500 entirely for survey data collection

Managing Offshoots

For many of us research is as much a creative as a technical endeavor. Good research always raises new questions and directions for future research. Good research management requires that these offshoots be managed efficiently in a way that renders them and their relationship to the previous project legible to you. Generally, my management strategy in organizing offshoots of research is about the intellectual relationship of the products rather than when the data collection or product begins and ends.

To provide a real-life example, I was working on a paper that went out for peer review, and a reviewer suggested an exciting analysis and research question on a separate but related topic that could be answered with different variables and methods within that same (secondary) dataset. That analysis was beyond the scope of the first paper, but it sparked some thinking, and I wanted to explore it further in depth. I had a folder as part of my system that was the first paper, and I originally was only going to write the one article from this data, the one I had sent out for review. When I began the new paper, I opted to designate a new stub name for this new project (despite it using a dataset I had used in another paper) and create a new folder, copy that same (de-identified) source data, and analyze it for this new paper.

One researcher I know organizes (and often that means reorganizing) their folders and work by products where data and paper drafts live in entirely different folders, each with their own naming conventions (e.g., they will not have a stub for a research project with all papers and data nested there, but rather a folder for each set of data and a folder for each paper that can call on any data, all with different names and no nesting; see Chapter 4). Papers will "call" on that data (sometimes one dataset, occasionally several) where each paper or report too has its own folder. Their system has less nesting than mine, and they have a separate research log for each dataset and product. You will want to pick a system that organizes your work in a way that is intuitive to you and works with your rhythm and data requirements while being legible and getting the research "right" in a way that prioritizes accuracy. In my case, offshoots often have their own folders. I organize them as either nested in the larger project or separate depending on how intellectually related they are to the overall project. For the scholar with different folders for each set of data and each product, offshoots that require new data collection lead to a new data folder with its own research log and other folders for products with their own research logs. Neither strategy is right or wrong; it depends on the type and rhythm of your work and how you think through extensions of existing projects.

The good news is that electronically, the costs of moving and reorganizing things are comparatively low. Gone are the days when you had to physically move papers and folders from filing cabinets around. You can change your mind about your organizational strategy and rely on your research log to point to where things are stored. To be sure, reorganizing will require time and effort, but be wary of falling into the fallacy of sunk costs described in Chapter 9; changing your system, a tool, bookkeeping, or workflow will be well worth your time if it can help you better organize and navigate your current and future research project(s) more efficiently, easily, and intuitively.

The Post-Project Reflection

Once you complete a project, it is helpful to **reflect on the successes and challenges of the research project** to learn as you move forward; this is part of the adjustment project and may require some system-level adjustment (Chapter 8, Worksheet 8.5). The idea of a post-project reflection (often called a post-mortem in corporate settings) is a retrospective assessment of how the project went and a prospective exercise to implement change based on lessons learned. I encourage adjustment continuously via check-ins, which means that only a few new themes or insights emerge in the post-mortem because they have already been addressed. However, a post-project check-in is especially important in collaborative projects—and serves as an opportunity for everyone to come together and reflect on the project. As a researcher, if you are managing a project with others, it makes sense to hold a post-project reflection meeting to thank your team members for their work, review what was accomplished, and provide space to share successes and challenges. Even if you are working on solo research, it helps to leave a moment for a post-project check-in—that is, a post-project reflection. Worksheet 9.2 invites you to do just this. You can also adapt it to share with any people working with/for you to elicit their thoughts and experiences as part of your project completion process!

The Future Directions Document

Front and center on my computer (for me this is in my overall Dropbox folder; see Chapter 3) is a future directions document, not nested in any folder. This is a prized location I rarely use in my own filing/organization system. The only things that live there are my signature (for inserting into documents), letterhead, and the future directions document because they cut across so many of my needs (personal and professional—in my case, everything lives in Dropbox, not just my work but also my cell-phone photos and tax documents). While I might put project-specific thoughts and

Worksheet 9.2 Post-Project Completion Reflection Worksheet

POST-PROJECT REFLECTION WORKSHEET

PROJECT STUB NAME: medtour

PROJECT GOAL
Examine Americans' experiences and perceptions of medical tourism via a nationally representative survey (n=1,000) and analyze discourse surrounding medical tourism in the media (discourse analysis of NYT articles from 2000 to 2020).

PROJECT OUTPUTS
[name] dataset, article1 citation, article2 citation, presentation1, presentation2, [name] blog post

BUDGET
$15,500 spent on survey collection in July 2021

TIMELINE
Planning and grant application: January–April 2021; data collection: June–October 2021 (originally supposed to end in August); data analysis: November 2021–April 2022; articles under review: June 2022, published in May and July 2023; blog post: April 2023.

WHAT WENT WELL
Successful publications in high-impact venues, building an understanding of medical tourism as it relates to public perceptions of health and medicine, inequality, privilege

WHAT COULD HAVE BEEN BETTER
Data collection and analysis was delayed, there were issues with our data collection, documentation, and analysis, which stemmed from lack of clear communication and protocols at the beginning.

WHAT CAN WE IMPROVE FOR THE FUTURE
Make sure that communication is really clear on naming and analysis conventions between co-PIs, budget timeline more realistically!

ideas into my pensieve (Chapter 4), I also keep a future directions document front and center. Because I work across many areas, I like to keep a centralized document with ideas that might refer to any one of my research streams and related to any single project (e.g., I'll make a note of a paper idea, and then note the stub name that the idea might be related to). For collaborative projects, I may also copy this into the research project's log because I want my co-author(s) to have access to these ideas.

To decide if you want such a document, think about where you have done your brainstorming, that is, is there somewhere or several places (e.g., a research log, notebook, pensieve document, a whiteboard, sticky notes) where you already keep ideas for future research projects? Would they benefit from being centralized somewhere (and again, this does not have to be a document, it can be sticky notes or a whiteboard, though I would recommend creating a document and pasting photos of the whiteboard or sticky notes into it regularly to catalog your thinking), and if in digital form, do you want one overarching file or one nested within projects? If you've made the decision to have a future directions document or location, go ahead and take a moment to decide where to store it and create it!

Works Cited

Alexander, Steven M., Kristal Jones, Nathan J. Bennett, Amber Budden, Michael Cox, Mercè Crosas, Edward T. Game, Janis Geary, R. Dean Hardy, Jay T. Johnson, Sebastian Karcher, Nicole Motzer, Jeremy Pittman, Heather Randell, Julie A. Silva, Patricia Pinto da Silva, Carly Strasser, Colleen Strawhacker, Andrew Stuhl, and Nic Weber. 2020. "Qualitative Data Sharing and Synthesis for Sustainability Science." *Nature Sustainability* 3(2):81–88. doi: 10.1038/s41893-019-0434-8.

Berg, van den, Harry. 2008. "Reanalyzing Qualitative Interviews from Different Angles: The Risk of Decontextualization and Other Problems of Sharing Qualitative Data." *Historical Social Research / Historische Sozialforschung* 33(3 (125)):179–92.

Feldman, Shelley, and Linda Shaw. 2019. "The Epistemological and Ethical Challenges of Archiving and Sharing Qualitative Data." *American Behavioral Scientist* 63(6):699–721.

ICPSR. 2023a. "openICPSR: Share Your Behavioral Health and Social Science Research Data." *openICPSR*. Retrieved October 20, 2023 (www.openicpsr.org/openicpsr/).

ICPSR. 2023b. "Start Sharing Data | Deposit." *Start Deposit*. Retrieved October 20, 2023 (www.icpsr.umich.edu/web/pages/deposit/index.html).

National Academies of Sciences, Engineering, and Medicine. 2019. *Reproducibility and Replicability in Science*. Washington, DC: The National Academies Press.

NIH. 2023a. "NIH Institute and Center Data Sharing Policies | Data Sharing." *NIH Institute and Center Data Sharing Policies*. Retrieved October 20, 2023 (https://sharing.nih.gov/other-sharing-policies/nih-institute-and-center-data-sharing-policies).

NIH. 2023b. "NOT-OD-21-013: Final NIH Policy for Data Management and Sharing." *Final NIH Policy for Data Management and Sharing*. Retrieved October 20, 2023 (https://grants.nih.gov/grants/guide/notice-files/NOT-OD-21-013.html).

NIH. 2023c. "Writing a Data Management & Sharing Plan | Data Sharing." *Writing a Data Management & Sharing Plan*. Retrieved October 20, 2023 (https://sharing.nih.gov/data-management-and-sharing-policy/planning-and-budgeting-for-data-management-and-sharing/writing-a-data-management-and-sharing-plan#elements-to-include-in-a-data-management-and-sharing-plan).

NSF. 2023a. "Proposal & Award Policies & Procedures Guide (PAPPG) (NSF 23-1)." *Proposal & Award Policies & Procedures Guide (PAPPG)*. Retrieved October 20, 2023 (https://new.nsf.gov/policies/pappg).

NSF. 2023b. "US NSF—GEO—Data Policies—EAR." *Earth Sciences*. Retrieved October 20, 2023 (www.nsf.gov/geo/geo-data-policies/ear/index.jsp).

Pascale, Joanne, Diane K. Willimack, Nancy Bates, Joanna Fane Lineback, and Paul C. Beatty. 2020. *Issue Paper on Disclosure Review for Information Products with Qualitative Research Findings*. Working Paper Number rsm2020-01. United States Census Bureau.

Timmermans, Stefan, and Iddo Tavory. 2012. "Theory Construction in Qualitative Research: From Grounded Theory to Abductive Analysis." *Sociological Theory* 30(3):167–86.

PART IV

Final Notes

CHAPTER 10

Finding Your Style

The Non-negotiables

As we discussed in Chapter 1, there are very few non-negotiables in your research project management approach and a lot of places where you can adapt things to your needs, preferences, pace, ethics, values, and circumstances. The non-negotiables include accuracy, legibility, reliability, and organization. However, there are as many ways as people to craft a research project management system that meets those goals. This chapter invites you to consider (or reconsider) the principles, ideas, lessons, and recommendations of the previous chapters in terms of your style and adapt them to your own life and rhythm.

Knowing Yourself

Many of the worksheets have already prompted you to think about the elements of your management and research style. For example, what values and ethical commitments guide your research (Chapter 1)? Do you prefer to write with pen and paper or electronically (Chapter 3)? Are you someone who is detail oriented? Do you tend to micro-manage? Or are you content to go with the flow? Do you prefer to work independently or collaboratively (Chapter 6)?

"Know thyself" and self-awareness are critical to any progress. For example, I know a faculty member who wakes up every weekday and works on research tasks from 6:00 to 7:30 in the morning. They limit their research work to those hours, leaving the other hours of the day for teaching, office hours, socializing, and other activities. As much as I wish I could hold such a schedule, I cannot, both because of external constraints as well as my circadian rhythm and preferences. It is simply not how I *can* work nor how I work *best*. The better you understand what of your habits and style are changeable and what is more fixed and, more importantly, what you are unwilling or unable to change, the easier it is to tailor your system not only in research project management but in life to your style (you can revisit your priority checklist/Eisenhower matrix in Worksheet 7.3 in Chapter 7 as well as the section about building your schedule).

There are always ways to tweak, adapt, and change your system. However, not all solutions work for all people or situations. As this book has emphasized, while there are some best practices, no one size fits all, and as I have discussed, I have come to my system (which I continue to refine) through much trial and error and adapting and following others' recommendations selectively. My north stars remain my values and ethical commitments, legibility, efficiency, and reliability. Perhaps not all but many roads can lead to Rome, so to speak. The experiences shared in the book, both mine and those from other researchers, are intended to give you additional data and information about *what* to prioritize in your research management system (legibility, efficiency, reliability) and *why* (to improve your research and research experience by making it more organized and accurate, to reduce mistakes, respond to employer and external demands, and help manage your workload and stress) as well as tools and approaches to help you figure out *how* to do so. But it is not intended as a prescription pad or dogma (see the Introduction), but rather as a guide. Your tools, system, rhythm, and style will be your own.

Knowing yourself will help you figure out where you might want to build some guardrails so that you don't fall off your research path entirely. The preceding chapters have worked to help you identify what your values are and where you might need help, where errors or issues arise. Building guardrails against the instincts and approaches that do not serve you will further help advance your research and well-being.

In Worksheet 10.1, I invite you to list the elements of your work style as it relates to research. As a starting point, list three to five **characteristics of your research work style**. Try to include both positive and negative attributes, such as perfectionist, detail-oriented, fast writer, or control freak. If you are struggling to identify your style I recommend asking professional contacts, ideally those you have worked with on research, for example, advisors, mentors, supervisors, co-workers, collaborators, co-authors, and

---

Worksheet 10.1 *Your Researcher Characteristics*

YOUR RESEARCHER CHARACTERISTICS

1. *Fast writer*
2. *Expansive thinker and lots of ideas*
3. *Interdisciplinary and cross-area interests*
4. *Collaborative*

---

research assistants, to describe your researcher characteristics. It can be as easy as an email or a hallway conversation asking, "I'm working through a book about research project management, and I'm working on ways to develop my system. As part of this, if you had to describe my style and characteristics as a researcher [or you can use scholar or PhD candidate or whatever descriptor you like here!], what would be three words you might use?" I always find it fascinating to hear how I'm perceived, and depending on the nature of the relationship (e.g., if it is horizontal or there's a lot of trust), you might even want to specify your best and most challenging attribute(s) rather than a general request for "characteristic." Above is an example of mine, and as always, blank worksheets are available at the book's companion website.

Adapting Your Research Project Management System to Your Style

Your system should take advantage of your strengths and shore up things that you find are issues or challenges but are not particularly good at. For example, one researcher I know is all about the details but sometimes loses sight of the big picture. Scheduling regular time to think broadly once a month—a "big-picture" meeting with themselves on their calendar, and time to "dream" alongside some graduate-school friends once a year to consider the direction of their research and their research career is an important complement to their strengths. They make time for their yearly meeting during their discipline's annual conference.

Regarding some of my challenges, I am a speedy writer and a very expansive thinker. This means that I often struggle to draw boundaries around analyses, projects, and papers. Similarly, my writing, while very fast, is also very sloppy. I know this about myself and accept it because, as with most things, there are positive and negative things about each characteristic. In terms of my writing, for example, I have to make time and force myself to carefully proofread my work before finalizing a manuscript, or if I have the funds, send it to a copy editor (though I've only done this twice I desperately wish I could always do so!). As another example, my expansiveness is very helpful in the planning phase (Part I), and it means I also have many ideas and directions I can go, which helps with adjustment (Part III), but this expansiveness often needs reining in during execution (Part II). When this is the case, I focus on the specific outputs for my research—trying to identify not only paper topics but even target journals earlier rather than later in my research process, which helps ground me and draw some lines through and around my big ideas.

Another researcher I know struggles mightily with perfectionism in their writing. This researcher is in a so-called book discipline where they are writing a solo-authored monograph, which they have been told they need to earn tenure. After reading many books about writing, working with their therapist (whom they already saw for other concerns), and being unable to move forward and send their work out for review, they started working with a writing coach, which has helped. Another researcher who struggles with perfectionism is in a branch of the natural sciences where collaboration is valued and common. Their approach has been to work with others in their department and at other institutions as a bulwark against their perfectionism. With someone else depending on them and helping set and enforce deadlines and their collaborators knowing the issue, the person is much more willing to send things out for review knowing that a respected co-author has signed off on it and taken the time to review it before external eyes see it. I, too, rely on co-authors to set "internal" or informal deadlines for myself and to help keep me focused on specific rather than big-picture research ideas.

These are some examples of how the issue (challenges with sending things out for review) is the same, but the preferred solutions (writing coach, therapist, co-authorship) differ depending on the researchers' goals and contexts. We worked through some of this in Parts I, II, and III of the book related to your research management approach, but here we are focusing more on your style and attributes and ways you can design or edit your system to deal with them.

Worksheet 10.2 invites you to identify the **benefits and challenges of each of your researcher attributes** you listed in Workshop 10.1 and begin

Worksheet 10.2 *Adjusting Your Management System to Your Style*

ADJUSTING YOUR MANAGEMENT SYSTEM TO YOUR STYLE

CHARACTERISTIC	BENEFITS	CHALLENGES	RESEARCH PROJECT MANAGEMENT ADJUSTMENTS
1. Fast writer	able to meet deadlines, can get preliminary thoughts out	sloppy, while I'm a fast writer I'm a very slow and reluctant editor, I'm super resistant to editing my own work	make time and force myself to read my own work out loud, send to a copy editor when possible
2. Expansive thinker	many ideas and directions I can go, which can help with adjustment	hard time drawing boundaries around analyses, projects, and papers	focus on quite specific outputs for my research—trying to identify not only paper topics but even target journals
3. Interdisciplinary and cross-area interests	creates exciting opportunities and ideally can help move areas forward, cross-pollination of ideas and theories	hard to place, need to fit into multiple communities, need to learn distinctive approaches and literatures	collaborate with others in other areas, budget time to develop expertise in different areas within timelines and planning phase
4. Collaborative	allows for exciting work, strong relationships, I learn a lot from co-authors and collaborators	I give up control, managing different work styles and communication challenges, some have been great, others difficult	enter into collaborations carefully and with preparation, make sure that work expectations and outputs are clearly defined

to think of ways to change your management system to account for those. As I mentioned, there are many ways to do so, and it might be helpful to consult some professional contacts for recommendations, especially if they understand your disciplinary and/or institutional context, on their strategies for tackling and managing any one issue or if they have any ideas for you.

I hope you can reflect on your unique attributes and strengths and determine how to flex those muscles more and rely on their benefits (this can also help you rethink the resources in the form of skills in the planning stage of research projects; see Chapter 2 and Worksheet 2.2). Ideally, effective research project management can help you play to your strengths. For example, if you are a talented writer and that is your favorite part of research, you can spend more time writing by streamlining your other duties, hiring others, or collaborating with them. On the other hand, there are likely some areas where you would benefit from more accountability or external help. You can adjust your system to account for this by getting work edited or proofread either by peers (and repaying the favor in some other way that plays to your strengths) or a professional, as one example.

The book's central argument is that your research project management system can and should help you achieve your goals. While many people think of project management as tedious and boring, about as exciting as an accounting binder (no offense intended to those who love accounting binders, I love a binder or spreadsheet of any kind), my argument here is that good research project management allows you to do the things you *like* to do: research the topics that are important to you, with reduced stress and increased efficiency and accountability.

In this way, it might help to think of research project management as the frame for your artwork that holds your work together and up, gives it structural integrity, and is changeable and adaptable. That is, any two artists may be doing similar (though never identical!) art, but they will want different frames to complement it and facilitate the display of that art. To continue the metaphor—the frame should complement the art, but there are many different ways to frame art, depending on the nature of the art and the preference of the framer (for example, color, size, kinds of backing, matting, and whether it needs glass). Similarly, any two researchers may do similar work in the same discipline but may have different research management systems depending on their own styles and goals. Ideally, these will reflect their ethics, values, and preferences while allowing them to manage their research effectively in the interest of legibility, efficiency, and reliability in the service of accuracy. In the next chapter, we focus on ways to make research project management more fun!

CHAPTER 11

Managing the Day-to-Day and Making Things Fun(ner)

For many of us, research, to use Marie Kondo's phrase, sparks joy (Lees 2021). However, managing research can also be joyful. I feel genuine satisfaction and joy when I can mentor someone in doing their research and know that I am helping contribute to their goals and development. Similarly, when everything is organized in its folder, my research log is clean and updated, and each of my three email accounts are at three emails or fewer, I feel immense satisfaction. For many, the administrative portion of research project management is sometimes less joyful, feels monotonous, and occasionally (or usually, depending on who you are) is boring. But there are ways to make this more fun.

This book has encouraged you to view these project management tasks as part and parcel of your research, not an extraneous and annoying add-on. When done right, effective project management can improve research—rendering it less error-prone but also more pleasant and less stressful. Even the administrative tasks spark joy for me at times: this happens when my files and folders are clearly labeled, and my weekly plans and calendar are color-coded. I approach the organization of my work, at least the outer package, with a spirit of curiosity, play, and joy whenever possible (though I, too, inevitably get grumpy and burnt out). Below, I offer you some ways I derive more enjoyment from the mundane and necessary research project management work. I hope some of these strategies inspire your own thinking. I hope you too can derive joy from research and its management.

The Aesthetics of Research Management and Organization

For me, color coding is not just aesthetic; it allows me to visually categorize my work and see where my time is going at a glance on my calendar; It also makes things fun. I derive joy from colorful displays. For me, this means that my calendar is color-coded by categories that work for me. While I know some folks who distinguish colors for research and teaching, for example, or meetings, as compared to data analysis, I use one color for all work-related tasks, including all of the above. I have separate colors for errands, one for personal, including family and friend commitments, and one for medical/health. Even with a few categories, I can look at my calendar and see where my time is going based on the colors on my screen. You might want to make your categories even more broad (e.g., personal versus professional) or more specific (separate out family and friends, or different family members)! My calendar is on my computer (I use Google Calendar), but you might derive great joy from finding the right paper planner and using it regularly. I went through a bullet journal phase for several years that I found very effective at that time, and I have used paper planners previously. Who knows, I may go back to them!

As discussed in Chapter 3, choosing the tools you will use is important, but even the "best" tool will not work if you won't use it. Making your tools fun will likely make you more willing to engage with them and to do so joyfully. For some technical and complex tools (e.g., data analysis), we may have limited options (though you can change the background and font color in many statistical analysis programs!) given that most of us are not software programmers willing to build our own tools. But, for the basic organizational tools, there are often many options, and they are often "tweakable" and customizable—for example, color-coding calendars.

Whether you are a maximalist or a minimalist, I hope you can find a way to make your work tools and environment aesthetically pleasing and joy-sparking for you. Whether that means big, colorful notebooks and fluffy pens or a monochromatic desk set, I find that having a work environment—and by this, I mean virtual as well as physical—that is as pleasant as I can make it helps motivate me to do my work. I am a person who spends several hours choosing a background for any new phone or laptop and matching cases to it. This may be something you don't care about at all, but whatever the thing is that makes things smoother and calmer for you—whether it's changing your default font, having a set of your favorite pens handy both at home and in the office, lighting a candle, or setting a new default color scheme in a program you use, I strongly recommend you find time to do those things. Combined with knowing yourself (Chapter 10), this will allow you to infuse some joy into your work via the tools you will use.

Managing Email

Email is a ubiquitous form of communication and a core function of many of our jobs. As I described briefly in Chapter 3, I have **three email inboxes**: personal, institutional, and professional accounts for the reasons I describe there. I try never to let my three inboxes get above 12 emails each (and most hover in the five to eight range at any given moment except first thing in the morning, when they're usually holding lots more emails that have come through in the evening/early morning, including newsletters), and emails only stay in my inbox if I need to take action (and note, that action can be reading, like a newsletter or link to news digest). Otherwise, they are deleted, tagged, scheduled, archived, or answered. I have a **label (the stub name)** in my email account for each of my research projects (others like to create a folder by research project, another good strategy!), and I sometimes use filters to send some listserv emails to their tag and review them when I'm ready. That way, I can prioritize personal (that is, specifically to me rather than a listserv or announcement) emails during the work day. I also try (and am mostly successful, but not always) not to check email after 5 pm and do not typically send emails before 8 am and after 5 pm—I like to think it reinforces workday boundaries and signals the same to others. I use the **schedule send** option for a weekday workday if I happen to be on email late at night or on a weekend. Another researcher I know checks email only at the start and end of their workday, which you can try! I tried it and didn't like it and instead check emails throughout the day (but not when I set my 30-minute pink sand hourglass to work on research; see Chapter 3), but it works great for them. Once I respond to emails, I **archive** them; if the person needs me again, they'll respond, and it'll pop back into my inbox. If I need to remind myself to follow up if they don't respond, I will **schedule** (or "snooze") the email to a week (or however long) from that date, and it'll pop back up in my inbox on the day I need it.

I've set a calendar **reminder to check my spam** (on all of my accounts) every Friday morning to ensure that I don't miss anything important (sadly, I know many people who have missed exciting professional opportunities, including a job offer once, because it went to spam and they checked too late). If I'm not answering emails (say, I'm traveling), I set an out-of-office and filter that funnels all new emails past my inbox. Then I put a note on my calendar to check my "All Mail" folder when I'm back to email, a way to avoid getting overwhelmed when I open my inbox during travel, if I need to, for example, send an email. I also have **template emails**: in response to students, for instance, with advising information and resources that contain information I find myself resending often.

Knowing I have a system makes email less stressful. Things do fall between the cracks, as always, but it's rare (I estimate I miss or don't respond to no more than three emails a year across all accounts since I started managing email this way). This system has seriously minimized forgotten requests and allowed me to deal with email effectively, making for less stress and time spent on email and more time for (other) important tasks. Email is sometimes urgent but not important, and occasionally important (see Worksheet 7.3 in Chapter 7), and developing an effective system allows you to deal with it appropriately.

The Freedom to Change Your Mind

As a person who values (and clings to) routine, I am often reluctant and resistant to change. My antidote to this is to try (alas, I am not always successful) to treat things with a spirit of curiosity and experimentation. I talk myself into trying something new by reminding myself that I can always go back to my previous approach and that exploration is not wasted time but rather a step toward knowing myself better and trying new things. This has been instrumental for my willingness to try new things. My response to change and new approaches or tools is often a reflexive no. I think, "I already know how to use this, and it's good enough," even if there are issues.

I have to work to counteract this knee-jerk reaction actively. I try not to get caught up in the fallacy of sunk costs (Chapter 8). Some of my favorite work strategies, like **working on research every day** and using the **Pomodoro method**, were things that I was initially unwilling to try for a long time (sometimes years). It was not until a friend challenged me to try something I didn't want to do for a week, telling me, "Just try it for this week; if it doesn't work for you, you can just stop." This lowered the stakes for me and delinked the behavior from an identity or fixed characteristic— trying something new did not have to be a lifelong commitment. Of course, some things are costly to change; in those cases, as discussed in Chapter 4, do some research before committing to, for example, learning and buying a new data analysis software.

Game-ifying Your Work

Research suggests that game-ifying your work may make it more fun for you, though designing and creating good games can be challenging to do effectively (Dale 2014). Some features of games that make them fun include positive reinforcement, achievement, and competition. You know yourself best, and it may be that some of these things are ineffective for your motivation and work, but they might work well for you and are at least worth considering.

For example, I find **tracking my achievements**, in my case with a colorful green checkmark every weekday I can work on research for at least 30 minutes, very rewarding. I derive genuine satisfaction from pasting in that green check mark where an empty black box lives if I do not "touch" my research daily. One researcher I know **assigns points to their personal and professional tasks** (cleaning data, writing, editing, eating a salad), with the tasks they like least rated as "higher" points. They then try to "earn" a certain number of points weekly or daily. Another researcher uses a similar system, but earning certain points over the course of a few weeks translates to a particular reward (e.g., dinner at their favorite spot), which keeps them motivated. I don't do either of these things, and this may sound stressful to you or antithetical to how you work or want to think about work, but perhaps there are other ways to make your work more pleasant for yourself. Whether or not you choose to game-ify it, you can try it for a week and see how you feel!

Time Tracking as Fact-Finding

Time tracking is one of those practices that generate data that may be helpful to you in understanding **where you are spending your time** and how to maximize your efficiency with one of our most limited resources as researchers: time! We discussed this briefly in the context of writing and time management tools in Chapter 3, but I think it merits a little more attention regarding what it can do for your research project management. You can track your time with a pen, paper, and basic watch, or do more complex time tracking with spreadsheets, categories, and dedicated applications (e.g., Toggl or Harvest). Another fun tool that some researchers I know love and use is TIMEFLIP, a 12-sided die that syncs with an app; you can track your time on up to 12 categories by turning the die so that the category you are spending time on is upturned (one scholar I know divides this by writing, data analysis, teaching prep, grading, and so forth). It is helpful to track your time on research projects to **understand what tasks demand most of your time and how long things take** as you plan future projects and craft timelines for them (Chapter 2). Sometimes, how long we think or feel we're working doesn't correspond to reality, and we are actually under- or over-estimating how we spend our time. Again, the goal is not judgment but fact-finding and data collection about how we work that will allow us to successfully manage our research. This may help with planning, execution, and adjustment. This may be a particularly promising direction if you are unsure where your time is going and want to reallocate your time to better correspond to your goals, values, and priorities.

Developing a Daily Research Habit and the Power of Rest

There are many books on writing, particularly academic writing, with excellent and helpful advice, and I leave the detailed advice to them. Generally, I recommend, if possible, **developing a daily research habit that includes writing**. Especially for those of us for whom research is only one component, and sometimes not the primary element, of our jobs, I find it essential to create space and time for "touching" your research each workday (which for most but not all of us is the workweek). Even on workdays where I teach for many hours or have other obligations, I "touch" my research. This involves setting a 30-minute timer (I like www.marinaratimer.com, which I am using at the moment after having taught away from home for four hours, to dedicate 30 minutes to writing this chapter) to work on my research and scholarship. This may or may not be writing in your case, but this habit has also helped me find the time to write. What this does for me is ensure that my research is never far from my mind, and it gives me the mental space and peace of mind to know that I will return to my research daily instead of panicking about when I will be able to write or work on research next.

As a recovering binge writer, I used to be quite precious and particular about my research and scholarship, especially in graduate school, believing I needed just the right conditions (then this was: quiet at home, coffee with lots of cream, nighttime), waiting for the muse to strike, and needing at least six hours (an entire workday essentially) of uninterrupted time to embark on research work. I got work done, but I was perpetually stressed out waiting for the muse and not quite knowing when the next time I would have or make time for my research was. To be sure, I got work done, but it was much less pleasant and, frankly, unrealistic in my current reality of many more demands on my time. Now, I consider writing as labor that needs to be scheduled daily on workdays.

This is not to say that you don't need some long stretches to focus on your writing, research, and thinking and hit a flow state (as discussed in the Introduction), only that most of us can ill afford to work *only* in that way. When I **set my timer**, I make sure to eliminate other distractions. I either write or do data analysis or something research-related, or I do nothing but stare at a blank screen (the latter rarely happens, thankfully). This is the only way I can get through writer's block; inevitably, I find something to write, do, or work on! Other scholars, I know, turn the internet off entirely or go somewhere without internet access.

You'll note that I mentioned the **workweek**. However, I also talk about **workdays** because one researcher I know likes to take their "Saturday" on Wednesday and run errands when everyone else is working, in the middle of the week. They then put in a full day of work on Saturday and take Wednesdays and Sundays as their "weekend." However you schedule your time, it is essential to take time to rest. **Rest** can increase your productivity and creativity and is important for your well-being and health (Hunter and Wu 2016; Smallwood and Schooler 2015). As with my binge-writing habit, I used to work through the weekend, seeking that uninterrupted time that was nowhere to be found during the week. I was always tired and not as productive as I am currently. I was also much more distracted when spending time with friends and family—always worried about the work I could be doing. I am now quite protective of my weekends as personal time (though I do find I have to work an occasional Saturday and Sunday) and force myself to **take breaks** during the workday, adapting the **Pomodoro method**. Rest allows me to recharge, recover, and think in the background (I have many breakthroughs in my thinking while walking my dog), which brings me re-energized and excited for my research when I once again engage with it.

Celebrate Effort

We live in a society that is very results-focused. And this makes a lot of sense; the proof is in the pudding, so to speak. And yet, the end product, especially in research, is often far outside of our control. By the end product, I don't mean what our research uncovers—our results, findings, and conclusions, which are naturally outside our control and subject to the data; I mean something beyond that: our outputs as evaluated by others (Chapter 1).

For example, many journals we submit to or grants we apply for have 90% or higher rejection rates. **Failure is statistically more common than success**. It is the norm, not the outlier, and rejection is a feature of the system, not a bug. Given that I can't control the outcome, my approach is to celebrate my effort. I treat myself to some time off or a good non-work book or something of the sort when I submit a paper or a grant (at least the first time!). This way, I provide **positive reinforcement for what I can control**: the submission rather than the outcome, for example, getting the grant or publication. Of course, I often celebrate the latter, too. Still, one way I "take back control" in areas where I feel I have little control is to focus on and reward my effort rather than sometimes arbitrary (e.g., Mayo et al. 2006; Pier et al. 2018) decisions made by others about my research.

Works Cited

Dale, Steve. 2014. "Gamification: Making Work Fun, or Making Fun of Work?" *Business Information Review* 31(2):82–90.

Hunter, Emily M., and Cindy Wu. 2016. "Give Me a Better Break: Choosing Workday Break Activities to Maximize Resource Recovery." *The Journal of Applied Psychology* 101(2):302–11. doi: 10.1037/apl0000045.

Lees, Eleanor. 2021. "What Does 'Sparking Joy' Mean? Marie Kondo's Method Explained." *Newsweek*. Retrieved September 3, 2023 (www.newsweek.com/marie-kondo-sparking-joy-konmari-method-netflix-1622959).

Mayo, Nancy E., James Brophy, Mark S. Goldberg, Marina B. Klein, Sydney Miller, Robert W. Platt, and Judith Ritchie. 2006. "Peering at Peer Review Revealed High Degree of Chance Associated with Funding of Grant Applications." *Journal of Clinical Epidemiology* 59(8):842–48.

Pier, Elizabeth L., Markus Brauer, Amarette Filut, Anna Kaatz, Joshua Raclaw, Mitchell J. Nathan, Cecilia E. Ford, and Molly Carnes. 2018. "Low Agreement among Reviewers Evaluating the Same NIH Grant Applications." *Proceedings of the National Academy of Sciences* 115(12):2952–57.

Smallwood, Jonathan, and Jonathan W. Schooler. 2015. "The Science of Mind Wandering: Empirically Navigating the Stream of Consciousness." *Annual Review of Psychology* 66(1):487–518. doi: 10.1146/annurev-psych-010814-015331.

Conclusion: Getting to It

I hope this book has convinced you that effectively organizing and managing your research is good for you, the research, and your organization/employment. I hope it has also shown you that what your research management system looks like can vary and suit your needs and priorities. You have hopefully begun working through the chapters and worksheets to craft your own research project management system: do not be daunted or discouraged if some of these tasks seem big and challenging! **You are capable and an expert in your field**. Research uncovers new information about the world but also about ourselves. Your system will likely never be complete; it will change alongside you and hopefully improve to best meet your changing needs.

Key Takeaways: How to Manage Your Work as a Researcher

There are some non-negotiables: **management and organization of research need to be legible, reliable, and efficient**; that is, it should allow you to organize information in a way that makes it understandable to you and those you are accountable to (perhaps journals, for reproducibility or replication purposes, or co-authors)—**legibility**. You should be able to quickly find what you need consistently—**reliability**; and easily, without stress—**efficiency**. In my experience, your management and organization will require trial and error and must be updated to accommodate new tools, actions, demands, collaborations, preferences, and developments.

As long as you can keep in mind your ethical commitments (Chapter 1) and set a timeline and secure resources (Chapter 2), you can select tools and build your system to suit (Chapter 3). As you execute your plans, be sure to keep track of what is essential: not only the workflow of your research, organizing and documenting what you do, and why and how (Chapter 4) but also the administrative information that is important to your organization, stakeholders, and gatekeepers (Chapter 5). In doing so, work to build accountability with yourself and your collaborators and co-authors (Chapter 6). Sadly, despite our best efforts at planning and execution, things go awry. The first step to addressing problems is recognizing their origin and deciding what is important (which is not always the same as urgent!) (Chapter 7). Then, we must figure out how to troubleshoot appropriately and effectively (Chapter 8). You will need to decide when your research project is complete. When you are ready to share the results of your research, you will need to think about dissemination, keeping in mind transparency, replication, and reproducibility (Chapter 9).

As you do all of this, you will want to develop a project management approach consistent with your style (Chapter 10) and make things as easy, joyful, and pleasant for yourself as possible (Chapter 11). Remember, **managing your research, like research itself, is a dynamic process.**

Further Exploration

There are many resources and tips to help us improve our work, including books about how to write more clearly, revise our writing, refine our methodological skills, and beyond. You can find advice that is not work specific but can help you with your research, for example, on improving time management (Morgenstern 2004); **temptation bundling**—coupling an activity you don't want to do with one you do want to do as motivation—to build good habits (Milkman, Minson, and Volpp 2014); and building in **nudges**, changes in the context of choices, that might steer you to good decisions that can be implemented via apps or other means (Sunstein 2014). You may also want to think about **habit stacking**—"stacking" or coupling a new habit to build one on top of one you already have (Clear 2018; Seaver 2023). So, for example, when I set my timer to work on my research, I have "stacked" the habit of closing my email tabs as soon as I set the timer, which helps limit my distractions.

I am an avid seeker of data and information; I'm particularly interested in how others do things, what they find compelling, and whether and how those approaches can fit into my work routine and life. I gather this information via formal and informal mentoring relationships as both mentor and mentee, podcasts, conversations with other researchers, articles, and more. This does not mean, however, that I take most or sometimes any of the advice offered to me, nor emulate the actions of even people I admire greatly. I know myself (Chapter 10), and not everything will work for me. I see advice and examples as data points I can sift through, examine, and sometimes adapt and implement.

That is how I invite you to use this book and how I encourage you to pursue additional advice and information about research project management: learn and try some new things, experiment with practices that address issues you've identified with your systems, take what is useful, and leave what doesn't work for you! **Happy researching; you can do this.**

Works Cited

Clear, James. 2018. *Atomic Habits: An Easy & Proven Way to Build Good Habits & Break Bad Ones*. New York: Penguin.

Milkman, Katherine L., Julia A. Minson, and Kevin G. M. Volpp. 2014. "Holding the Hunger Games Hostage at the Gym: An Evaluation of Temptation Bundling." *Management Science* 60 (2): 283–99.

Morgenstern, Julie. 2004. *Time Management from the Inside Out: The Foolproof System for Taking Control of Your Schedule—and Your Life*. New York: Holt McDougal.

Seaver, Maggie. 2023. "Habit Stacking Is the Easiest Way to Make New Habits Last— Here's How It Works." *Real Simple*. Retrieved October 20, 2023 (www.realsimple. com/work-life/life-strategies/inspiration-motivation/habit-stacking).

Sunstein, Cass R. 2014. "Nudging: A Very Short Guide." *Journal of Consumer Policy* 37:583–88.

Appendix A

At the time of this writing, a helpful list of templates by funder is available at DMPTool at https://dmptool.org/public_templates, while examples can be found at ICPSR at www.icpsr.umich.edu/web/pages/datamanagement/dmp/resources.html.

The following are some places where you can pre-register your studies:

AEA RCT Registry

    www.socialscienceregistry.org/

AsPredicted

    https://aspredicted.org/

Center for Open Science

    www.cos.io/initiatives/prereg

ClinicalTrials.gov

    https://clinicaltrials.gov/

ICTRP Registry Network for Clinical Trials by the WHO

    www.who.int/clinical-trials-registry-platform/network

Registry of Efficacy and Effectiveness Studies (REES)

    https://sreereg.icpsr.umich.edu/sreereg/

Appendix B

Select Popular Tools

Below is a non-exhaustive list of some popular programs. This is because: first, tools and their functions change and new tools are always being developed; second, many research tools are very specific to certain fields and areas of inquiry, and I do not know about all niches; third, because you want to find tools that can/will integrate and fit your system, which, again, will depend on your goals, their functions, availability, price, integration with your other tools, and a myriad of other considerations that may be specific to you (for example, aesthetics, what collaborators are using). This Appendix is not intended to be a catalog but rather a place to start your exploration and provide some ideas as you search for tools.

Writing and Focus Tools

Flow

Website: https://flowapp.info/

Features: A focus and Pomodoro timer app, only for Macs, provides statistics on your work.

Cost: Free, $1/month for Pro version

Forest App

Website: www.forestapp.cc/ (can only be downloaded as an app)

Features: Works to help you stay focused and partners with real tree-planting organizations.

Cost: Free, $3.50/month for broader capabilities

Freedom

Website: https://freedom.to/

Features: A digital distraction-blocking program.

Cost: Free for Android ($1.99 for the paid version, iOS is $3.99 paid

Google Docs

Website: https://docs.google.com/

Features: Google Docs is particularly effective for collaboration, is easily shareable with a link, and has many of the functions of Word documents. I find the headings and navigation menu particularly useful for getting an outline overview of my documents.

Cost: Free with a Gmail account

LaTeX

Website: www.latex-project.org/

Features: LaTeX is a popular typesetting program that allows for advanced mathematical formulas, sectioning, and cross-referencing and works with a citation manager (with additional plugins).

Cost: Free

Microsoft Word

Website: www.microsoft.com/en-us/download/office.aspx

Features: Microsoft Word is commonly known and available, with many capabilities, including symbols and equations for publications and other information. It integrates with the citation software listed below. Office365 allows for online collaboration.

Cost: Office365 $69.99/year

Overleaf

Website: www.overleaf.com/

Features: Overleaf provides a LaTeX environment that is user-friendly and allows collaboration.

Cost: Free for a single user, a Professional license is $38/month

Pen and Paper

Website: Many. My favorite pens are TUL Retractable Gel Pens, Needle Point, 0.5 mm—smooth, come in fun colors, and write like a dream; my current favorite notebooks are Sunnee spiral notebooks, graph-ruled paper, 100 sheets, 11" x 8½"—I like a spiral-bound notebook so I can tuck my pen in the spiral and get it to lay flat on a single side. I like grid paper for writing anything, because I find it easily accommodates lists, doodling, and working across the entire page, especially for brainstorming and diagramming. My favorite sticky notes are Post-it Super Sticky Notes, 4" x 6", white with blue grid lines, but as of late I'm also a big user of Post-it Transparent Notes, 2.8" x 2 .8", on books and other things I'm reading, especially to annotate it. **They are the inspiration for the book's cover.**

Features: Versatile

Cost: a few dollars to much more, depending on the pen and paper

RescueTime

Website: www.rescuetime.com/

Features: Seeks to help you focus and limit distractions and set a timer to focus, allows calendar integration and other features and collects data on your time-use.

Cost: Free, $12/month for premium subscription

Scrivener

Website: www.literatureandlatte.com/scrivener/overview

Features: Scrivener is particularly popular for longer projects and allows for nesting and easy reorganization of texts, images, and documents, and integrating background material with writing in a single platform. Organizationally, Scrivener has several formats for both viewing and integrating documents and pieces of writing.

Cost: Free 30-day trial, $49 license

Reading and Reference Management

Academia.edu

Website: www.academia.edu/

Features: A repository of academic articles/

Cost: Free with subscription, $9/month for premium content

Beeline Reader

Website: www.beelinereader.com/

Features: This is a plug-in that creates eye-guiding color gradients for text, enhancing focus.

Cost: $4.50/month for five browsers

Connected Papers

Website: www.connectedpapers.com/

Features: This finds papers related to a paper you search to get a visual overview of the field via citation networks.

Cost: Free

Endnote

Website: https://endnote.com/

Features: This provides reference and citation management and annotation, citation add-in for Microsoft Word, and collaboration.

Cost: $249.95 for an individual license

Feedly

Website: https://feedly.com/

Features: This web feed allows you to subscribe to websites and blogs, as well as journal tables of contents and other professional information.

Cost: Free for online personal use

Mendeley

Website: www.mendeley.com/

Features: This provides reference and citation management and annotation, citation add-in for Microsoft Word, and the ability to work with groups.

Cost: Free (with a cost for additional storage)

Paperpile

Website: https://paperpile.com/

Features: This provides reference management, built for Chrome apps (Google Docs, Drive, etc.).

Cost: $2.99/month for academics

reMarkable

Website: https://remarkable.com/

Features: This tablet allows you to read, annotate, and write and export that information as images, PDF, or handwriting to text. It "feels" like paper, allowing you to draw, write, doodle and so on in a close digital imitation of pen and paper.

Cost: Starting at $299 for reMarkable2

ResearchGate

Website: www.researchgate.net/

Features: A social networking site to share and find papers, as well as answer questions and communicate.

Cost: Free with account creation

Research Rabbit

Website: https://researchrabbitapp.com/

Features: This finds and recommends papers related to a paper you searched for to get a visual overview of the field via citation networks.

Cost: Free with an institutional email

Zotero

Website: www.zotero.org/

Features: This is a reference manager with the ability to cite and organize references. It allows you to work collaboratively and share and contribute to shared libraries. It works with Microsoft Word but can also be made to work with LaTeX and other writing software.

Cost: Free up to 30mb (with a cost for additional storage, e.g., $20/year for 2GB)

Brainstorming and Communication

Email

Website: Varied (Gmail, Hotmail, Yahoo, etc. My institutional and personal emails are both Gmail, but I have also used Outlook; your work account is typically determined by your institution)

Features: Many programs offer archiving, tagging, filtering rules, out-of-office replies, and more.

Cost: Free

LucidChart

Website: www.lucidchart.com

Features: This is a diagramming application, with additional mind-mapping features available in an accompanying program (separate pricing) called "LucidSpark"; allows for collaboration.

Cost: Free with limited diagrams, then $9.95/month for an individual

Slack

Website: www.slack.com

Features: This is a workplace messaging program; you can create channels for different aspects, exchange files, and more.

Cost: Free (unlocking more features requires monthly payments)

Xmind

Website: www.xmind.net/

Features: This creates mind maps, enables brainstorming, and allows for collaboration across teams.

Cost: $59.99/year for a single user (discounts for educators, those working at NGOs, and more)

Tools for Project Management

Acuity

Website: www.acuityscheduling.com/

Features: The platform allows for online scheduling across multiple schedules including appointment slots, syncs calendars, and allows online payment.

Cost: Free for a trial version ($16/month per single user)

Asana

Website: www.asana.com

Features: The platform allows for collaboration, creation of timelines, goal setting, and team communication features.

Cost: Free for a trial version ($15/month per user for paid version)

Basecamp

Website: https://basecamp.com/

Features: Creates a page per project with various features including messaging, to-do lists, and more.

Cost: Free for the basic version ($5/month for Unlimited)

ClickUp

Website: www.clickup.com

Features: This integrates documents, goals, and tasks with chat for communication.

Cost: Free for the basic version ($5/month for Unlimited)

Confluence

Website: www.atlassian.com/software/confluence

Features: A team and collaborative workspace.

Cost: Free for the basic version ($11/month per user for Premium)

Evernote

Website: https://evernote.com/

Features: This uses boards to manage to-do lists, tasks, deadlines, and meetings; additionally, it integrates with Google products.

Cost: Free for the basic version ($14.99/user/month for Evernote Teams)

Git

Website: https://git-scm.com/

Features: While different than the other more comprehensive project management tools listed here, Git is an open-source distributed version control system meant to manage and track changes in files, popular among programmers developing code.

Cost: Free

monday projects

Website: www.monday.com/project-management

Features: The platform allows for collaboration, creation of timelines, goal setting, and team communication features.

Cost: Projects with up to two members free, then billed based on additional member access, depending on the version ($9–20/month)

Microsoft Project

Website: www.microsoft.com/en-us/microsoft-365/project/project-management-software

Features: Uses dashboards for projects that allow the creation of tasks, file sharing, team communication, and more.

Cost: Project Plan 1 (the lowest cost option) is $10 per user per month.

Notion

Website: www.notion.so

Features: This is a flexible workspace that allows for integrating documents, tasks, roadmaps, and more.

Cost: Free for the basic version ($10/month for Team)

OpenProject

Website: www.openproject.org/

Features: Offers tools to create budgets, Gantt charts, and more.

Cost: Free "Community" version without access to some features while Basic is $7.25 per use per month with a minimum of five users.

Trello

Website: www.trello.com

Features: This uses boards to manage communication, to-do lists, and tasks.

Cost: Free for the basic version ($12.50/month for Premium)

Storage and Backup

Backblaze

Website: www.backblaze.com

Features: System backup that allows collaborating and managing content.

Cost: Free trial, then $7/month per computer

Box

Website: www.box.com

Features: This facilitates collaboration, signatures, and workflow (e.g., for contracts).

Cost: Free for up to 10GB ($10/month for 100GB)

Dropbox

Website: www.dropbox.com

Features: This allows you to save, share, sign, and access files across multiple machines.

Cost: Free for 2GB of storage ($11.99/month for 2TB for an individual user)

Google Drive

Website: www.clickup.com

Features: This allows for file storage and collaboration in Google products, including Docs, Sheets, and Slides.

Cost: Free for up to 15GB ($12/month for 2TB)

Commonly Used Tools for Social Science Data Analysis

As discussed, I am a social scientist and focus on commonly used tools for data analysis in that area. Below, you'll find a list of some of these. However, you should be able to get a good sense of the tools that are available and preferred in your discipline from your department and publications in your area.

Quantitative Data Analysis

I use Stata for my own work, for the most part, because that's what I was trained and am most comfortable in. I also appreciate its technical support. However, I have used Mplus and R for functions unavailable in Stata (and more specialized software for social network analysis, such as Pajek and UCINET), and I teach statistics in SPSS. All of these software programs offer training, often in the form of short courses offered by the software company itself, and numerous online forums, tutorials, and more, which is helpful if you get stuck.

Excel

Website: https://support.microsoft.com/en-us/excel

Data analysis information: https://support.microsoft.com/en-us/office/analyze-data-in-excel-3223aab8-f543-4fda-85ed-76bb0295ffc4

Cost: Usually bundled with Microsoft Office but $160 separately

MATLAB

Website: www.mathworks.com/products/matlab.html

Data analysis information: www.mathworks.com/solutions.html#applications

Cost: $500 for a single education perpetual license www.mathworks.com/pricing-licensing.html?prodcode=ML&intendeduse=edu

R and RStudio

Website: https://cran.r-project.org/bin/windows/base/ and www.rstudio.com/products/rstudio/#rstudio-desktop

Data analysis information: Contained in packages across the web.

Cost: Free

Mplus

Website: www.statmodel.com/

Data analysis information: Particularly suited for latent variables.

Cost: $595 for a single-user Base Program Educational pricing (different pricing available for non-profit/government/commercial and student pricing) www.statmodel.com/pricing.shtml

SAS

Website: www.sas.com/en_us/home.html

Data analysis information: www.sas.com/en_us/software/stat/features-list.html

Cost: Individually determined, but about $9,000 www.sas.com/ en_us/software/how-to-buy/request-price-quote.html

Stata

Website: www.stata.com/

Data analysis information: www.stata.com/features/

Cost: $295 for a single academic, BE license (licenses vary across size of datasets but also across occupations, such as educational versus business) www.stata.com/order/

SPSS Statistics

Website: www.ibm.com/products/spss-statistics

Data analysis information: www.ibm.com/products/spss-statistics

Cost: $76 for 12 months for a single academic license www.ibm.com/ products/spss-statistics/pricing

Tableau

Website: www.tableau.com/

Data analysis information: www.tableau.com/products

Cost: $70/month for Tableau Creator www.tableau.com/pricing/ teams-orgs

Qualitative Data Analysis

I use ATLAS.ti but have some experience with each of the below programs. While I like ATLAS.ti, I use it primarily because my institution provides it to me at no cost. Many of these programs' capabilities are similar, and if one is available to you at no cost, I recommend going with that one and possibly enrolling for training via the company to learn its capabilities, although many free and excellent online resources exist.

ATLAS.ti

Website: https://atlasti.com/

Data analysis information: https://atlasti.com/why-atlas-ti; allows for coding, analysis, and memos and can be used for mixed methods research.

Cost: $20/month for a single education user https://atlasti.cleverbri dge.com/74/catalog/category.92842/language.en/currency.USD/ ?id=uFYijIdtbR

dedoose

Website: www.dedoose.com/

Data analysis information: www.dedoose.com/home/features; allows for coding and analysis and mixed methods research (integration with quantitative data).

Cost: $14.95/month for an individual license www.dedoose.com/ home/pricing

NVivo

Website: www.qsrinternational.com/nvivo-qualitative-data-analysis-software/home

Data analysis information: www.qsrinternational.com/nvivo-qual itative-data-analysis-software/support-services/customer-hub/ nvivo-academy/nvivo-core-skills; allows for coding, organization, memo-writing, and transcription (the latter can be added on for a cost).

Cost: $849 for a single academic license for Windows or Mac www. qsrinternational.com/nvivo-qualitative-data-analysis-software/ buy-now

MAXQDA

Website: www.maxqda.com/

Data analysis information: www.maxqda.com/interview-transcription-analysis; allows for coding, visualization, and transcription (and modules for quantitative/mixed methods research at extra cost).

Cost: $253 for a single academic license www.maxqda.com/pric ing#role-institution

Index

Note: Figures are indicated by *italics*.